E. C. R. Baker was born and educ  where he attended Dudley College a keen scholar and writer on the pile through which he became aware of Pat Pattle's remarkable ... Through his work he was made an honorary member of 80 Squadron in February 1966 at the squadron's reunion in London. He retired from teaching after more than 30 years in 1980. He died in 2002, aged 74 after battling cancer. He was the author of two books – *Ace of Aces* (originally titled *Pattle: Supreme Fighter in the Air*) and *The Fighter Aces of The R.A.F.*

ACE OF ACES

E. C. R. Baker

SILVERTAIL BOOKS • *London*

First published in Great Britain by William Kimber & Co. Ltd in 1965
This edition published by Silvertail Books in 2020
www.silvertailbooks.com
Copyright © E. C. R. Baker 1965 and 1992
The right of E. C. R. Baker to be identified as the author
of this work has been asserted in accordance
with the Copyright, Design and Patents Act 1988
A catalogue record of this book is available from the British Library
978-1-913727-01-7

Contents

Prologue

At the side of the coastal road some sixty-five miles west of Alexandria in Egypt stands the El Alamein War Cemetery. Above the entrance to an enormous limestone cloister, which forms the northern boundary of the cemetery, is a dedicatory inscription which commemorates those of the Commonwealth forces who lost their lives in the Second World War and who have no known graves. On the inside walls of this cloister are fixed hundreds of Portland stone panels bearing the names of almost 12,000 soldiers, sailors and airmen, who gave their lives. About halfway down the 239th column appears the name of Squadron Leader M T St John Pattle, DFC. Apart from the decoration after the name there is nothing else to distinguish it from the thousands of other names on the columns; unless one was searching for this particular name one could quite easily miss it. It seems so unobtrusive and insignificant for such a distinguished flyer, and yet is compatible with the character of the man. Pattle's natural reticence, modesty, and avoidance of the limelight, are probably the main reasons why so little has been heard of his exploits; and yet this man was a superb pilot, a deadly accurate marksman, and in the opinion of many, the most successful Royal Air Force fighter pilot during the whole of the war.

That he has never officially been acknowledged as the top-scoring fighter pilot is due to the fact that the Air Ministry were never in a position to confirm his victories in aerial combat. The last official score ever credited to Squadron Leader Pattle was for twenty-three victories announced in the citation to the award of a Bar to his Distinguished Flying Cross early in March 1941. No official records of his activities during those last few weeks of intensive operations in Greece exist today, because all official records were destroyed when Greece was evacuated by the British forces towards the end of April 1941. The only semi-official record is the Operations Book of 33 Squadron, which is held by the Air Historical Branch of the Air Ministry, and which is merely a summary of operations written from memory, aided by such information as could be gleaned from Middle East Intelligence Summaries many months after the evacuation; these actually bear out the fact that Squadron Leader Pattle destroyed a large number of German and Italian aircraft during the few weeks that he commanded 33 Squadron.

Squadron Leader Pattle was certainly Commanding Officer of 33 Squadron during the months of March and April 1941; the hundreds of officers and airmen who served with the squadron at this time all state that not only was Pattle the Commanding Officer of the squadron, but that he was the finest leader the squadron ever possessed, both as a pilot in the air and as an administrator on the ground; but even this point is not officially recorded; Squadron Leader Pattle's personal and confidential Certificate of Service gives no indication that he ever served with 33 Squadron. The official records or even semi-official records relating to those last few hectic weeks of operations in Greece are by no means absolutely correct, though this is certainly not the fault of the Air Ministry authorities.

When I wrote *The Fighter Aces of the R.A.F. 1919-45,* I naturally assumed that all these records kept by the Air Ministry were, in fact, complete and, consequently, in the chapter concerning Squadron Leader Pattle, gave him credit for thirty-four confirmed victories, which placed him second in the list of top-scoring Royal Air Force pilots, immediately below that great Spitfire pilot Group Captain (now Air Vice-Marshal) J E 'Johnny' Johnson, DSO, DFC. It was only much later when I met and talked to ex-members of 80 and 33 Squadrons that I realised how much I, and I have no doubt many others, too, had underestimated the efforts of this incredible South African fighter pilot – who should perhaps be recognised as the outstanding Allied fighter pilot of the Second World War.

When one remembers that these victories were scored in less than nine months of active warfare – almost half of them whilst flying in an obsolete biplane fighter, the Gloster Gladiator – only then can one realise the greatness of this magnificent achievement, and wonder why this courageous, skilful and devoted airman was only awarded a Distinguished Flying Cross and Bar, whilst pilots of far less distinction on the Home Front received decorations galore. Perhaps if Squadron Leader Pattle had lived to come back to the United Kingdom he would have been given some of the recognition which he deserved. I am convinced that, had he lived, his name would have become as well known as Bader, Malan or Cunningham.

So many pilots showed great courage, but lacked discretion; it was only a matter of time before they fell by the wayside unless luck remained on their side. Squadron Leader Pattle was a tactician who regularly outmanoeuvred his opponents in clearly thought out, well planned moves, taking into account the elements of height, surprise and cloud cover, and the advantages of his own aircraft when compared with the aircraft being flown by the enemy.

He was far too sensitive and imaginative ever to be reckless in the air. Always he drummed into his fellow flyers the fact that they should temper dash with discretion, and constantly he told them that air fighting was as safe as crossing the street providing one thought ahead, thought quickly, and did not take any unnecessary risks. He was fully prepared, however, to take a risk when the life of a friend was in danger.

His successes in the air were by no means the result of brilliant tactical flying alone. His perfect eyesight, which enabled him to spot enemy aircraft when they were pinhead specks in the distance, was a big contributing factor. Never once was he surprised in the air; long before the enemy had seen him he was in a position to make his own attack. With some fighter pilots the spotting of aircraft at long distances was undoubtedly a gift, but many became proficient at it merely through constant practice. Pattle had perfect vision, which had been trained to an exceptional degree through intensive and untiring practice.

Perhaps Pattle's greatest attribute, however, was his ability to shoot accurately. The way he used to send heavy Italian bombers hurtling earthwards in flames with merely two short bursts from his guns was uncanny. He had evolved a technique in dealing with Savoia 79's which all his colleagues copied with success. Attacking from the rear, he would fire a half-second burst at the tank situated between the fuselage and the port engine. Then he would formate in line astern with the bomber for about ten seconds to give the petrol time to leak out. Another brief burst with his guns into the petrol vapour, and down would go the aircraft in flames.

On the ground he was a quiet, calm and reflective man of integrity and great conscientiousness, devoted to the task of defeating the enemy. He set himself high standards, and through his own efficiency and example commanded the respect of everyone. All the members of his squadron admired him and trusted his judgement implicitly. As the new young commanding officer of a very tired squadron, battling against great odds, fighting against a falling-off in morale, he was superb. At this pressing time when he was called upon to carry such a tremendous burden of responsibility on his young shoulders, when the great pressure from the enemy would have made the stoutest heart feel fear, Squadron Leader Pattle provided that lively spark which gave everyone all the confidence they needed to face the terrific opposition which just continued day after day.

A tired and sick man, he defied the orders of his Medical Officer and the protests of his Adjutant, in order to lead his tiny, battle scarred unit to take on an armada of Luftwaffe fighters and bombers; and in the end he made the supreme sacrifice while trying to save the life of a friend. In so doing he left his name in a place of honour amongst the immortals of the air.

E. C. R. BAKER

1

Early life and family background

In the early morning of 23 July 1914 Jack Pattle paced restlessly up and down the waiting-room at the hospital in Butterworth, a small town in the South African Transkeian native territory. Several cups of coffee and many cigarettes later the white door swung open and a smiling midwife entered the room. She proudly announced: 'It's all right, Mr Pattle. You can tell Cecil he has a bonny, bouncing brother.' And, as the look of relief on the young man's face changed to an expression of inquiry, she anticipated his question: 'Your wife is fine. You can see Mrs Pattle and your son in a short while.'

They called the youngster Marmaduke Thomas, after his grandfather, but his name was not the only thing he inherited from the old adventurer. Captain Thomas Marmaduke Pattle, son of a lieutenant general in the British Army, had given up his commission in the Royal Horse Artillery to emigrate to South Africa in 1875. Fighting was in his blood, and very soon he was appointed to lead the Fingo levies in the Kaffir wars. His courage and tenacity in action is shown by the fact that to this day he is still remembered by these people as 'Mlelo' (Fiery) Pattle. Subsequently he settled in the Transkei after that country had become more peaceful, raised a family, and became the first military magistrate of Butterworth.

His son Jack, who was born in Butterworth on 5 September 1884, followed in the traditional military footsteps of the Pattles by joining the army when he was only fifteen years old. He fought on the British side during the Boer War and later on also took part in the short episode of South African history known as the Natal Rebellion. He came to

England as a member of the South African contingent for the coronation of King Edward VII, and on his return to the Union left the army in order to study law. He set up as an attorney at Willowvale, a few miles from Butterworth.

In 1909 Jack Pattle met an attractive nursing sister during a visit to Butterworth Hospital. Edith Brailsford, a young Englishwoman from Bishop Auckland, had come out to South Africa with her parents when she was about five years old. She had wanted to be a nurse for as long as she could remember, and was endowed with all the attributes one associates with the nursing profession – kindness, faith, loyalty, quiet courage and fortitude, and a quality which she shared with Jack Pattle, a deep and sincere devotion to King and Country. They were married in Butterworth in 1912, and the union was blessed a year later with the birth of a son, who was christened Cecil.

Barely three weeks after the arrival of Cecil's brother, Marmaduke Thomas, the world erupted into conflict – the Great War. Mrs Pattle courageously held back the tears and clung to her two baby sons as her husband went off to do battle against the Kaiser's troops in South West Africa. It was to be four long years before Jack Pattle was to see his children again, but he knew they would be in safe, loving hands.

During the lonely months of waiting Edith Pattle inculcated into the minds of her two young sons a loyalty and devotion to duty which were to stand the brothers in such good stead in later life. Telling them true stories of British gallantly and achievement, she delved into British history as far back as the reign of King Canute. The boys were fascinated by their mother's descriptions of the exploits of Robert the Bruce, Raleigh, Drake, and Scott; their favourite story was that great epic of the late Jack Cornwell which made a vivid and lasting impression on the minds of the two boys.

When the Kaiser finally surrendered Jack Pattle decided to remain in South West Africa, where he had been offered a commission in the newly formed Police Force. Mrs Pattle and her two sons joined him and the family settled in Keetmanshoop, a town situated in the arid wastes of southern

South West Africa, with a population of one and a half thousand white people, mostly of German descent.

The boys were sent to the local school in Keetmanshoop, and for the first time in their lives were able to mix freely with children of German and Afrikaans descent; this broadened their outlook on life, giving them an insight into the problems and traditional way of life of other people. Tom had an exceptionally quick-thinking brain and a retentive memory, and this combined with a great interest in mathematics, and a natural aptitude for getting into trouble with his childish pranks, soon brought him into frequent contact – sometimes painful – with the principal of the school, Mr O. P. Tarr, an Oxford graduate with a rather eccentric but fine personality, who was later to give his life rescuing two girls from drowning.

In 1921 Jack Pattle relinquished his commission in the Police Force and started a practice as an attorney in Keetmanshoop in partnership with a certain Mr Oliff. Although a popular and likeable character, Jack Pattle was slapdash in his business dealings and soon the partnership was terminated. He took on the job of Assistant Town Clerk in Keetmanshoop and within a couple of years was able to buy a small farm on the banks of the Auob river, about five miles outside the town. The boys were both given pellet guns, an indispensable part of a South African boy's equipment, and during the weekends and vacations from school, their father took them out on hunting expeditions, teaching them how to look after themselves in the wild, rugged country that surrounded the farm. Their father's first-hand knowledge of guns and shooting was quickly assimilated by the boys, and the time spent on the farm with its sunny days and blue skies soon developed in young Tom a sharpness of vision and unerring skill with a gun that was to serve him well later on in life.

The fact that Keetmanshoop is nearly 500 miles from Windhoek, where the next school was situated, meant that at Keetmanshoop School there was very little sport. With no outside competition there was little incentive to play really hard at cricket or rugger, so Tom concentrated on swimming. He spent a great deal of his time by the dam four miles outside the town and soon became a fine long distance swimmer. Two of his other schoolboy occupations were boxing and scouting – a movement which he joined as a Cub. He was full of grit at boxing and ready to take on anyone, even bigger boys than himself, whenever he was given the opportunity.

Mechanical things were a great attraction for Tom and he spent hours with a Meccano set, making all sorts of working toys. On one occasion whilst in the quadrangle of the school he heard for the first time the sound of an aeroplane engine. He looked upwards and was fascinated by the sight of an airliner winging its way towards Windhoek. For several months afterwards his Meccano set was used exclusively to make models of aircraft – biplanes, monoplanes, planes with one, two, three, or four engines, planes with wheels, planes without wheels, planes of the past, planes of the present, planes of the future – his creative and intelligent mind knew no bounds, until the interest was finally absorbed by other more immediate attractions. His father had bought an old Ford motor car and immediately Tom developed a passion for engines of every kind. He was 12 years old at the time.

One morning the old car refused to start. Jack Pattle wasted half an hour checking the petrol, battery, plugs and points, swinging the starting-handle, and finally getting his sons to give him a push in a futile effort to get the engine ticking over. Eventually he persuaded a neighbour to give him a lift into town, leaving Tom still tinkering with the dead engine, a spanner in one hand and the Ford instruction book in the other. With the aid of a native helper, Tom hauled the engine out of the chassis, and after much thought and experiment at last traced the trouble to an ignition fault in the flywheel dynamo. He repaired the short and put back the engine ... an experienced mechanic could not have done a better job. He jumped into the driving seat and switched on. The engine instantly fired, ticked over healthily and roared out in short, sharp, rhythmic bursts as Tom's foot prodded the accelerator. The surge of pleasure that filled his body at the success of his efforts also went to his head; the next moment, before his mother could stop him, he moved the gear lever, let out the clutch and slowly accelerated down the road, heading towards Keetmanshoop. Although he had never had a driving lesson, he drove the Ford the five miles to town without undue incident and pulled up outside his father's office in time to take him back to lunch. Mr Pattle was too astonished to say or do anything ... until they got home.

Tom never swotted hard at school, nor did anything extra after ordinary school hours on the academic side other than the usual homework, but he had an intelligence above average and therefore it came as no real surprise to the family in 1929 when he passed the Junior Certificate Examination at Keetmanshoop in the first class and thereby qualified to go as a boarder to the Victoria Boys' High School in Grahamstown.

After the initiation ceremony – he had to sing a song and then run through a corridor of boys armed with folded towels – *Never fear*. he wrote home, *I stood it like a man. All did except three who gave way to tears*. Tom settled down quickly and because of his smiling good nature soon made a lot of friends. There was so much to do and so much to see in Grahamstown that although he was a thousand miles from home he seldom felt homesick. He studied conscientiously, played games with gusto, and at the end of his first term was able to report that *the school and the climate evidently seem to suit me for I am gaining in weight, have a much bigger appetite and have not been sick since I have been here!*

Like most boys he was fond of pranks and occasionally incurred the displeasure of his housemaster, Mr Rabie. On one occasion, he was confined to his room for several days after printing his name in large, bold letters on the boards of the passage outside the classroom. But on the whole he behaved himself reasonably well, especially after becoming a member of the Students' Christian Association. He also enjoyed a game of chess and this undoubtedly kept him from more boisterous pursuits.

Although never excelling at sports and outdoor games, he enjoyed taking part in them, particularly rugger. During his last year at Victoria High School he was made skipper of the Third Rugger Fifteen, playing in the position of fly-half. The team seldom won a match, always *owing to a considerable amount of cheating on the referee's part,* but nevertheless Tom was a true sportsman and always gave a good cheer for both opponents and referee.

Tom matriculated from Grahamstown at the end of 1931, during the middle of the world depression; the slump had hit South Africa pretty hard and jobs were few and far between; it was not a case of choosing a profession to enter in those days; one had to be content to do any job that could be found. Although Tom had made up his mind to fly and, in fact, had already sent in an application form to join the South African Air Force, he realised it might be some considerable time before he heard from the authorities. Early in 1932 he began to earn a few shillings a week as a garage assistant at a filling station in Komgha, Eastern Province, owned by his uncle.

After many months the official invitation to attend for interview at Pretoria arrived and on 12 March 1933 Tom walked into the waiting-room at Air Force Headquarters. It was full of big, hefty-looking chaps, much older than he was, and Tom immediately felt rather insignificant, especially when he learned that of the thirty applicants present only three would be accepted. Nevertheless, Tom reassured himself with the thought that height and weight were of no consequence to a pilot, especially a fighter pilot; he recollected reading somewhere that many of the famous pilots of the Great War, Ball, Bishop, McCudden, Fonck, and Richthofen were all small men. Perhaps they wanted men of short stature. He was convinced that he would be one of the lucky ones when, three hours later, his turn came and he was ushered before the Selection Board. They fired all sorts of questions in both English and Afrikaans and Tom felt at the end that he had given a fairly good account of himself. He was told to wait outside. Ten minutes later he was recalled and Tom knew from the expressions of the members of the Board that he had been rejected. Later he learned that the three chaps who had been selected had all had over twenty hours' solo flying time. His dreams of getting into the Air Force shattered, he felt very disappointed, but not downhearted. He remembered the Pattle family motto

'Perseverance', and decided there and then that he would never give up until he had achieved his ambition to fly.

On returning to Johannesburg, Tom began a course at one of the local commercial colleges. He felt that this would not only brush up his knowledge of English grammar, which he knew was one of his weak subjects, but that the mathematics, shorthand and typing would also be of use to him in finding temporary employment until the Air Force again began to accept aspiring flyers.

Finding a job was easier said than done at this time in South Africa, and on several occasions Tom went along for an interview only to find that the vacancy had already been filled before he arrived. On other occasions he was far too modest and self-conscious to give a good opinion of himself at an interview, and consequently the job always went to someone else. This would never do, thought Tom, and made up his mind that the next time he was interviewed he would be the 'know-all'.

The opportunity came shortly afterwards. He had gone to college as usual and sat down to do shorthand. About five minutes later another fellow tapped him on the shoulder and said: 'The head wants to see you.'

Now previously whenever the headmaster wanted to see him it was for an explanation of his latest bit of mischief. Tom wondered what it could have been, as he slowly made his way towards Mr Norris's study. The day before he had sketched the features of a pal on the blackboard, all over the head's carefully worked out balance sheet. That must be the reason for old Norris wanting him, he decided. Before he could think of an adequate excuse, Mr Norris came round the corner of the corridor.

'Ah! Pattle. I want you.'

Tom put on his most innocent air. 'Yes, sir,' he said, prepared for the worst.

'Do you want a job, Pattle?'

It was several seconds before Tom could mutter, 'Yes, sir.'

Mr Norris handed him a card. 'Go to this address. They want an assistant, and I believe you are the only boy in the college capable of doing the job at present.'

Tom could not decide whether it was a compliment or merely a bit of rather cheap sarcasm. He hurried off to the address on the card.

He was admitted into the office without delay, and sat down on the offered chair in front of the manager, who eyed him keenly. The usual formalities, name, age, previous experience, references, etc., were soon dispensed with and they got down to business.

'Can you drive a car?' the manager asked.

'Yes.'

'Can you type?'

'Better than the typist I noticed as I came into your office.' Rather presumptuous, but Tom didn't care. It was the truth, anyway, for she was using the two-finger system.

'Do you think you could manage salesmanship?'

'Yes. It was born in me.' Tom was warming to the task now.

The manager grunted. 'Do you know anything about mechanics?'

'Yes,' Tom answered. 'I worked for six months in a garage, and besides I'm told I have a mechanical mind.'

So the interview continued, Tom answering everything most emphatically and praising himself as he had never done before. For once he felt quite at ease, and he made sure the manager noticed it.

'Can I see a sample of your handwriting?' the manager asked, handing Tom pencil and paper.

Tom wrote – *You had better take me, for you will not find a more efficient fellow anywhere.*

The manager laughed. 'Pattle, I am greatly taken with you, and although a friend of mine has asked me to take in his son at no salary at all [Tom did not believe that, but just smiled blandly], I am giving you the position if you want it. The salary is seventeen shillings and sixpence per week.'

It was not much, hardly enough to live on, but Tom accepted without a moment's hesitation. It would at least keep him occupied until something better turned up.

Tom had to do a bit of salesmanship, clerical work and fix up refrigerators which came in for repair. He also had to drive himself round the reef in the firm's van, collecting payments and doing a bit of canvassing. This brought him into contact with several companies and ultimately led him to the Sheba Gold Mine at Barberton. Towards the end of 1933 there occurred a vacancy in the assay office at the mine, and Tom was given the job.

He liked the work immensely and would probably have made a great success of assaying had he stuck to the job. He was kept very busy, which helped the days to pass quickly and pleasantly, but was not overtired when the day's work was done, and was often able to enjoy a game of tennis. After a few weeks he was elected secretary of the company's tennis club and found this to be a great mental stimulant. The surface of the court was in a very bad state and Tom had to find ways and means of getting the court in a decent condition with the minimum of expense. He was assured by the manager of the mine, Mr Mitchell, that the company would give the money to have the court put in order provided that the members of the tennis club showed enthusiasm. They were enthusiastic enough about playing tennis, but not so enthusiastic when it came to paying subscriptions or attending meetings. At first Tom was lenient ... asking, cajoling, pleading. Then he decided to exert his authority in the interests of the club. He stuck up a notice at the court 'Members Only'. It opened a few eyes and Tom was able to collect some long overdue subscriptions. He followed this up with a list of rules which, together with his own exuberant enthusiasm, soon gained the respect of all the members – and a cheque from the company for the relaying of the court.

Besides the ordinary routine assaying, which he found extremely interesting, Tom did much chemical research work in the laboratory. His own boss, Mr Lee, the reduction officer, began to teach him analytical work and this came in very useful when the company decided to build a swimming pool for its employees. The water for the pool was to be pumped from an old mine and a sample of it was sent to Johannesburg for analysis, to see if it was fit for swimming. Tom took a sample himself and analysed it just to see how his results compared with the expert results of the analytical chemist from Johannesburg.

He did very well. Of course, there were a few substances in it of which he had never heard; for instance, he had found ammonia, whereas the expert had found ammonia and three other compounds of it, but in spite of this the percentages were almost identical. Tom was very proud of his efforts.

The tennis, swimming, and the work in the open air kept him very fit, and although he had not grown any taller, he had broadened considerably. At his mother's suggestion he began to rise an hour earlier each day in order to do a few physical exercises. His fitness and endurance were tested to the full one weekend when he went hunting with a friend. They walked for twenty-five miles without seeing a single buck, and returned to Barberton, thoroughly disappointed at about 9.30 p.m. They could not sleep in a strange bed that night, and so the two of them decided to walk the ten miles back to their quarters at Sheba. The hills were steep and each one resembled the next, with the result that they soon became hopelessly lost. They wandered around the hills all night, their packs becoming heavier with each stride, before the sun rose and they eventually arrived at Sheba at 7.15 a.m. The two of them were in such good trim, however, that after an hour's sleep they were both able to play tennis for the rest of the morning, and then enjoy a couple of hours in the swimming pool in the afternoon.

Tom thought less and less about flying as the time passed with no further news from the Air Force; after a very encouraging talk with Mr Mitchell, he had almost made up his mind to study for a mining degree, when something happened to revive his obsession with flying.

One day an aeroplane landed at the mine in order to collect some samples of ore, which were required in Johannesburg rather quickly. Tom, who had never been so close to a real aeroplane before, was fascinated as he slowly walked around it again and again, his deep set grey-green eyes, sparkling with excitement, taking in every little detail of the weather-beaten and rather flimsy-looking biplane.

'Would you like a flight?' a voice inquired behind him, and Tom turned to face a tall, good-looking young man, wearing a brown flying helmet, and swinging a pair of flying goggles in his left hand.

Tom nodded. He was too astounded to speak.

'Okay, son. Jump in.'

The flight lasted about half an hour, but it seemed only a minute or two before they were once more on the ground. For days, weeks afterwards he could think of nothing else ... the smell of the petrol fumes, the wind whistling through the wires, the propeller spinning like a huge Catherine wheel, the people and the huts on the ground becoming smaller and smaller, and then disappearing altogether as the filmy white mass of a cloud enveloped the plane, the sun glinting on the wing tips ... over and over he relived the ecstasies of that flight, and more determined than ever to achieve his goal, his whole being longed for an opening into this wonderful new world.

A new military unit known as the Special Service Battalion had been formed in South Africa, mainly through the efforts of Oswald Pirow, the Minister of Defence. Its aim was to enlist school-leaving youngsters who were unable to find jobs, and to discipline and mould them into trained cadets capable of being absorbed later on into the regular services of the Union.

When Tom heard about the SSB he thought this might be a possible door into the South African Air Force, and at the beginning of 1936 he relinquished his rather lucrative position as assayer to become a cadet in the SSB at the meagre pay of a mere 'bob' a day. He soon found it was a hard-earned shilling, with few opportunities for leisure from the time he rolled out of his bunk for Reveille at 5.30 a.m. until Lights Out at 9.30 p.m. Physical training and drill kept him fully occupied during the mornings, whilst the afternoons dragged with 'spit-and-polish'. Every little piece of equipment had to be shined so that he could see his own reflection in it. Rifles, bayonets, boots, buttons, plates, water bottles, everything had to undergo the constant attention of the Brasso rag and the elbow grease. Even the blanco and polish tins themselves had to be relieved of their coat of paint, and rubbed and rubbed until they gleamed.

After tea the time was officially the cadets' own and they could do as they wished; Tom always found plenty to do, as did all the other cadets.

Washing and ironing took up part of the time and then there was always some special item which would be selected for inspection the following day. One day it would be rifles, the next tunics and kit. Another day the cadets' feet would be thoroughly inspected to make sure they were standing up to the strain. At weekends the cadets finished early, because there was a weekly inspection, and they had to have the time to scrub out the barracks and put out their kit. Then the Colonel would arrive, the cadets standing at the foot of their beds with a shirt in one hand and a pair of socks in the other. As the officer passed along the avenue of clean laundry each cadet jumped to attention and bawled out his name and number at the top of his voice.

In spite of the monotonous and continuous strain of the training, Tom was prepared to put up with it, even to make himself enjoy it, provided it would lead to his becoming a flyer. But it soon became obvious to Tom that few if any of the cadets were going into the Air Force. Most of them were posted to the artillery, and the rest were returning to the Special Service Battalion as instructors and NCOS. A note of despondency crept into Tom's letters, but as usual his mother was kind and understanding, and for ever a source of comfort and inspiration to him.

In 1935 the Royal Air Force began its long-overdue expansion scheme. At long last the growing danger from the rapidly expanding forces of the dictators of Germany and Italy had penetrated the density of the politicians' minds, and only two years after preparing a disarmament plan the nation's leaders decided that the strength of the Royal Air Force, at this time numbering approximately 30,000 officers and men, should be trebled within the next three years. The announcement inviting young men with school certificate or the equivalent to join the finest service in the world went out to the newspapers, and eventually found its way into the South African editions. Thus one day in March 1936 Cadet Tom Pattle picked up the *Johannesburg Star* and read with increasing excitement the great news. At once he picked up pen and paper and wrote to the Recruiting Officer requesting an interview.

A week or so later he met Mr Rockie, the Recruiting Officer, who gave him all the details about the Royal Air Force's short-service commission scheme. Of course, he would be expected to make his own way to London, where he would have to pass a medical examination and get accepted by a Selection Board, but Mr Rockie assured Tom that he was just the sort of person the Royal Air Force was looking for, young, keen to fly, intelligent, extremely fit, and with the necessary academic qualifications. Furthermore, the Royal Air Force was particularly keen to obtain pupil pilots from the Empire. He would be given a commission straight away with a salary of £25 per month, plus an allowance for uniform. The short-service commission was for a duration of four years and after that he could either go into civil aviation or be absorbed permanently into the Royal Air Force. At the end of the four years he would receive a gratuity of £600, and undoubtedly he would be offered a job as an instructor in the South African Air Force. He would have the topmost fellows in the Royal Air Force backing him, and would receive the finest training in the world. If by some remote chance he failed the medical examination when he arrived in London, Mr Rockie told him they would almost certainly be able to fix him up with some job which would enable him to be near aeroplanes.

It took Tom less than a minute to make his decision. No matter what his chances of success were in South Africa, he told himself, he would be a fool not to accept this offer. He might never get the opportunity again. As for failing the medical examination, or not getting past the Selection Board, well he would worry about that when the time came. He filled in the application form, and signed his name with a flourish.

By the time he returned to the camp at Roberts Heights he had calmed down a little and realised there were several obstacles to be overcome. He was still a member of the SSB and the only way out of that would be to purchase his discharge. Then he had to find the money for his fare to England. He counted his savings ... nearly £5 ... that would not go very far! There was only one thing he could do. He sat down and wrote:

Mom Darling,

I simply must go over. I am writing to Uncle Sam [Brailsford] to see whether he can. manage to fix me up with a job on a boat. If I could get a boat I reckon about thirty pounds ought, to be plenty to see me through and anything I have over I could return.

Mom, couldn't you possibly manage it? I know how hard-pressed we all are and if it can't be managed I'll give up the idea. But it wouldn't take me long to get on my feet there and I could return it all.

Tom.

P.S. I'm going to the Royal Air Force even if I haven't got a penny in my pocket. I'm going to put the Pattles in the limelight again.

His mother as usual gave him every encouragement and the necessary capital to purchase his discharge from the SSB, as well as a few extra shillings to make sure that he did not go short of anything. Her brother, Sam Brailsford, a senior official in the East London branch of the Union Castle Line, bought his ticket and booked a berth for him.

On the last day of April 1936 Tom boarded the SS *Llandovery Castle* at East London and set sail on his great adventure. Although his tangible possessions, comprising one suitcase and a letter of introduction to the Air Ministry, were not much to look at, they were supplemented by Tom's own great faith in his ability to do well in the profession for which he and his family had sacrificed so much.

2

Training

When the *Llandovery Castle* arrived in London, Tom hurried along to the house of Charles Colbourn in North London. Charles was a fellow South African from Keetmanshoop, who had emigrated a few years earlier, on retiring from his post with the South African Railways. He and his family had settled in London and now welcomed Tom with open arms, eager to learn the news of the folks back home. Tom enjoyed the company of the Colbourns and quite naturally soon linked up with the sons Basil and Cecil, who had been his chums at Keetmanshoop School. During the next couple of years Tom enjoyed the hospitality of the Colbourns quite frequently.[1]

Within twenty-four hours of his arrival Tom was at the Air Ministry in Whitehall with his letter of introduction. He filled out an application form and was told that he would receive further instructions by post. He went back to the Colbourns, passed away the time by reading a number of books about aviation from one of the local libraries, and by making the rounds of the aerodromes in the southern counties astride the pillion of Cecil Colbourn's motor-cycle. After a week of impatient waiting for the postman, he could stand it no longer, and hurried round to the Air Ministry to make a few inquiries. He was politely but firmly told that his 'application was receiving attention through the usual channels and that in due course he would be informed'. It was about a

---

[1] Cecil followed in Tom's footsteps at the outbreak of hostilities by joining the Royal Air Force. He became an observer and was attached to No. 15 Bomber Squadron. His aircraft was shot down over Holland during the night of 18 May 1940 and Cecil was killed instantly.

fortnight later before he was requested to attend for interview, by which time he was looking around for a job to supplement his meagre resources, which were fast disappearing.

Dressed in his best flannels and sports coat and resolved to put up a good show, Tom arrived in good time for his interview. He sat down and turned the pages of an old edition of *Flight* as he nervously awaited his turn. His heart beat faster, and his mouth dried up as the minutes ticked slowly away, but outwardly he looked cool, calm and collected, a characteristic which was to prove of inestimable value to him later. After what seemed like hours, yet in actual fact was less than ten minutes, his name was called and Tom entered the room where his fate was to be decided. He sat down on what was to him a rather uncomfortable chair facing a large elliptical mahogany table at which were seated several impressive-looking Royal Air Force officers glittering with gold braid, and three rather stern gentlemen dressed in immaculately tailored suits. An Air Vice-Marshal in the centre of the group, who was apparently acting as Chairman of the Board, opened the interview by welcoming him, introducing him to the other members, commenting on the 'healthy tanned appearance of this undeniably enthusiastic youngster who has come all the way from South Africa', and concluded with the assurance that he hoped Tom would not feel nervous, because the Board were there, not to catch him out, but to help him make a career of the Air Force, providing Tom had the necessary ability, interest, attitude and intelligence to make a success of it. He asked Tom to give the Board an outline of his career to date and to explain why he had come so far to join the Royal Air Force. Tom told them briefly and modestly, but with increasing confidence, the highlights of his life. As he concluded he wondered why he had been asked this question, because he could see that each member of the panel had a copy of the application form containing all this information. He did not realise until later that it was purely and simply a tactical move employed by the Selection Board to help each applicant to get over the initial nervous tension which quite naturally was prevalent in most youngsters attending for interview. It worked perfectly on this occasion, since by the time he had completed his outline Tom had settled down, and was ready, able and willing to answer the questions that were fired at him from all angles across the table. There was a brief pause and then the Air Vice-Marshal spoke again.

'Thank you very much, Mr Pattle, for answering our questions so readily. I think we are all agreed that we can offer you the opportunity of training to become a pilot in the Royal Air Force. You will be receiving an official confirmation of this within the next few days, together with further details of where and when you will carry out your training. Congratulations and good luck.'

The Civil Flying School at Prestwick in 1936 was merely a rather large grass airfield with a couple of hangars to house the Tiger Moths, and several wooden huts of varying sizes which served as quarters for the trainees and the staff. The flying instructors were all civilian pilots employed by Scottish Aviation Limited, who ran the aerodrome. At this time there were many of these Civil Flying Schools directed by the Air Ministry for the initial training of pilots, principally because the Royal Air Force had not enough flying schools of its own to cope with the increased numbers of trainees being accepted under the new four-year short-service commission scheme.

The First thing that happened to Tom on arrival at Prestwick as a pupil pilot on 29 June 1936 was that he acquired a nickname. To avoid the possibility of having to explain that the M T was short for Marmaduke Thomas and envisaging some leg-pulling over the Marmaduke, he introduced himself as 'Tom Pattle, but most of my friends call me Pat'. It was a name which was to stick throughout his service career, although to his family and friends in South Africa he would always be Tom. For the purposes of our story, I shall follow the example of the Royal Air Force and henceforth refer to him as Pat.

Most of the trainees of No. 3 Course were English. Pat was the only South African, and this fact made him very self-conscious at first, because he thought that the English chaps had the edge on him as far as education was concerned. This was possibly a blessing in disguise, however, for he studied more conscientiously than the others, and as a result when they wrote their first examinations Pat came out top, with 99 per cent for Gunnery and Bombing, and 91 per cent for Airmanship.

Flying was simply grand. He would have been quite happy cruising around in a Tiger Moth above the clouds for the rest of his life. To him it was a sport, the finest sport in the world, and he would never regret taking it up. He did well right from the start. Four days after his arrival at Prestwick he was due to go solo after only four and a half hours' dual instruction. But unfortunately the Chief Flying Instructor had to take up all pilots first before they could go solo, and he was away in London. On the Monday morning, exactly a week after arrival and with only six and a half hours of dual instruction, Pat experienced his first introduction to the clouds alone. He had the second shortest time out of the whole of the twenty-eight trainees.

After that his instruction went forward fast and furiously. Plenty of hard work was the order of the day at Prestwick. The trainees were being rushed through their training at a terrific pace and anybody who could not keep up the pace had to go. This did not worry Pat, who quickly mastered all the intricacies of flying. He liked aerobatics best of all; loops, rolls, inverted flying, flick rolls, stall turns, half-roll off the top of a loop – it was all great fun and gave him a new kick out of life.

He was duly presented with his 'A' Licence, which meant that he was now a qualified pilot, and he considered it to be the best birthday present he had ever received – the fulfilment of a long, long dream.

Towards the end of July he went on his first cross-country test, and experienced for the first time the trial of flying alone in bad weather. He had to fly from Prestwick to Turnhouse aerodrome near Edinburgh and back again. He set off in high spirits, but after about twenty miles ran slap bang into a fairly big storm, which tossed his little Tiger Moth about like a cork on a rough sea. He could hear his heart beating as he lost sight of the ground. Soon the rain was pouring down so heavily, and the clouds had become so dense, that he could not see even the wing tips. He was on the point of turning back; but then, rather than admit defeat on his first cross-country flight, he determined to carry on flying by compass alone. At the moment when he estimated that he should be over his destination he closed the throttle and glided down. At about 500 feet he broke through the clouds and saw the aerodrome about two miles off his port wing. He was as pleased as punch and that helped him to make a perfect three-point landing. When he jumped out he was greeted by a fellow trainee who had taken off about half an hour earlier, so he felt very glad he had not turned back. After all, he reasoned, a Pattle could not accept defeat where another chap had succeeded.

Actually flying in rain and cloud was not such a big ordeal as Pat had thought and much later, as his experience of flying grew, he came to regard it as very elementary and simple. But at the time – this was the first time he had ever been out of sight of his own dear old aerodrome – it had seemed to be quite an undertaking. 'I felt something like a little fledgling leaving its nest for the first time and meeting up with old Poppa Hawk,' he said.

A few days later he made another cross-country flight to Abbotsinch, this time without undue incident, and was fascinated by the sight of the huge cranes in Brown's shipyards, where the *Queen Mary* had been built, and where soon her sister ship the *Queen Elizabeth* was to be laid down.

The course at Prestwick lasted for two months, at the end of which the trainees had a series of examinations on the Theory of Flight, Air Navigation, Airmanship, Rigging of Aircraft, Engines, Aerial Photography, Administration, and Armament. Pat passed each examination with ease.

As for his flying, the confidential report by his instructor was by far the best of the entire course. It said that *he is a fine aerobatist*, that *his air sense is highly cultivated*, and that *this coupled with an exceptional use of the controls should make him an outstanding service pilot.* How true that forecast was to prove!

The official report on his character summed him up as: *A quiet young South African of the better type. Is very conscientious and has a determination above the average.*

Pat now became an acting pilot officer and went off to No. 1 Depot at Uxbridge to collect his uniform and to do a fortnight's square-bashing.

Early in September he began his flying training proper at No. 10 Flying Training School at Ternhill in Shropshire. This consisted of two squadrons, the Initial Training Squadron (ITS) and the Advanced Training Squadron (ATS), each of which was split into two flights containing thirty pupils. The candidates, if they were successful in passing all their examinations, spent one term of three months in the ITS, and then three more months in the ATS. This system, of course, led to great rivalry between the two squadrons, and the Station Commander, Group Captain Darley, utilised this to good purpose in organising numerous sporting activities. Soon after the arrival of the new course Group Captain Darley arranged a boxing tournament, as a direct result of boisterous mêlées in the mess between the new-comers and the Senior Term. All those not taking part were promised fatigues, so naturally everyone put down his name to have a bash. Pat was drawn against an officer from the ATS by the name of Thewles; knowing very little about the rules of the noble art, he advanced to the centre of the ring when the gong rang; when Thewles extended his gloves for the handshake, Pat promptly floored him! It was then explained that the idea was to touch gloves before battle commenced. The gong went again. This time Pat walked from his corner smiling an apology, and eager for a firm handshake to show there were no ill feelings, whereupon Thewles touched his gloves and knocked Pat down. There is no record of the eventual result of the fight.

One night there was a fire in the camp. The officers' quarters, for some unknown reason, went up in flames and were completely destroyed. Unfortunately it happened on the officers' night out and, with most of the trainees out of camp, very little was salvaged. Pat lost practically everything except his service uniform and the clothes he was wearing. The trainees were placed in temporary quarters until a new mess could be built and for a time were rather cramped. The long barrack-room, inside which eighteen of them were billeted, was large enough only to take a bed and a washstand for each. There were no cupboards or wardrobes, in fact nothing in which to keep one's clothes – what clothes were left – and Pat's few remaining belongings reposed in a drawer under his bed. All his books and notes had also been lost in the fire, so for several weeks Pat was very busy making out new notes, and swotting for the first of the examinations taken early in November. He was amply rewarded for his efforts by scoring 98 per cent for the Engine examination, 96 per cent for the Meteorology test, and 95 per cent for Applied Mechanics.

Pat had very quickly realised that on the first few months of his training depended his whole career. He was trying for a distinguished pass or even a special distinction, as he knew he would then stand a splendid chance of getting a permanent commission, as well as being relieved of writing a promotion examination in a year's time. He knew that if he could obtain either of these averages he would automatically be promoted to flying officer without any fuss or bother later on.

Brains were not enough, however, as a Royal Air Force pilot must excel in many practical subjects, too – in fact, the academic subjects formed only a fraction of the total marks. In addition to theoretical knowledge, 500 marks were allotted for flying, 500 towards ability as an officer, 250 to drill and discipline, 250 to ability on the range – that is the handling of guns, shooting at targets and dropping of bombs.

After the usual Armistice Day parade, the trainees were dismissed and given five days' leave. So Pat travelled up to London to stay with the Colbourns. He had very little money to spare, having to provide about £100 to replace the things he had lost in the fire – though he hoped that the insurance would cover this – and because of this and the cold and wet late autumn weather, which he was experiencing for the first time, he spent most of his leave either eating, sleeping or reading.

On his return to Ternhill he studied harder than ever, and his flying improved by leaps and bounds until fog kept the aircraft grounded for three weeks. Then Pat went down with a dose of influenza. Eventually a fine day rolled along and the trainees were rushed through their final flying test. Pat, still feeling far from well, was told that he was first on the list. His own particular aeroplane was being overhauled, so he had to take a strange one, with the result that in the words of his own instructor, 'Pat did not do as well as I had expected.' The Chief Flying Instructor, Squadron Leader Bowen-Buscarlet, who put him through the test, seemed quite pleased, however, and gave him an assessment of *Above Average.*

The Initial Flying Training Course came to an end in December, and Pat finished third with an average of 88.5 per cent – a special distinction pass. He was duly presented with his pilot's wings and thus, according to the very high standards of the Royal Air Force, he could now classify himself as a fully qualified pilot. He felt that he had really achieved something, though he also realised that he still had much more to learn in the important Senior Term.

Pat spent the first week of his Christmas leave at a house only twelve miles from Ternhill. His hostess was a Miss Harrison; she mothered him to such an extent that he almost felt himself at home again; he had a wonderful time. The house was a magnificent affair with sixty-eight rooms run by a staff of twenty-six servants. It was Pat's first experience of high society and he found it extremely interesting. Every night there was a party with many young guests and Pat never once had a dull moment. Miss Harrison was Master of a local Shropshire pack of hounds and invited Pat to join in, but he declined politely and followed the hunt lying at ease in the back seat of the family Rolls-Royce. Christmas dinner was all that he had expected an English Christmas dinner to be. There were about thirty guests and it was really a gay affair, in the true spirit of the festive season.

The lavish attentions of his hostess made Pat feel a little homesick. It had not occurred to him before that it would be in all probability at least four years before he would be able to see his family again. He began to feel very much alone in the world. The excitement and glamour of the first few months had overshadowed this feeling, but now that he was away from flying, though only for a short period, he realised that four years can be a very long time.

He was glad when his leave ended and he returned to Ternhill to the Advanced Training Squadron. This was run just like an operational squadron, except, of course, they were still in training. Now his time was fully occupied with his flying and his ambition to achieve that special distinction pass.

Pat normally only left camp on Wednesday afternoons or weekends, when a crowd of trainees usually went into the nearest large town, Shrewsbury, which was barely sixteen miles away; then he did nothing worse than see a film or watch a play. On the whole he found life out of camp rather dull, when compared with the excitement of flying.

When there was no night-flying he was usually to be found in the mess playing games or generally fooling around in the traditional Royal Air Force manner. Most of the trainees went to bed early and Pat was no exception, for, like all the trainees, he was very tired after being up in the air for a few hours. He began to appreciate the stamina required by the record-breaking flyers, Amy Johnson, Bert Mollison, Alan Cobham and a dozen others, whose names were constantly in the news at this particular time. Pat was not unaware that flying could be dangerous, as well as exhilarating, though like most pilots he never thought a great deal about it. During February 1937, however, the perils of flying were brought home rather forcibly, when there occurred two crashes, although on each occasion the pilots escaped without even so much as a scratch. The first accident happened during night-flying training, and as Pat was on duty on the flare path at the time, he saw the whole thing. The aircraft was undershooting badly and the pilot, instead of opening up his engine until he was within gliding distance of the aerodrome, tried to stretch his glide. The inevitable happened – the plane lost flying speed, stalled and tumbled fairly heavily to the ground. The pilot was ticked off for his foolish action and, as Pat said, 'he fully deserved it'. This incident was only one of many which soon convinced Pat that a high percentage of flying accidents are caused by lack of common sense on the part of the pilot. Every pilot who has gone solo should realise that he cannot take chances when near the ground.

Pat's flying was now so good in comparison with the other trainees that his Flight Commander, Flight Lieutenant Pearce-Harvey, told him that he would probably be selected to give an exhibition of aerobatics to entertain the Air Officer Commanding on passing-out day at the end of term; because of this he had to put in extra practice in order to put on a good show. On one of these practice flights the danger of taking risks in the air was again rather forcibly brought to his notice. He was flying at 6,000 feet, which is 4,000 feet higher than the minimum height allowed by regulations, and was doing an upward roll with the nose of his Gloster Gauntlet pointing straight up to the heavens. When he was halfway round the engine conked out from petrol starvation; the speed required for the stunt – over 250 miles an hour – had put too much drag on the fuel system. The machine immediately stalled and the propeller stopped dead, as there was no rush of air to keep it rotating. As soon as he managed to get the plane out of the stall Pat pushed the control column forward and dived in an attempt to get the propeller turning again. With such a high-compression engine it took some diving, but finally the airscrew starting turning and the engine fired. Pat pulled back on the stick, levelled out, and then suddenly realised that he was down to 2,500 feet. He hardly dared to think what would have happened if he had been practising at the minimum height of 2,000 feet.

During March the trainees should have gone to the Armament Training Camp at North Coates, but owing to the persistent showers and the heavy flooding which resulted the camp was under 6 feet of water, so they were redirected to the AT Camp at Penhros in North Wales. They flew there in a mass formation of thirty-four aircraft, with Pat leading the fighter group, which consisted of five Gloster Gauntlets.

Pat thoroughly enjoyed the fortnight's stay at Penhros for several reasons. For a change, the weather was kind and there was a spell of spring sunshine which made the hills of North Wales seem more beautiful than ever. The friendly local Welsh villagers who knew everyone by their first name reminded Pat very much of the people in Keetmanshoop, although he was very surprised when he heard them conversing in their native Welsh language. For some unknown reason he had always thought the language obsolete.

As far as the work on the range was concerned, he felt very satisfied with the results – he easily obtained the highest scores. Many of the instructors were surprised at his astonishing marksmanship with the aircraft's front guns; his percentage of hits was higher than the scores of experienced pilots from some of the crack fighter squadrons. Flight Lieutenant John Davies, the gunnery instructor recorded:

Pattle was a phenomenally good shot. Most of the trainees were very indifferent performers and the airmen stationed on the range had very little to do in the way of patching holes in the air-to-ground front-gun targets; but Pattle was the exception and the airmen used to pretend to curse whenever he was on a detail, because he used to cut the target to shreds as he got such a high percentage of hits with the bursts he fired. Quite apart from his skill as a marksman, he was also a well above average pilot.

On returning to Ternhill the trainee pilots received their assessments. Most obtained an *Average*, a few received *Above Average*. Pat was rated *Exceptional* for flying and *Exceptional* as a navigator-pilot; he was the only one of the fighter flight to achieve such a high standard.

Pat was not a natural born pilot, who felt perfectly at home in an aeroplane the first time he grabbed the joystick – he himself did not believe there were such pilots. His success he attributed to the fact that he had worked extremely hard during the past year and, as he said in a letter to his mother,

... because I left no stone upturned in an endeavour to improve my flying. In spite of past failings I really have followed in the foot steps of 'Percy Verance' this time. You see, mom, I do not want you to feel any misgivings in my suddenly trotting over here. I realise that I threw up a good job with sound prospects to dash over here on a short course of jour years with nothing definite afterwards. I know perfectly well that is an angle a mother would take. To get a permanent commission I will have to continue working just as hard and even then I cannot be dead

certain. But I'm willing to tackle the job. I am not brilliant and my success proves what it has meant to me taking what I sometimes wonder if you ever term, 'this wild escapade'.

He got his distinguished pass all right, but was a little disappointed when the Air Officer Commanding expressed a wish that there should be no flying display when he came for the passing-out inspection.

He received his orders to report to No. 80 Fighter Squadron at Henlow, but before going there he returned to the Colbourns for a short leave, during which he wrote a letter giving his impressions of England and comparing them with conditions in his native land:

FOOD – Very much the same. Miss rice and South African fruits such as pawpaws and mealies.

WEATHER – Gets me down. When bad weather, i.e., fog and rain persists for several days I feel terribly homesick and swear lustily at the cruelty of fate. Have you ever heard: 'Oh to be in England, now that April's here?' Poet ought to be in a mental hospital.

PEOPLE – Very friendly and easy to get on with except the 'Old School Tie' type – cannot stand them. Have one with us and kick him in the pants regularly every day. The true aristocracy are a great crowd. Our Commanding Officer is an earl – a great sport.

INTELLIGENCE – I think they have less. They think I have less. Quits!

PLACES OF INTEREST – Country abounds with them. Too many to prove interesting. Impossible to see everything without having Graecian stamina, so usually do not see any at all. Wide open spaces trumps every time.

ENGLISH TOWNS – Too dirty. Too many people. Streets far too narrow. Buildings interesting and varied. Too much smoke – no horizon, even on a comparatively clear day. Cafés better than in South Africa, but coffee always lousy. Country towns are terribly backward as far as modern improvements are concerned, even in comparison with South African small towns. Good tarred roads even to smallest villages.

DRESS – Less conservative than South Africans. Wear what they like here especially at Oxford and Cambridge.

3

Fighter Squadron

Pat thought himself very lucky when he joined No. 80 Fighter Squadron. It was not a new squadron, having been originally formed in Scotland in August 1917, but it had established a fine reputation during the closing months of the First World War in France, under the able command of Major Bell. Soon after the Armistice it had been disbanded, but now it was re-forming at Kenley as a unit of No. 11 Fighter Group. Within a few weeks it was transferred to Henlow in Bedfordshire, where Pat joined it with two other pilots from Ternhill FTS, Sergeant Brett and Sergeant Pond.

The squadron was still in the process of formation, having only a nucleus of seven officers from Nos. 3 and 46 Squadrons, and forty airmen who had been posted *en bloc* from No. 17 Squadron. But from the very beginning Pat sensed that it was going to be a fine squadron. There was a spirit of keenness that had not been present at Flying Training School; this was even noticeable amongst the airmen. The discipline from the start was first-class. Flight Lieutenant Oliver, who was acting as Squadron Commander, and the other officers, Gordon Jones, Algy Schwab, Percy Oldroyd, 'Old Man' Evers-Swindell, Terry Webster, and Jones-Bateman were all regulars, young and inexperienced, but keen and ambitious flyers who very quickly commanded respect from the airmen. The ground staff responded by keeping the squadron's aircraft in spotless and perfect condition, and by doing their other tasks in a most efficient manner. Pat decided that it definitely had the makings of a crack squadron.

Compared with training days, however, squadron life was rather lazy.

28

The atmosphere was more relaxed and one was generally left to one's own devices. Because they were not yet fully equipped, there were few rules and regulations to be obeyed and the pilots could more or less come and go as they wished. Pat did very little each day, apart from occasional flying, but this did not upset him unduly, because he consoled himself with the thought that things would improve as soon as they settled down. After all, they were just filling in time really until their new Commanding Officer was appointed and their few outdated Gloster Gauntlets were exchanged for more modern aircraft.

For the first few weeks all Pat's flying was either in formation or solo aerobatics. He practised so assiduously that very soon he felt that he could do most of the stunts with his eyes shut. He frequently did, too, for owing to the high speed of the planes he flew he often blacked out when doing a steep turn or pulling out of a dive. It was a queer sensation, only the eyes being affected. One went completely blind for a few seconds. For instance, when doing a roll off the top of a loop Pat sometimes blacked out when pulling up for the loop and only came round just in time to see the horizon in front of the nose before he turned right side up again. This blinding, although alarming at first, was only temporary and had no permanent effect on the eyes.

Squadron Leader P. S. Blockey – soon to be known throughout the squadron by the nickname of 'Papa' – arrived to take command of 80 Squadron on 19 May 1937 and, before the end of the month, many more new faces were to be seen in the mess. The squadron also began to re-equip with the Gloster Gladiator, which was the newest and fastest fighter in squadron service with the Royal Air Force at this time.

A development of the Gauntlet, the Gladiator was the last of the biplane fighters. Designed by Mr H. P. Folland, it had several ultramodern features, including a sliding cockpit canopy and a streamlined undercarriage with a new type of oleo leg. It was extremely manoeuvrable and very light on the controls, and consequently was an excellent machine for aerobatics. It also had another quality which soon endeared it to all pilots who flew in it. Most aircraft, however well designed, always seemed to have some fault, but the Gladiator appeared

29

to have no vices at all. It was a true thoroughbred, the descendant of a long line of single-seater fighters designed and built at the Gloster Aircraft Company. A Bristol Mercury Mark IX 800 hp engine, which turned a two-bladed wooden propeller, gave it a maximum speed of just over 250 mph and enabled it to cruise at around 200 mph. It could climb to 15,000 feet in about five minutes, and reach its absolute ceiling at 32,000 feet. Its armament consisted of four 303 machine guns. Two guns were situated in the fuselage firing forward through the path of propeller blades; the propeller was protected from the bullets by means of an oil-controlled interrupter gear. Two more guns, which also fired forward, but outside the arcs of the airscrew, were mounted in blisters under the lower mainplanes. In 1937 the Gloster Gladiator was probably the best single-seater fighter in service with any air force in the world, but within a year it was to become sadly outdated with the appearance of the new monoplane fighters, the Supermarine Spitfire and the Hawker Hurricane, which were already undergoing a thorough testing, before being produced in ever increasing quantities.

Pat went up for his first flight in a Gladiator one fine morning towards the end of May. There was no dual control on a single seater, so he listened intently to the few words of advice offered by the flight lieutenant who had already been checked out on the Gladiator. He put on a new flying helmet with a microphone buttoning across his mouth and listening apparatus fitting snugly around his ears. He adjusted his oxygen mask and when he pulled down his flying goggles all that remained visible of his face was the tip of his nose. He practised taxiing first, and when he had satisfied himself that he knew where all the controls were and how they worked, he decided to try a take-off. He did not have to obtain permission to take off from the control tower, but he had to obey the rule of taking off on the left and landing on the right of the airfield; he also had to make sure that there were no other aircraft landing or taking off. Having satisfied himself on these points, he opened the throttle, loosed the brakes and, as he gathered sufficient speed, gently pulled back on the control column, rising gracefully into the cloudless sky. The Gladiator handled very much like the Gauntlet, except that it had a more powerful engine, so he had very little difficulty in turning and managing a good three-point landing. He flew several more times during the day and before dusk had mastered the aircraft and was able to throw it about with ease. The following day Pat painted the family crest and motto at the side of *K 7913*, which was the number of his brand-new silver fighter. He would have liked to have added the squadron badge, which consisted of a gold bell in the middle of a white circle with a thin blue edging, but could not do so because the crest had not yet been approved by the College of Heralds.

The Squadron moved to Debden in Essex in June, and Squadron Leader Blockey, determined that 80 should be the finest squadron in Fighter Command, soon had all the pilots hard at work at squadron training. This was more like it, thought Pat, and enjoyed his flying tremendously. Although the least-experienced pilot in the squadron, his flying was so good that he was very quickly acknowledged to be the best formation pilot in 'B' Flight.

On the ground he shared with the other commissioned officers the duties of Officer in Charge of Night Flying and the Watch Office, and he was also the Messing Officer. These routine chores kept him fairly busy and he always seemed to be running about on some job or other.

Periodically mock air raids were carried out on London by Royal Air Force bombers, and the fighters had to go up to intercept them, using camera guns instead of the real thing. The squadron took part in their first combined exercise in August, and for the purposes of the exercise had to move temporarily to Duxford. It was all very exciting.

The pilots gathered together in the crew room, and when the signal to stand by went they rushed out to their waiting Gladiators lined up on the tarmac and got them started with the aid of their hardworking groundcrews. They taxied into position, took off in threes and joined up into an immaculate close squadron formation as they circled over the airfield. They were tuned in by radio-telephone to the aerodrome and received information from the control room as to where and when to intercept an incoming raid. The Commanding Officer, Squadron Leader Blockey, immediately acknowledged the information, and led his squadron to the sector given, where they all split up into sections and flights and patrolled up and down at different heights, keeping their eyes open for the approach of the bombers. Once the enemy was sighted the order to form *Line Astern* would be given over the radio-telephone, and the pilots would then line up behind the leader and dive down one by one to the attack.

Unfortunately things did not turn out quite like that in practice. They patrolled the sector without spotting the enemy and finally had to return to the airfield as quickly as possible, doing a very tight circuit and side-slip landing in order to save fuel – and to make sure that they could land on the airfield should the engine cut through lack of fuel. Altogether during one day Pat put in five hours' flying without once making contact with the enemy force. Most of it was in formation, which made it extremely tiring, and by the time the pilots were released for the day Pat felt like turning in early. Before he went off to sleep he heard that London had been badly bombed. He turned to his room-mate Percy Oldroyd and commented: 'It just goes to prove how difficult it is to prevent an aerial attack on the capital.'

Percy nodded and remarked: The defence of London is not as perfect as some people blissfully believe.'

The exercise lasted for a week altogether, and in the official summing-up was described as *very successful, a large number of interceptions being made.*

Soon after returning to Debden the squadron suffered its first accident; Pat's room-mate Percy Oldroyd was involved. Percy had taken off in a Hawker Hart, with one of his groundcrew, Aircraftman Isaacs, as a passenger, to fly to Northolt to pick up some three-lobed gun cams for use with the new three-bladed propellers. It was a lovely summer afternoon, but it also happened to be a Wednesday afternoon, which was regarded by all and sundry as an afternoon of complete freedom. Percy did not want to waste time and landed the Hart rather too near the hangars. As soon as he touched down Percy realised that he had misjudged the distance and would finish up in the Watch Office. He therefore opened the throttle, pulled back hard on the stick and managed to stagger into the air once again. Unfortunately he was unable to gain sufficient height in time, and flew the Hart on to a hangar roof. Neither Percy nor his passenger were hurt in the crash, though the Hart looked in a very sorry state. Isaacs, undoubtedly shocked by the accident, hurriedly evacuated the rear cockpit and, in his anxiety to reach terra firma again, jumped from the roof of the hangar and broke both of his legs. Poor old Percy, who waited patiently for a ladder to make a safe descent, had his leg pulled unmercifully for several days afterwards, not to mention a ticking-off from Blockey.

The Gladiators flew to West Freugh to No. 4 Armament Training Camp for annual shooting practice in September and Pat for the first time used four guns simultaneously. He was astonished at the results, since the targets were torn to shreds after only a few rounds had been fired. He wondered what would be the effect when the new eight-gun fighters, the Spitfires and Hurricanes, came into squadron service with the Royal Air Force. Some of the Gladiators, including Pat's, were equipped with a new reflector sight, but several minor technical details went wrong and the results of the firing practices were only fair. Later, when they reverted to their old sights, the shooting improved, and once more Pat was able to give a display of first-class marksmanship. When firing at the square canvas ground targets he used the methods which had been proved time and again since the first strafing raids in the Great War of 1914-18 – dive on the target, come in very low and hold your fire until the very last moment. In this way he was usually able to get an almost 100 per cent score.

With the air-to-air firing tests he was more unorthodox, employing his own method of sighting and firing. When the towing aircraft approached with its drogue billowing out 1,000 feet astern Pat would fly to meet it head-on, but at a slightly greater height. As it passed by he would roll over and dive towards it from the side and rear. Normally this would mean that he would have to use deflection, the art of aiming in front of a moving target in order to obtain a hit. Deflection shooting entailed the calculation of the speed of the target, making an allowance for one's own speed and direction of attack, and then deciding the exact moment at which to open fire. This was all very well in theory, but in practice the drogue usually went past the sights in a flash with no time to make all these complicated calculations. Pat never made any calculations, at least not consciously; he fired instinctively, as he had been taught by his father many years earlier. He did, however, remember and put into practice one golden rule that had been handed down by the great flyers of earlier times – get in close and do not fire until the very last split second. This enabled him to do very much more damage to a target with the least possible amount of ammunition, an asset which was to prove of extreme value to him on operations.

In October, Pat was made Adjutant of the squadron, in which capacity he was a sort of secretary to the Commanding Officer. The aim of an efficient Adjutant is to cut down the paper work for the Squadron Leader, to deal with many squadron matters such as correspondence, orders, leave, postings, promotions, charge sheets and so on, and to leave to the Commanding Officer only those things which need his signature or a decision which has to be made by him.

Pat was kept extremely busy and sometimes the work piled up at such a rate that he did no flying for days on end. Squadron Leader Blockey had such a high opinion of Pat's capabilities as an administrator that he sometimes left details to Pat to which he normally would have attended himself. Pat found himself remaining in the office long after duty hours, clearing up correspondence and making out orders. During November his flying time dropped to half his usual number of hours. Squadron Leader Blockey quickly noticed this and told Pat that in future he must put flying before his duties as Adjutant. They soon organised a system whereby Pat could carry out his work efficiently and at the same time still do plenty of flying.

It was not long before the unfortunate Percy Oldroyd was in trouble again – another crash, although it was not his fault. Pat and Percy and two others were practising formation flying at the time and were making a circuit of the aerodrome preparatory to landing. Suddenly Percy broke formation and dived away in a steep turn. Pat, realising that something was wrong, immediately broke as well and followed him down. Percy's Gladiator flew in a wide spiral, losing height all the time, until it eventually crashed in a field. Fortunately he managed to get the machine more or less on an even keel just before hitting the deck and his crash was converted into rather a heavy landing; the Gladiator finished up between two trees which folded the wings back on both sides of the cockpit. The Gladiator was written off, but Percy suffered no personal damage, apart from a severe shaking up.

There was a Court of Inquiry over the accident and it transpired that an insulator had broken away from the aerial and jammed the starboard aileron, with the result that Percy had no lateral control over his aircraft. If he had been flying at a greater height, he might have been able to clear the jam, but as it happened so low down, he did very well to get the Gladiator down in one piece. He was completely exonerated from any blame for the accident, although he had to put up with a few witticisms from his comrades. But they had to admit to themselves that this was a case in a million and that they all had good reason to thank Percy because, as a result of the crash, all the aerials on the Gladiators were modified so that this sort of thing could never happen again.

Pat went off to the Colbourns for his Christmas leave, but had only been there long enough to enjoy the Christmas festivities when a telegram arrived recalling him to Debden. When he returned he was met by Squadron Leader Blockey, who informed him that Fighter Command had given instructions to draw up various plans which, in an emergency, were to be brought into instant operation. The strictest secrecy had to be maintained and consequently only the Commanding Officer and Pat, as Adjutant, knew anything about it. Naturally the other officers got suspicious at the sudden activity in the office, and Blockey and Pat had quite a difficult time in trying to put them off the scent. All sorts of rumours were going round the camp and Pat was very glad when at last Blockey was able to pass on the news to everyone. Pat paraded the squadron one morning in March 1938, and handed them over to Blockey with a snappy salute. The Commanding Officer stood the flights at ease and proceeded to give them a lecture on discipline for about fifteen minutes. He ended his talk and was just about to hand the squadron back to Pat, when as an afterthought he added: 'By the way, the 80th sails for Egypt at the end of April!'

The ensuing excitement was terrific and it took an hour or so to get everybody back to work again.

Pat himself was tremendously excited about the move and looked forward to it immensely. Not only would it be one more country for him to visit, but he would be much nearer home, and he hoped that either his family would be able to come up to Egypt to see him, or that he could perhaps spend a leave in South Africa.

The squadron was a beehive of industry for the next fortnight, as they prepared to depart. Officers and airmen arrived daily from squadrons and training schools, were supplied with tropical kit and suffered the consequences of the inoculation needle. In a week the personnel had been doubled and the squadron had become completely self-contained, with medical, accountant, and equipment staffs. The aircraft strength was brought up to forty-two Gladiators, which were all modified for tropical service and fitted with the new Browning machine guns, a big improvement on the old Vickers. The Gladiators were thoroughly overhauled from top to bottom, back to front, oiled, greased, cleaned and polished until they were spotless and gleaming silver in the pleasant spring sunshine. Then they were flown to the packing depot at Sealand, dismantled, packed into crates and loaded into the holds of a transport vessel, where they were joined a few days later by the forty-six motor vehicles allotted to the squadron. By 30 March, Squadron Leader Blockey was able to report that Air Ministry Expansion Scheme 'F' was complete, and the officers and airmen proceeded on embarkation leave.

Pat took his last look at England from the seat of his motor-cycle. Perhaps the poet had been right after all – it was pleasant in the country in the spring, especially as he would soon be on his way to his own continent. He was happy and proud. Happy because he was doing what he had always wanted to do – fly an aeroplane. Proud because he belonged to a fighter squadron, not just any fighter squadron either, but No. 80, the only fighter squadron to be sent overseas, charged with the most responsible task of defending the Suez Canal.

When the squadron returned from leave on 28 April one face was missing – that of Percy Oldroyd. He had suffered another crash, this time in a motor-car, and was lying miserably in a bed in Uxbridge Hospital contemplating his bad luck. Eventually he left the hospital and was posted to another fighter squadron, where he enjoyed a much happier time, having apparently left the gremlins in hospital.

The squadron, complete to the new establishment, paraded at Debden for the presentation of the squadron badge by Air Chief Marshal Sir Hugh Dowding, GCVO, KCB, CMG, Air Officer Commanding in Chief Fighter Command, and then boarded a special troop train for Southampton. Early the next morning, 30 April 1938, they sailed on H.M. troopship *Lancashire,* bound for the Mediterranean and Ismailia.

4

The Middle East

Ismailia was a pleasant little town, with open-air cafes and many little bars. The European part of the town and the main shopping centre was well laid out with attractive trees planted at intervals along the pavements, and there were scores of good shops in the many small side streets. The native quarter, however, was a complete contrast, filthy, stinking to high heaven, with dirty, straggling mud huts bundled together and domestic animals wandering inside, outside and all over them. Around the town for as far as the eye could see stretched the wilderness of the desert. It was quite different from Pat's expectations, for there were no sand dunes and palms. It was dead flat, an immense waste ground consisting of yellow grit, hard smallish stones, sand and, here and there, a patch of spiky camel thorn. At the edge of the town was the Royal Air Force station, which was in the process of being reconstructed when 80 Squadron arrived, so for the first fortnight they had to manage with temporary accommodation. Until the building operations were complete all the pilots spent most of their time at the United Services Club, a large bungalow surrounded by trees and overlooking Lake Timsah. It had everything; a bar, showers, changing-rooms, and an enormous lawn which stretched right down to the edge of the lake. But the best thing about it was that everything was free, or at least one did not need any money; at the time one just signed for a book of tickets – the cost of the book was then added to the mess bill at the end of the month.

When the squadron moved into its new quarters each of the flights was allocated a separate hangar for the servicing and maintenance of its aircraft, a flight office where all records of flights, fuel and equipment were kept, an armament workshop and office, and a maintenance store, so that for the most part each flight was a self-contained unit which could, more or less at a moment's notice, be packed up and moved out on detachment into the desert. No. 80 was a mobile squadron, which meant that, in an emergency or in time of war, all the flights would be pushed off into the desert and controlled by the squadron headquarters, which would remain at Ismailia.

As soon as the flights were acclimatised to the new flying conditions which, owing to the reduced density of the air over the hot, blistering sand, were slightly different from England, they were sent out on detachment, so as to acquaint themselves with life in the wilderness.

As Adjutant, Pat did not belong to any particular flight and normally would not have had the opportunity of experiencing such conditions. However, realising that this would be extremely valuable experience, especially in the event of war, he badgered the Commanding Officer to such an extent that finally Squadron Leader Blockey allowed him to give up his duties as Adjutant and take three other pilots and the necessary ground mechanics into the Western Desert. Pat was made Officer Commanding the detached flight, whose job was primarily the patrolling of the frontier between Egypt and Italian-occupied Libya. They had also to act in liaison with a flight from a bomber squadron which was making an aerial survey of the district.

Pat and his flight existed in the desert for six weeks. The torrid heat of the day caused them to perspire until their shirts and shorts were clammy and wet, turning the clinging sand into a muddy paste and attracting every fly and insect from miles around. By way of a change, some days it was cooler, but then the wind picked up the sand and dust and deposited it in a film over everything, including the food. Sleep seemed out of the question as the wind howled across the desert wastes and tore at the flaps of the tents. Some of the airmen contracted desert sores, patches of raw flesh which were impossible to protect from the sand, and others went down with 'gippy tummy' and fever, but nevertheless their morale remained at a high standard throughout the ordeal, much of it undoubtedly due to the example set by Pattle. He had realised that the success of any mission depended on the officer in charge and the response he obtained from his men. This mission convinced him that the men would respond to any demand put upon them provided they could see the necessity for it. Subsequently he always showed a great interest in the men he commanded and was ever aware of their welfare requirements.

The detachment, having accomplished its allotted tasks successfully in spite of the trying conditions, returned to Ismailia towards the end of July. A few days after their return Pat had to make a forced landing. He was testing the flaps on his Gladiator, flying at a height of 50 feet, when the engine suddenly spluttered and stopped. The aircraft struck the ground rather heavily and bounced back into the air. The impact with the earth restarted the engine, and Pat was able to open the throttle and continue his flight. He decided that he had better get down as quickly as possible, before the engine packed up again. He completed one circuit of the field, approached the aerodrome and was just about to put down when much gesticulating from the ground personnel warned him that something was wrong. He opened up the engine, climbed up over the control tower and got into touch with his radio-telephone. The Commanding Officer's voice came clearly through the headphones:

'Blockey to Pattle. Don't look now, but your port wheel is missing!'

There was an ominous silence for a few seconds as Blockey waited for the news to sink in; then his voice, still clear, but quiet and reassuring, once more came through the headphones:

'Blockey to Pattle. Keep calm and keep on flying until you exhaust the main fuel supply. Keep within sight of the aerodrome, because you will have to glide in without the aid of your engine.'

Pat acknowledged that he understood and proceeded to fly around the airfield until he had used up all his petrol. He knew this would minimise the risk of fire when he did land, but at the same time it also meant that he could not use his engine if he got into trouble with his final approach. He continued his circuits and watched the excitement going on below. Airmen and pilots were rushing around, making sure of a ringside seat at the side of the runway, whilst the soldiers who were stationed at the nearby Army Garrison all gathered around the perimeter of the aerodrome to obtain a good view of the landing. The soldiers were there to see the crash, but the Royal Air Force personnel, knowing that it was Pattle who was flying the crippled Gladiator, were there because it promised to be a superb display of flying skill. They knew Pattle and they had complete confidence in his ability to land the aircraft safely.

Pat had about an hour before his petrol gave out, so he had plenty of time to figure out how best to make the landing. A crash seemed inevitable and, as he saw the ambulance manoeuvre into a handy position, he had visions of lying on an operating table and spending weeks in a military hospital.

At last the engine spluttered and then stopped: the moment had come. He switched off, turned and approached the aerodrome in a fairly steep dive to keep up his airspeed and prevent the aircraft from stalling. He judged his speed and height perfectly, concentrating hard on the control stick and holding it well over to starboard to keep his port wing up. There was a slight bump as he touched down and he felt the Gladiator running along the ground, balanced on its two remaining wheels by his slight but skilful movement of the controls. The Gladiator rolled almost to a standstill before there was a lurch, as the wing finally dropped and the port oleo leg dug into the ground.

Pat calmly unbuckled his straps and climbed out of the cockpit, to be met by a cheering crowd of pilots and airmen. He felt awfully shy, as they gathered around him.

'It was an amazing piece of flying,' commented Pilot Officer John Lapsley. 'The only damage to the machine was that the tips of the propeller blades were missing, and the fabric was torn off the tip of the bottom mainplane.'

Pilot Officer Jimmy Kettlewell agreed: 'It was a perfect touch-down, the finest landing any of us had ever seen.'

Later in the day, after the damaged Gladiator had been repaired, Pat took off again and completed his testing. He was able to report that Gladiator *K 8009* was in perfect flying condition.

Within a few days Pat was on detachment again, this time with Pilot Officer Pete Wykeham-Barnes, two Gladiators and five ground-crew members. They went to Palestine and were stationed first at Samakh, a small landing-ground on the southern shores of Lake Galilee. The Arabs had started a rebellion and the Gladiators were there to co-operate with the ground forces of the army against the rebels. The work consisted mainly of message-dropping and reconnaissance, although Pat and Pete were occasionally called upon to machine-gun rebel positions or drive off the Arabs when they attacked convoys on the roads. For the first time Pat realised what a lethal weapon a Gladiator could be. The four Browning guns poured a shower of lead in the direction of the enemy and there was not much chance for the poor Arab if he was selected as a target, especially when the guns were under the expert control of such excellent marksmen as Pattle and Wykeham-Barnes. On the other hand, the Arabs themselves were extremely good shots. They had been taught all about deflection by Lawrence of Arabia and they used their knowledge with expert skill. In four engagements during one week three Royal Air Force aircraft were brought down by their accurate Fire. On another occasion, when an assortment of twelve bombers, Fighters and reconnaissance aircraft were sent off on a mission, nine of them had to force-land, having received bullets in the engine or fuel tanks.

Pat and Pete were lucky, for although their Gladiators received their fair share of bullets during these engagements, they were never seriously damaged and were always able to fly safely back to their own landing-ground. However, Pat soon had to make another forced landing, though this was not due to action taken by the Arabs. It happened on 12 September when he was searching for some native policemen who had been driven from their post at Zuweira by Arab tribesmen. When he arrived over the area he discovered that the police were already back in their fortifications, but were expecting another attack. He was just about to drop a message to them when the engine started giving trouble. There was another plane formating with him and, rather than risk flying back to the nearest aerodrome which was fully fifty miles away, beyond a wilderness swarming with Arabs, he

42

landed in a valley in full view of the other plane. Unfortunately the ground was covered with small, jagged pieces of granite which cut the tyres of the Gladiator to ribbons and smashed the tail-wheel. The situation was certainly not very pleasant. The police post had just informed him that the enemy were located only about two miles away and all Pat had to comfort himself was a service revolver and fourteen rounds of ammunition. The Gladiator was useless, in fact, if anything it was a thorough nuisance as it stood there like a well-planted landmark, inviting attention from the rebels. The other plane had set off for home, so Pat had nothing to do but wait until help arrived in the form of three Arab policemen. After about two hours, during which he imagined he saw Arabs behind every boulder, he saw two aircraft approaching. He had not expected help from the air, because the ground was not suitable for landing. While he looked on helplessly, one of the planes came in to land. Fortunately it was fitted with extra large desert tyres and a tail-skid, so the rough ground could not do much damage. No sooner had it landed than the other plane, a Hawker Hind, which had orders to fly around and keep the rebels away, also came in to land. Pat tried to wave it off, because he knew the Hind was equipped with very thin wheels and a rather flimsy undercarriage, but it was useless. Immediately the wheels struck the ground the undercarriage folded up and the Hind went over on to its nose. It was carrying a dozen bombs mounted in racks under the wings. They were scattered all over the terrain. Not one of them exploded, which was fortunate for both the pilot and observer, who scrambled hurriedly out of the wreck and dashed over to join Pat and the occupants of the Fairey Gordon.

They inspected Pat's Gladiator and decided that the Gordon would have to fetch some spare parts. The bomber attempted to take off, but it was a massive old machine and it did not have the necessary power to clear the surrounding hills. The pilot throttled back and managed to put it down on the side of a hill, without doing too much damage to it.

Now they really were in a mess. Three useless aircraft and their crews stuck in the middle of Palestine, in an area which was infested with rebel Arabs.

By means of the wireless/telegraphy set which was one of the few things that still worked on the crashed Hind, they managed to contact headquarters, who were not at all pleased with the situation.

The pilot of the Gordon was a flight lieutenant and therefore the senior officer; he had to decide what to do. He was a stout-hearted type who did not want to risk losing the three aircraft; he gave orders that the married fellows would be sent to the police post, which was about two miles away, whilst he and Pat and another pilot officer would remain to guard the planes. After the others had disappeared the three officers and the three Arab policemen built themselves a small emplacement from the numerous boulders strewn around, dragged the Lewis gun from the Hind and mounted it in a satisfactorily commanding position in the centre of their dug-out. Then they sat down to await developments.

When the sun went down the policemen packed up and went back to their camp. They absolutely refused to stay outside after dark. So Pat and the others took it in aims to do sentry duty through the night. Not one of them expected to see the sunrise again and they were all dead scared, but they were determined to carry out their orders in spite of their fears. As if by instinct no one mentioned the word 'Arab' and they never once spoke of the predicament they were in. They talked of everything under the sun except Palestine and the Arab rebellion.

At about half past one they heard a body of men approaching from the direction of the police post. They knew that a detachment of the Black Watch was being sent out in armoured cars, but hardly expected them much before dawn. The flight lieutenant yelled a warning as the shadowy mass came closer to the emplacement and all three flyers breathed a sigh of relief as the reply came back in a broad Scots accent. The detachment consisted of thirty kilted soldiers armed to the teeth. So Pat and the others were able to sleep fairly comfortably for the rest of the night. The much-talked-of attack did not materialise after all and Pat actually felt a little disappointed.

The next morning the soldiers cleared a runway for the Gordon and this time it managed to get off safely. Orders were then received from headquarters to fire the Hind and abandon the Gladiator, as the district was considered too dangerous. Pat was bitterly disappointed. After all the trouble he had gone to in looking after his plane, he now had to leave it. He knew it would not survive another couple of hours if it was abandoned, and for some time he seriously contemplated trying to take off on bare wheels. However, the elevator was too badly damaged and he quickly realised that he could not keep it in the air even if he managed to get it off the ground.

He left the area in an armoured car, taking one last look at his plane in the valley a mile away. It looked so forlorn and lonely standing beside the burnt-out wreckage of the Hind. Pat never saw it again, for it was fired by the Arabs soon after he left.

The whole of the way back to Jerusalem Pat and his rescuers were sniped at from the hillsides. Armoured cars were not designed to provide much shelter for the passengers and judging by the sound of some of the bullets, they came pretty close. About fifteen miles from Jerusalem they ran into a scrap. Pat soon picked out Wykeham-Barnes in the other Gladiator swooping down on the rebels. Seeing him in action and hearing the rat-tat-tat of his machine guns made him feel very proud of the Royal Air Force. It seemed to take the army ages to sort itself out and decide what to do, but once they had worked out their method of attack they did not waste much time. Pat grabbed a rifle and went charging up the hillside with the Black Watch soldiers yelling Zulu war cries. They fairly rushed the remaining Arabs off their feet. Very few shots were fired and most of the rebels were taken prisoner. An hour later Pat was in Jerusalem, still brandishing the rifle and bayonet, which he was allowed to keep as a memento of the time he joined in a charge made by the famous Scottish Regiment.

Within a few days Pat and Pete were recalled to the squadron, but by the time they reached Ismailia, the rest of the squadron had moved. A state of emergency had been declared because of the crisis in European affairs over the cession of the Sudeten province of Czechoslovakia to Nazi Germany.

Using four Vickers Valencia troop-carrying aircraft from No. 216 Squadron and the station motor transport, 80 Squadron, hilly equipped with aircraft and personnel, had moved to their war base at Amriya in a little over twelve hours. When Pat and Pete caught up with them they found things quite different. The squadron had been put on a full war basis; all aircraft had been camouflaged and the squadron crests replaced by code lettering; the guns were all filled with live ammunition.

Amriya was not a proper Royal Air Force station such as Ismailia, or Helwan. It had been an aerodrome in the First World War, used for the training of Australian pilots, but was now almost derelict. There was one large wooden building which had been recently repaired and this was used by the officers both as a mess and a dormitory. The food, however, was quite good and there were hot showers. Many of the pilots preferred to sleep in the open air, although it became quite chilly after sunset and there were hordes of persistent insects who stung and bit throughout the night.

All personnel and aircraft were constantly at Readiness or Standby. This was done on a rota system with one flight at Readiness and two flights on Standby. When at Readiness the aircraft was on the landing area, the pilot sitting with parachute and Mae West fastened, his radio switched on and ready for instant take-off. There was a fleet of over twenty naval vessels in Alexandria harbour and they would have to give aerial protection to these; if the pilots did have to take off they knew it would be up to them to hold up any Italian attacks until reinforcements arrived.

The European situation looked grim. Everybody hung around the radio in the mess each evening listening to Daventry and discussing the Sudeten problem at great length. There were a number of wild speculations as to what the solution would be. Pat personally thought *Alles Sal rig kom* – a 'this can't happen to me' sort of feeling.

Chamberlain waved his piece of paper at London Airport after his meeting with Herr Adolf Hitler in Munich, declaring 'Peace in our time', and things returned to normal. The aggrieved Sudeten Germans came under the protection of the Führer, and 80 Squadron flew back to Ismailia.

In December 1938 Squadron Leader Blockey was posted to the Royal Air Force Staff College, and Squadron Leader R C Jonas assumed command of 80 Squadron. All the pilots were sorry to lose Papa Blockey, because he had been a first-rate Commanding Officer who had seen the squadron through its early trials and had moulded it into a fully competent and efficient squadron. 'Jonah', who had come from No. 29 Squadron at Debden, was to prove an equally good Commanding Officer; capable, conscientious and determined to build on the good foundations laid by his predecessor.

Soon after Jonah's appointment it was decided by higher authority to transfer the squadron to Helwan. Pat welcomed the change and so did everybody else in the squadron, because now they would be within easy reach of Cairo. They had heard also that there was an excellent club with a swimming pool at Maadi, only five miles from Helwan.

Two bomber squadrons, Nos. 43 and 211, moved to Ismailia from Helwan at the same time and to celebrate the change-over a cocktail party was organised. It started at half past six. There was a bar in the ante-room and tables covered with food; the dining-room had been cleared for dancing. More than 200 guests were invited, including army personnel from the nearby garrison, the staff of No. 4 Flying Training School from Abu Suweir and enough local French girls to make it a splendid show. It lasted until well after midnight.

It was the last late night that 80 Squadron had for some considerable time, for at Helwan they became a relatively dry squadron, with very little drinking and always early to bed. Apart from this, they were back to normal routine with the formation practice every morning and night-flying practice every Thursday just before supper. Pat usually flew along the River Nile, which showed up clearly in the moonlight, reflecting his lights on its smooth, silvery surface.

All the officers automatically became members of the Gezira Sporting Club in Cairo. There was polo and horse-racing, but neither of these had a great attraction for Pat. He was more interested in the swimming pool and the tennis courts. He had bought a big American car secondhand, an Auburn, firstly because he considered it was a real necessity, secondly because cars were so cheap both to buy and to run, and thirdly because he was now a flying officer and could afford one.

Frequently he went into Cairo, usually with Jimmy Kettlewell or Old Man Evers (Evers-Swindell), where they would do a little shopping, have tea at the Continental Savoy on the terrace overlooking the street, and end up with a pleasant bathe in the swimming pool at the Gezira Club.

On one occasion he went up to Cairo with Kettlewell, and after their usual routine Pat pulled the Auburn into a filling station for petrol. Egyptian garage proprietors were noted for not being over-honest in their dealings and Pat was always very careful when doing business with them. He checked the petrol, decided that he had been given short measure and politely said so. The wily Egyptian denied the accusation, but Pat refused to pay the full price. They argued vehemently for several minutes. Pat offered what he considered a fair price for the petrol, but the other pushed the money away, shouted and demonstrated, and finally jumped on to the bonnet of the car. Pat, still outwardly calm, decided that he must be taught a lesson. He jumped into the driving seat, started the engine, put his foot down and never gave the man a chance to get off until they reached Helwan, some thirteen miles away. Pat's punishment, although harsh, was very effective; he never had to complain about short measure again.

'Summer dress' came into operation on 1 April and the pilots and airmen changed into khaki drill clothes, reminding Pat of his scouting days. A week later the squadron began its summer exercises, for which purpose it moved out to the desert station at Amriya. The headquarters staff, however, went to Dekheila, where they received information about bombing attacks from a system of strategic outposts. This information was passed on to Amriya, where the pilots were at readiness in the cockpits of their Gladiators from five o'clock in the morning to six o'clock in the evening, except for twenty minutes for breakfast and twenty-five minutes for lunch. When the alarm sounded, usually three short bursts on a machine gun, the planes took off immediately and patrolled over the sea to the west of Alexandria. It was quite pleasant at Amriya at this time of the year, much cooler than at Helwan, with a cool sea breeze. The pilots were comfortable in their cockpits, dressed in shorts and shirts, both on the ground where the sun was hot and pleasant, cooled by the sea breeze, and in the air, where the sun was still quite warm. It was tiring work, though, up in the air four or five times a day, and most of the pilots, Pat included, went to bed immediately after supper, because they would be up again at 4.30 a.m. next morning. The exercises were completed by the beginning of May and the personnel had an easier time, since they only worked during the mornings. It was as well, because it was now getting hotter, sometimes up to 105 degrees in the shade. The Khamsin wind, coming across a thousand miles of desert, was like the blast of air from a fiery furnace and the Gladiators were almost too hot to touch. It seemed unbelievable that the aircraft could stand up to the heat and dust, especially as they were in the open night and day. They were parked in rows on one side of the road that ran right through the middle of the camp; there were no hangars or sheds at Amriya.

Before the end of the month the squadron was once more split up, 'A' Flight remaining at Amriya, 'B' and 'C' Flights returning to Helwan, where they found a new fighter squadron had arrived. No. 112 Squadron had been hurriedly formed in England, and like 80 Squadron had come out to the desert fully equipped with aircraft and motor transport. The pilots were all officers, thirty-one of them altogether, and most were raw kids direct from Flying Training School. It was a bit of a crush for the time being, because there was not enough accommodation for two squadrons at Helwan, so some of the 112 pilots had to sleep on camp beds and to share rooms. No. 80 had already taken possession of the best accommodation.

A week later there were more arrivals. Two lieutenants from the Royal Iraqi Air Force were attached to 80 Squadron for experience of advanced fighter training. They only stayed for a very short period, owing to the fact that they crashed two Gladiators during landing. They apparently needed basic training first!

Pat seemed to have a particularly restless spirit about this time. He was all right during the mornings when there was plenty of flying, formation practice and so on. But in an afternoon when he had not anything in particular to do he just could not sit still. He made innumerable trips between the mess and his own room for no apparent reason. When he got tired of that he jumped into his car and drove aimlessly about for half an hour, still feeling just as restless. Although as a general rule he was very fond of reading, he could not even settle down to that unless it was a book of special interest.

This restlessness soon disappeared when he had to take 'B' Flight to relieve 'A' Flight at the desert station. He was now Flight Commander of 'B' Flight, and in this capacity he arranged a strafing attack on the motor vehicles containing the groundcrews and equipment. He wanted to see how the airmen of his flight responded to such an attack and consequently he managed to lead the road party himself. He detailed three pilots to do the ground strafing and gave orders to the convoy party that as soon as the Gladiators were sighted, the vehicles were to spread out and the Lewis gun crews were to take up positions to repel the attack.

The convoy was about four miles north of Wadi Natran, on the narrow tar-sprayed track which was the main road from Cairo to Alexandria, when the trio of Gladiators appeared. Immediately the trucks shot off the road in different directions and the gun crews jumped to action stations. The three aircraft tore out of the blue in a screeching dive. Then came disaster. The leading Gladiator carried straight on with its dive, bounced off the ground in a ball of fire and exploded into a thousand pieces. The pilot could not have known anything about it. His body was found at least a hundred yards away from his head, which had apparently been severed on impact with the ground. Later it was discovered that a small attaché case, in which the pilot carried a few personal items, had worked itself loose during the dive and jammed the elevator controls.

He was buried next morning, about two hours before Jimmy Kettlewell was married. It is incredible to outsiders how casually the Royal Air Force accepts a death. But it is not callousness; it just has to be done that way so that the squadron can carry on with its duties, unaffected by the influence of any individual.

By the time the wedding had started the pilots had forgotten all about the funeral. It was a quiet wedding in the little English church in Helwan, but afterwards the pilots chased around the streets of the town with a big squadron flag flapping from the top of a car. They held the reception at Jonah's, where Jimmy's girl had been staying since she came over from England. The champagne flowed freely until the supply ran out, so they all drove into Cairo to continue the party. Pilot Officer and Mrs Kettlewell drove off to Alexandria for the honeymoon, whilst most of the others arrived back at Helwan in time for breakfast, which the majority did not in any case want.

'B' Flight returned to Helwan in July, and Pat was soon off to Abu Suweir to collect a Fairey Gordon, which was to be used for general communications and passenger work. It was the first time Pat had been to Abu Suweir and he was most impressed. Every pilot had a room each, with electric fans, mosquito nets and a loudspeaker connected to the radiogram in the mess. The food was excellent, consisting of the usual English dishes, served by Egyptian waiters dressed in white robes, with multi-coloured sashes, and fez. The station was also equipped with a first-rate cinema, an excellent open-air swimming bath, and a fine Officers' Club. Pat thoroughly enjoyed his few hours at No. 4 Flying Training School.

When he landed the Gordon at Helwan he found the pilots in a state of great excitement as a result of orders just received from the headquarters of 'B' Group. Because of the renewed threat of Hitler's ambitions, the whole squadron had been ordered to proceed to Amriya.

On 3 September 1939 mobilisation was ordered.

5

Prelude to battle

At the outbreak of the Second World War, Pat's father immediately joined the Eastern Province Battalion of the South African First Reserve Brigade, the equivalent of the British Home Guard, and was made a sergeant-major, in view of his vast soldiering experience. He had tried to join the South African Army, but much to his regret was classified as too old for active service. He was 55 years old.

Pat's elder brother Cecil also volunteered for active service with the South African forces, but was not accepted. His position in the Special Branch of the Criminal Investigation Department was considered a far more important contribution towards South Africa's war effort.

His mother was matron of the Keetmanshoop General Hospital, in which capacity she served faithfully throughout the war.

Pat was very proud of his family's contribution to the war effort, though he had some misgivings about how much he himself was doing towards the defeat of Germany. At Amriya things went on normally, except that the radio in the mess now used some new words – 'evacuation', 'rationing' – words which seemed quite unreal to Pat. It seemed to him that the squadron was doing no good at all in Egypt, and he could not understand why they had not been sent back to England or to the front line in France. When the inactivity continued he put in an application for a transfer to a fighter squadron in England, but nothing came of it, except that his efforts made him unpopular with the staff of Middle East Headquarters. Pat was not the only pilot in the squadron, however, who wanted action. Nearly everybody had the perpetual blues, because they all seemed to have far too much spare time, which made the days drag.

In order to while away the leisure hours everybody at the station turned to various hobbies and pastimes. The variety in hobbies was an amazing instance of the individuality of the human mind in general and the versatility of the average airman in particular.

One pilot spent his time riding around the aerodrome on a sand yacht made from bits of aeroplane and a derelict car. Two airmen made remarkable miniature petrol engines only about one inch in height and fitted them to model aeroplanes. Another chap collected snakes, scorpions and such like, and soon had a fully inhabited snake park that would have been a credit to many a zoo. One airman turned to sculpture and made a bust which was a remarkable likeness of Hitler, with the appropriate *R.I.P.* inscribed below. Another trained a goose to such effect that it was almost human. Two non-commissioned officers from the motor-transport section bought a chicken one day in Alexandria to put a little extra flavour into their Sunday dinner. Their efforts at fattening it were so successful that they very soon had a farmyard in the middle of the camp, its inmates including turkeys, geese, and poultry of several varying breeds. LAC 'Darky' Howell proved to be an excellent caricaturist and very soon his handiwork was framed all around the officers' mess.

The war also brought forth a producer from amongst the ranks. Flight Sergeant Morris got a few enthusiasts together and in October put on a variety show. It was a huge success, the whole house being in fits of laughter from beginning to end. The masterly way in which the sergeant introduced the comedy acts throughout the show, indicated a latent 'Hollywood' ability. It was decided that the squadron should be likewise entertained every four weeks.

The lesser-talented hobbies included carpentry, miniature golf, kite-flying and photography; Pat took up the last-named occupation, but without much success except in helping to pass the time.

Hobbies and pastimes were forgotten on 25 September, which was a day of great excitement. Flight Lieutenant Fry of No. 112 Squadron flew to the Maintenance Depot at Abu Suweir and returned with a Hawker Hurricane. It was an early type with a fabric-covered mainplane and a badly worn engine, but it was the first Hurricane the pilots had seen. Everybody was delighted when it became known that it had been allocated to 80 Squadron and that others would follow as soon as they became available. It was to be a long time, however, almost a year, before the squadron received its next Hurricane and much was to happen in the meantime.

Squadron training went on as usual and many exercises were carried out during mock air raids on Alexandria by the Blenheim bombers of No. 211 Squadron. Although only training exercises, these mock attacks gave the Gladiator pilots invaluable experience in interception, and many lessons were learned which were to prove of extreme importance when eventually the real thing did come along. For example, the Blenheims were much too fast to allow the Gladiators to make more than one attack; when it was realised that the Germans and Italians also had bombers with a similar or even faster maximum speed than the Blenheims, it became evident that the pilots of 80 Squadron, if they were still equipped with their now out-of-date Gladiators, would have to work out new methods of attack.

The difficulty of sighting the modern camouflaged bomber, especially from above, was also brought home to the pilots, and as a result arrangements were made to carry out extensive practices in searching for, and sighting, aircraft. Pat recalled the importance attached by the pilots of the First World War to seeing the enemy first and quickly realised that this was the key to successful aerial combat. The pilot who saw the enemy first had the advantage of being able to get into a good position from which to make an attack. Pat practised identifying objects at great distances quickly and accurately, so that before long he was always the first man in the squadron to sight the enemy, be it a Blenheim on a mock raid on Alexandria or, later on, a Savoia Marchetti S. 79 attacking Sidi Barrani.

The very elementary and mediocre scientific instalments used by the Observer Corps personnel at this time for determining the position and height of an enemy raid led to great discrepancy in the estimation of the altitude of the attacking machines. Although in many cases raiders were seen, the difference between the estimated height and the actual height of the raiders made it impossible for the Gladiators to catch them; only if they were higher than the Blenheims were they able to intercept. Pat decided that he could intercept and attack faster machines than his Gladiator only by flying higher, much higher, than the raiders; he would then dive and build up his speed, which would enable him to keep up with the bombers at least long enough for him to get in a few bursts of gunfire. This he reasoned, because of his outstanding skill with his guns, would be quite sufficient for him to shoot down the raider.

He put his theories to the test during the interception exercises and was overjoyed to find that most of them worked perfectly well. Whether they would work when the real thing came he would have to wait and see.

On one occasion, towards the end of October, Pat's quiet calm deserted him for once. He was doing a little local flying over Amriya with a box of safety matches in the hip pocket of his shorts. Unfortunately the safety matches were not very safe and ignited themselves. The groundcrews who witnessed the resultant display of aerobatics declared it was the finest exhibition they had ever seen, or were ever likely to see.

The exercises also brought disaster for the squadron. One day in November a section of four Gladiators – flown by 'Imshi' Mason, Charlie Lamb, Sergeant Barker and Sergeant Brett – intercepted a formation of Blenheims about two miles south-east of Amriya aerodrome and split up for a practice attack in pairs. Imshi and Sergeant Barker dived on the bombers from the starboard beam and then climbed up in the hope of being able to make another diving attack from astern. As they swung over the Blenheims, Charlie Lamb and Sergeant Brett came down in a dive, roared past the two climbing Gladiators and attacked the Blenheims from the port beam. Both broke away, but for some inexplicable reason towards each other. There was a blinding flash as the two Gladiators collided. Charlie Lamb's aircraft burst into flames immediately; the pilot was either killed or knocked unconscious, since he made no effort to get out of his blazing fighter as it fell leaving a trail of thick black smoke. The other Gladiator did not catch fire, but descended in a flattish spin. George Brett's legs had been broken in the crash and he was unable to get out of the plane. He pulled his parachute ripcord whilst still in the cockpit, in the hope that it would open and jerk him free, but, although it opened, it soon became hopelessly entangled around the rudder and tailplane. The pilot and the aircraft hit the ground together. Both pilots were buried in Alexandria the next morning.

Flying was curtailed during the winter months as the weather gradually deteriorated. The wind swung round from south-west to north and began to blow stronger, the temperature slowly dropped and there were showers or dust storms several times each week. In January there was mist during the night which thickened to fog at dawn, and frequently the aerodrome was unserviceable, which meant that all aircraft were grounded.

As soon as the weather began to show signs of improvement plans were made for an intensive programme of air-to-air firing. A Towed Target Flight, consisting of six pilots and Five Fairey Gordon towing aircraft under the command of Squadron Leader Barclay, arrived at Amriya and was attached to 80 Squadron for this purpose. The first detail was flown on 19 February, when the Gordon towing its drogue flew over Alexandria on its way to the target area. It must have been observed by a keen-eyed newspaper reporter, since the very next morning, an Arabic daily solemnly reported that *a small Zeppelin yesterday chased a British aircraft out to sea.*

The air-firing tests once again proved that Pat was an outstanding sharp-shooter. Squadron Leader Barclay commented that Pat's scores in both quarter and astern attacks were the best that had so far been obtained throughout the whole of the Middle East Command.

Towards the end of the practice period for attacks from the quarter, which is the most difficult practice of all, since deflection must be allowed for, the highest number of hits to be recorded on the conical target was sixty. Pat was one of the last to fire, and prior to his taking off there was a discussion in the flight office. Sixty was an excellent score for a quarter attack and Flight Sergeant Richens was bold enough to wager a bottle of champagne that this score would not be beaten. An hour later Pat made his attempt and, intent on winning the bubbly, went in even closer than usual before opening fire. He used up all his ammunition and flew back to Amriya to await the arrival of the drogue. Fifteen minutes later the Gordon appeared. It flew low over the aerodrome and released the target, which was gathered up by Sergeant Battle and two armourers, who began to count the holes. They had worked out the score by the time Pat and Richens arrived.

'How many, Sergeant?' Pat asked.

Sergeant Battle beamed. 'I believe Flight Sergeant Richens owes you some champagne, sir. You got exactly one hundred.'

In the spring of 1940 Italy was still officially neutral, but it seemed fairly obvious from her actions that she fully intended to come into the war as soon as the time was ripe, with the object of taking a share of the spoils. If Mussolini openly declared his hostility, he would undoubtedly order his forces in Libya to attack Egypt and try to obtain possession of the Suez Canal. Foreseeing the danger, the British Government sent out troops to reinforce the units already stationed in the area. Consequently during March and April the ground personnel of 80 Squadron was almost trebled, bringing guard duties every eighth night instead of every third. The general efficiency of the technical personnel was greatly increased, as it had been found that the airmen were unable to concentrate on their work in the flights after being on guard duty every third night. At the same time the security of the camp, which had been previously a very difficult problem, was much improved.

Also during April, Wing Commander Pearson-Rogers from Air Staff Headquarters, visited Amriya, inspected the defences and arranged for the complete wiring of the camp. On the same day Flight Sergeant Casey, the Squadron Disciplinary NCO, who incidentally had been at Lieutenant Colonel Smith-Barry's No, 1 School of Flying at Gosport in 1917, was promoted to warrant officer. Soon afterwards, an Indian regiment, the Fourth Battalion of the Sixth Rajputs, arrived to take over the defence of the camp and the aerodrome.

In spite of all these changes, which completely altered the outlook of the station, life went on very much the same. The most significant change as far as the pilots were concerned came when orders were received from Middle East Headquarters to conserve fuel and cut down on flying time. As a result of this, most of the pilots, Pat included, took up golf in an attempt to pass away the extra leisure hours. They soon had the golf craze, and the mess echoed with talk of 'slices', 'greens', 'rough' and all the general golf jargon.

Italy's aspirations, together with the significant changes going on at Amriya, brought a rising hope into the hearts of the pilots. They felt that Italy was now their main hope of getting some definite action and very soon wagers were being made on the date of Italy's entry into the war.

For a few days, however, towards the end of April, Pat and eight other pilots were able to stop their speculations and enjoy a short stay at the Royal Air Force station at Lake Habbaniyah in Iraq. They had gone there with the object of ferrying some new Gladiators from storage, and while these were being assembled, checked and serviced, the nine pilots had plenty of time to benefit from some of the luxuries provided by this most unusual of all Royal Air Force stations.

Situated within a bend of the River Euphrates some fifty miles west of Baghdad, it was more like a large town than an air station. Covering an area of something like four square miles, it contained all the usual buildings of a big station, plus several repair shops, an aircraft depot and over a thousand houses, from luxurious villas to mud huts. It was pleasantly laid out with straight, tarred roads, bounded by masses of flowering trees and patches of emerald-green lawn. Within its perimeter fence the station offered a better selection of amenities for the desert-weary airman than any other place in the Middle East. It had the finest swimming pool in the Royal Air Force, over fifty tennis courts, a golf course, a polo ground, a racecourse, the finest gymnasium Pat had ever seen, and an open-air cinema which showed all the latest films.

In addition, just beyond the perimeter fence, there was Lake Habbanryah, where the enthusiast could either swim, row a boat, sail a dinghy or, if he was of a less energetic nature, lie in the sunshine and watch the big Imperial Airways flying boats alighting on the calm, blue water.

All too soon it was time for Pat and the others to leave. They collected the Gladiators and returned in formation, led by the giant Bombay from No. 216 Squadron which had flown them down. When they landed at Amriya they found the international situation had worsened to such an extent that Squadron Leader Jonas, who had been on leave in Palestine, had been recalled and one flight was required to stand by round the clock for interception.

The Italians were now ferrying hundreds of aircraft through the country and orders were issued by headquarters that, whenever any Italian aircraft was sighted, it was to be escorted to ensure that it kept to the recognised corridors.

On 3 May, Pat was doing a little local flying in the Hurricane, when he noticed six three-engined aircraft flying a few hundred yards off his starboard wing at about the same height. He immediately went to investigate, and as he approached the formation he recognised them as Italian Savoia Marchetti S. 79's. They flew on, keeping to the same course, and still flying at the same speed, so Pat positioned his Hurricane about 100 yards behind the last of the S. 79's, and about 50 feet above it. He escorted the bombers all the way to the border, and then returned to headquarters at Helwan to make out a report.

It seemed that Mussolini was on the point of committing his country to war; the Royal Air Force in the Middle East made its preparations for defending Egypt and the all-important Suez Canal. At Amriya the operations room was manned day and night, complete blackout was brought into force and precautions were taken against sabotage with twenty-four hour sentry duty, aircraft guards and Bren gun posts. One day the Air Officer Commanding in Chief, Middle East Command, Sir William G Mitchell, KCB, CBE, DSO, MC, AFC, visited the station to inspect the defences. He chatted informally with the pilots and the groundcrews, and stayed for tea with Squadron Leader Jonas. He seemed quite pleased with both the spirit and discipline of the squadron, and said the defence schemes were most impressive.

On 22 May, Squadron Leader Jonas led eighteen of the squadron's Gladiators for a massed formation display over Cairo, as a token of reassurance to the people moving about in the streets that the Royal Air Force would be there to guard the city against any bombing attacks by the Italians.

The tension continued to mount with a practice air raid on Amriya. As soon as the alarm sounded everybody donned his gasmask and ran to his allotted station. The pilots dashed for their Gladiators and took off hurriedly, but in formation. The groundcrews made for their dug-outs, the Indian regiment on aerodrome patrol took up defensive positions, and armed tenders roared off to their prearranged points of vantage. Fifteen minutes later the aircraft returned, making a dummy bombing attack in waves of six aircraft, from a height of less than 100 feet. It was an exhilarating test and excellent practice for both pilots and ground staff. Everyone thoroughly enjoyed it, even though it did bring home the full ominous implications of what in all probability would actually be happening with live ammunition in a very short time.

On the evening of 10 June the squadron heard that Il Duce had finally made up his mind, to come out into the open. The declaration of war had been handed to the Ambassadors of Britain and France; at midnight a state of war came into being between Italy and the two countries without whose aid and friendship Italy could never have been united into one state. The squadron was instantly brought to readiness, the guards were doubled, the men armed and the Gladiators loaded with live ammunition. The Operations Book was completed by the Duty Officer. He wrote: *A complete feeling of readiness and calmness prevailed amongst all ranks.*

6

War in the Desert

Pat's first ambition in life prior to the war was to obtain security by making a success of flying in the Royal Air Force, and thereby winning a permanent commission. Now that war had come, like a true patriot, his first thoughts were to do his utmost to defeat the enemies of his country. At the same time he realised that if he could manage to go through the war uninjured, with a good record of victories, a permanent commission would be assured, because there would inevitably be many vacancies and much promotion after the war, even in a much-reduced peacetime Air Force. He was fairly confident about his own ability to do well, provided that he could manage to survive. However, there was an element of luck in war, the stray bullet or shell burst, which meant that a pilot could always be shot down every time he went into action, regardless of his skill or courage as a flyer. Pat was not unduly perturbed by this latter consideration, because there was nothing that he could do about it.

But there were many other things that could be done to improve his chances of success in the air. In the first instance he decided that physical fitness was of primary importance. He could not expect to give of his best in an aerial combat unless his eyesight was perfect, trained so that he was able to see the enemy before being seen. His hands and feet had to be in perfect condition to enable them to work in instant co-ordination with the demands of the brain. His stamina had to be built up to meet the stresses and strains of a dogfight or even a series of dogfights. Although he was probably the fittest pilot in the squadron already, because he did a lot of swimming, smoked and drank only moderately, and was usually early to bed, he also began to do a few physical exercises, including extended practice in training his eyes to pick out minute objects at great distances, which he regarded as being the greatest asset of any fighter pilot.

Next, although no less important, his aircraft had to be in perfect condition. This was primarily the job of his groundcrew, but nevertheless Pat took an intense interest in his Gladiator, so that the engine was tuned to perfection, the controls were in excellent working condition, the guns loaded and well oiled, and the whole aircraft cleaned so that it was spotless. It was to pay great dividends, for whenever the occasion demanded, Pat was always able to coax a few extra miles an hour out of his Gladiator. It gave him those split seconds which meant all the difference between advantage and disadvantage in a combat, split seconds that could mean the difference between life and death.

Pat was not a fatalist, and neither could he be accused of being afraid of the enemy in the air. His caution was the result of his scientifically based reasoning, the same reasoning which had enabled him to obtain his first job, to make a success as the secretary of the Barberton Tennis Club, and to do his aerobatics at flying training school at 6,000 feet instead of the regulation 2,000 feet. It was a reasoning which took into account all the evidence, weighed up the pros and cons, and then came out with an answer which would enable the task to be carried out with the least possible amount of risk.

By the same logical reasoning the squadron's Gladiators were obsolete, sadly outdated by the more modern machines of the Italians, and Pat would have been much happier if the squadron had been equipped with Hurricanes or Spitfires, as were most of the fighter squadrons in England. But what the Gladiator lacked in speed and firepower, was made up to some extent by its excellent manoeuvrability, its robust construction which allowed it to stand up to any amount of battering, be it either from the Regia Aeronautica or the sheer bad-weather conditions of the desert; lastly there was the skill and courage of its pilots, with their background of Royal Air Force training.

At the commencement of hostilities 80 Squadron had twenty-two Gladiators, in addition to the solitary Hurricane, and at dawn on the first day of the desert war three Gladiators flown by Flight Lieutenant 'Tap' Jones, Flight Sergeant Tom Morris and Flight Sergeant Vaughan carried out the squadron's first war patrol west of Alexandria. They returned to Amriya without seeing any enemy planes and were relieved by 'C' Flight, who were promptly told to look out for an enemy aircraft reported to be approaching Alexandria. The enemy plane, a reconnaissance machine flying very high, turned and headed back for Libya, before the Gladiators could even catch a glimpse of it. They were recalled to Amriya, where Pat was just taking off with his 'B' Flight for their first wartime operation. He took them to a position some twenty miles west of Alexandria where they patrolled up and down for seventy-five minutes, hoping to contact the Italians. They were unsuccessful and so were all the other patrols flown by the squadron that day. Evidently Mussolini was in no hurry to risk his intrepid Abbysinian-conquering eagles encountering the men and machines of the Royal Air Force. Or perhaps the odds were not sufficiently favourable yet, since the Italian aircraft only outnumbered the British aircraft in the ratio of about five to one.

The following morning Pat, John Lapsley and Sergeant Casbolt were at readiness in their machines when they were alerted.

'Control to "B" Flight. Unidentified aircraft flying five miles southwest of Amriya at 10,000 feet on an easterly course. Take off immediately and investigate.'

Pat acknowledged the message and looked over his shoulder to see if Lapsley and Casbolt had also received the news. Lapsley, smiling broadly, was holding both thumbs in an unmistakable gesture of affirmation; Casbolt had already waved away his chocks and was pulling the cockpit hood over his head.

Pat opened the throttle, loosed the brakes and rolled over the gritty surface of the airfield, closely followed by the other two Gladiators. The propellers sent a miniature sandstorm over the tents and groundcrews, as the planes accelerated to flying speed. The wind whistled through the wires and the wings vibrated as the tails of the Gladiators rose. Then the bouncing ceased and they climbed away, banking slightly as Pat led them round to head towards the south.

Within a few minutes Pat's sharp green eyes had spotted the raider about a mile away, 1,000 feet lower down and flying across the path of his aircraft from right to left. He shouted a warning to his companions and changed direction slightly so as to converge on the aeroplane, which was still only a speck in the vivid blue sky. As they drew nearer, Pat noticed the sun reflecting from the silvery surface of the aircraft and thought that this was a peculiar colour for a bomber or a reconnaissance machine. A few seconds later he was able to pick out four large letters on the fuselage of the plane – *M.I.S.R.* – and his excitement turned to disappointment as he realised that the aircraft was not Italian after all; it was, in fact, only a large twin-engined airliner of the Egyptian M.I.S.R. Airline Company. The Gladiators returned to Amriya, their pilots bitterly disappointed and thoroughly browned off with what had promised to be an exciting release from their normal routine.

Within a few days Pat and the whole of his flight saw their first enemy aircraft. Unfortunately, they were on the ground at the time, having just returned from an early-morning patrol, and consequently were unable to engage it in combat. The raider, a Savoia Marchetti S. 79, had been first sighted by the Observer Corps heading towards Aboukir, and 'A' Flight led by Tap Jones had taken off in an attempt to intercept it. The wily Italian, anticipating trouble, had changed course several times and as a result the Gladiators were unable to sight it. 'B' Flight's Gladiators were being refuelled and the pilots were making out their reports to the Intelligence Officer when they heard the unfamiliar sound of the Italian bomber approaching from the south. Not being in a position where they could do anything about it, they merely stood and gazed at the large three-engined machine as it passed directly overhead, flying at a great height. The anti-aircraft guns blazed away, but the gun crews had no time to make corrections for height and speed, and their attempts to shoot it down were futile; it disappeared out to sea, flying at maximum speed. 'C' Flight, who were on standby when the bomber was sighted, had immediately dashed to their Gladiators and taken off, but were unable to catch up with it.

As a result of this incident it was quickly realised that the standby flight must be kept readily available at all times and the pilots as near to their aircraft as possible. It would be humanly impossible to keep the pilots inside the cockpits, unless they were at readiness, and they could not be at readiness twenty-four hours each day. Pat came up with the solution one day when he returned from the depot at Aboukir, which was the base where all the stores for the Middle East – from nuts and bolts to aeroplanes and hangars – were kept. He arrived at Amriya with a heavy truck carrying a couple of very large packing-cases, which were dumped, at the aircraft dispersal point. With the assistance of some local native labour, a huge hole was dug in the ground by the pilots of 'B' Flight and the two cases were erected inside it and covered with a layer of sand. It proved to be an efficient and comfortable air-raid shelter and, from the time it was completed, all standby pilots were able to sit or sleep at dispersal, perfectly sheltered from the hot, burning rays of the sun.

One morning, soon after the outbreak of hostilities with Italy, there was a pleasant drone from the west and three Hurricanes and a Hudson appeared out of the morning mist. They came in to make a perfect touch-down at Amriya. The four aircraft had flown from England via the Bay of Biscay, the Gold Coast and the jungles of darkest Africa. They were fitted with special long-range fuel tanks, stripped of all guns and other operational equipment, and forced to fly at the slower cruising speed of the Hudson, which carried the equipment and also acted as an escort in case any of the Hurricanes was forced to make a landing; they would have been easy meat if they had been intercepted by enemy fighters. The pilots of those Hurricanes, members of the Air Transport Auxiliary, were brave and devoted flyers, who were denied the spasmodic excitement of the dogfight enjoyed by the combat pilot, but whose nerves nevertheless were tested to the limit by the constant tension they were subjected to, in flying unarmed aircraft in areas where there was always the possibility that they would meet a swarm of Italian or German fighter planes. They handed over the Hurricanes to 80 Squadron, stayed to sample a sandy-flavoured meal and then returned in the Hudson, by the same arduous route, to carry on with their thankless but most valuable contribution to the war effort.

Before the end of the month more ATA pilots arrived with three more Hurricanes. The squadron was now the proud possessor of seven of these modern eight-gun fighters, and Squadron Leader Jonas decided to form a Hurricane Flight. The officer in charge of 'A' Flight, Flight Lieutenant Tap Jones, was chosen to lead the Hurricane Flight, with Pat as his deputy. The other pilots allotted to the Hurricanes were Flying Officer Jimmy Kettlewell, Flying Officer Pete Wykeham-Barnes, Flying Officer John Lapsley, Pilot Officer Imshi Mason, Flight Sergeant Tom Morris, Sergeant 'Nobby' Clarke, and Sergeant 'Claude' Hulbert.

Pat had mixed feelings about this new move. Although he wanted to fly the new Hurricane, he still wanted to retain command of his Gladiator flight with the people he knew intimately. The members of the new Hurricane Flight were mostly chosen from the old 'A' Flight and although Pat knew them very well indeed, it was not the same as being in command of the pilots whom he had come to regard as 'his' flight. Men like 'Shorty' Graham, Syd Linnard, 'Heimar' Stuckey, Flight Sergeant Richens, and Sergeant Casbolt, who had been in Pat's 'B' Flight for nearly two years. They had become so accustomed to each other's company both on the ground and in the air that they were now a sort of family with Pat as the father and guide. Each, although of different physique, mentality and background, when brought together under the control and direction of a natural leader such as Pat combined to make a perfect team, each confident in his own ability, and each having complete faith in the abilities of the other members of the unit.

Pat's problem caused him to lose very little sleep, however, since it was soon solved for him. The Hurricanes were passed on to another squadron and he returned to his old beloved 'B' Flight. But, in the meantime, the war was going on and the squadron had had its first action and scored its first victories.

Flying Officer Pete Wykeham-Barnes had been sent forward to Mersa Matruh with his Hurricane, for duties with No. 202 Group. He was flying with No. 33 Squadron which, incidentally, was envious of the reputation already gained by 80 Squadron. No. 33 had been the undisputed premier fighter squadron in the Middle East until 80 Squadron arrived to challenge their supremacy, and now there existed a bitter rivalry between the two squadrons, each endeavouring in its own particular style to outdo the efforts of the other.

Pete was patrolling with four Gladiators from 33 Squadron during the morning of 19 June over the desolate wastes between Buq Buq and Sollum, when they sighted a formation of nine Fiat C.R. 42's, Italian fighters of a similar appearance and performance to the Gladiator. The 42's were slightly below and to the port side of the Royal Air Force fighters, who were in an ideal position to make an attack. Pete shot down the leader of the Italian fighters whilst he was doing a vertical turn, with a short burst at full deflection. Two more C.R. 42's were shot down by the Gladiators, but in doing so one of the Gladiators was also hit in the engine and fell in flames, the pilot being killed.

Although the enemy were superior in numbers, they lacked the aggression of the Gladiator pilots and gradually retreated towards the Libyan border. Pete found it difficult to get his sights on the Fiats, because they were so very manoeuvrable, but eventually one of them made a mistake and Pete was able to get in a good burst of shells which caused the 42 to dive away with smoke trailing behind it. He did not actually see it crash, but it was later confirmed as being destroyed by the land forces. The Gladiators and the Hurricane were then forced to break off the combat by lack of petrol and ammunition; on their way back to Mersa Matruh they had to land at Sidi Barrani to refuel and rearm.

Very shortly afterwards Pat had an opportunity to show his skill as a pilot. On 22 June, during the early hours of the morning, Alexandria experienced its first night bombing raid. The Italian bombers came from the west in a clear moonlit sky, with the obvious intention of bombing the British fleet in the harbour. Old Man Evers and Pilot

Officer 'Twinstead' Flower took off from Amriya in an attempt to intercept the S. 79's, and were followed a few minutes later by Pat, John Lapsley and Heimar Stuckey. They headed towards the searchlight beams and the anti-aircraft shell bursts, and sighted one of the bombers caught by one of the searchlights. It disappeared before they could get within half a mile of it and although the Gladiators searched for almost an hour they failed to contact any more of the raiders. The Gladiators had become separated during the search and returned singly to Amriya, where they found the airfield was obscured by a thick mist. Pat alone was able to make a successful landing. Evers-Swindell flew on and landed on a track twenty miles south-east of Amriya. Flower, Lapsley and Stuckey awaited until it was sufficiently light and then landed at Dekheila, returning to Amriya when the mist had lifted. Squadron Leader Jonas flew out to Evers-Swindell, assisted to start the Gladiator, and both pilots returned to Aanrrya at nine o'clock, by which time Pat was sleeping peacefully in his camp bed.

Two nights later Evers-Swindell made the first successful night interception for the squadron. After an alert he took off and was vectored successfully on to the raider. Just as he was about to open fire he noticed the aircraft was decorated with Royal Air Force roundels. Deciding to investigate further before pressing the gun button, he closed in and was astonished when he identified the 'raider' as a Blenheim of No. 211 Squadron.

Pat was becoming rather dejected again. The war with Italy was now a fortnight old and he had still not been given the chance to show his skill as a fighter pilot. He wanted action and, in an attempt to get it, he volunteered to go to relieve Wykeham-Barnes. His request granted, he took off in his Hurricane in high spirits and joined 33 Squadron at Mersa Matruh, which was much nearer the border and therefore the chances of meeting the Italians there seemed to be excellent, particularly as 33 Squadron had been encountering the enemy several times each day. Fate was unkind, however, since as soon as he arrived the weather deteriorated. On several days there were high winds which caused sandstorms and made flying impossible and on the other days the weather, although not sufficiently bad to keep the Royal Air Force fighters on the ground, was not good enough to entice the Italian aircraft into the air. He was not sorry when he was recalled to Amriya – until he jumped out of his Hurricane and heard the news. Whilst on his way back six Gladiators of 33 Squadron had engaged nine Fiat C.R. 42's and shot down seven of them! A few minutes later his own 'B' Flight landed and reported that they had encountered ten Savoia Marchetti bombers north of Alexandria, and had probably destroyed one and damaged another, before the superior speed of the Italian bombers had enabled them to escape out to sea. Pat cursed the cruelty of fate, glared at the 'Perseverance' crest on the side of his plane and stormed across to the operations room to make out his report.

Squadron Leader Jonas left the squadron in July to go to Malta and was replaced by Squadron Leader 'Paddy' Dunn, who was already well known to the squadron because he had been at Ismailia when 80 Squadron were stationed there. A small and tenacious fighter pilot, he was very keen on physical fitness and soon made arrangements for all personnel to take more exercise. Football was organised in the evenings and bathing tenders took the airmen swimming each day. He also stepped up the pace of the flying training, many practices in attacks, formation and night flying being earned out each evening. All the pilots were extensively trained in the newly arrived Hurricanes, carrying out attacks on different formations of Gladiators. After each exercise Squadron Leader Dunn would hold a conference of all the pilots, to discuss the merits of the different forms of attack. His object was twofold. First he wanted to prevent the pilots from becoming demoralised by their inability to come to grips with the Italians – although this was not due to any lack of trying on their part. Secondly he was trying to find the best method of attacking the faster Italian bombers.

Although the Italians made only a very few night raids on Alexandria harbour at this time, two Gladiators were kept at readiness all through the night. When an alarm was sounded Squadron Leader Dunn usually also took off in his Gladiator to try to spot the enemy. One night he slipped his flying kit on over his pyjamas and took off and landed without the aid of a Chance light or the flare path. On landing he asked his groundcrew to fetch his carpet slippers from the rear of the fuselage – he said he had kicked them off because he could manipulate the rudder far better with his bare feet!

Towards the end of the month the squadron was honoured by a visit from Sir Arthur Longmore, KCB, DSO, the Air Officer Commanding in Chief, Middle East, and a few days later Admiral Sir Gerald Cunningham, Commander in Chief, Mediterranean Fleet, passed through Amriya on his way to the front. Immediately rumours of a big push by the Allied armies in the desert began to get around and the pilots looked forward to the prospect of action in the air with great expectancy.

On 29 July, Squadron Leader Dunn sent for Pat, and gave him the gen.

'Since the Italian Air Force has failed to take the initiative, headquarters have decided that we are ourselves going to take the offensive. Consequently we have been ordered to send one flight up to Sidi Barrani, and to carry out offensive patrols from the satellite field there. Tomorrow morning you and I will fly over to Sidi Barrani, and make all the arrangements for the detachment there of "B" Flight. You will leave the Hurricane Flight, which will remain here for the defence of Alexandria, and will assume command of your old flight. In the meantime, make all the necessary arrangements for the transfer of the groundcrews by road.'

7

On the offensive

A cluster of whitewashed mud hovels lay at the end of the macadamised road that ran from Alexandria along the northern coastline of Egypt, surrounded on three sides by the desert, and on the other by the blue Mediterranean Sea; this was Sidi Barrani, the tiny village sixty miles from the Libyan border which was to assume such great importance during the many fierce battles that were fought in the Western Desert.

'B' Flight's eight Gladiators, flown by Pat, Wykeham-Barnes, Cholmeley, Stuckey, Lancaster, Vaughan, Casbolt and Rew, circled over the village and headed for the satellite aerodrome five miles farther south. They landed and taxied towards the assortment of tents which sheltered the ground staff, who had come by road in lorries and jeeps the day before. Although it was early in the afternoon, the hottest part of the day, with the fiery sun blazing down from the cloudless sky, the fitters and riggers moved quickly towards the aircraft. They had already received orders that the Gladiators were to be refuelled and serviced ready for instant take-off. Being acquainted with the offensive spirit of their Flight Commander, they had already guessed that Pat would be anxious to get to grips with the enemy as quickly as possible. They were quite right, too, for within a couple of hours of arriving at Sidi Barrani, Pat was in the cockpit, leading four Gladiators over the desolation of wadis and camel thorn, towards the wire which marked the boundary between Libya and Egypt. Bursts of anti-aircraft fire greeted them, but they were wild and caused no anxiety, so the Gladiators pressed on, searching for Italian aircraft. They followed the wide coastal *autostrada* built by Mussolini's engineers to carry heavy fast-moving traffic towards the Egyptian frontier. They failed to make contact with any of 'Il Duce's eagles of the skies' and Pat was just about to turn back towards the border when his attention was attracted by a cloud of dust moving along the road. Diving down to investigate, he found a convoy of Italian motor vehicles, presumably bringing supplies or reinforcement troops up to the front line. He detailed one of the Gladiators to remain as a look-out in case they were disturbed by Italian fighters, put the remaining Gladiators into line astern and dived towards the transport concentration. He lined up the leading lorry in his sights, steadied the Gladiator as tracer bullets curved towards him from the ground, and pressed the gun button. He saw the lorry slither across the road and Italian soldiers scrambling from the back of it. He flashed over the convoy, instinctively ducking down inside the cockpit as the ground fire increased and tiny holes appeared in the fabric covering of the mainplanes. He climbed away, looked back to see the two Gladiators following closely behind, and beyond them saw the remains of the convoy. Vehicles were scattered all over the road, some lying on their sides, one completely turned over, its rear wheels silhouetted against the sand, its front wheels nowhere to be seen. A few yards away another lorry was blazing furiously, a cloud of dense black smoke ascending vertically above it. Italian soldiers were lying in dozens on the road, and others were scrambling over the sand on either side, trying to find some cover amidst the sand dunes before the Gladiators came down in another blistering attack. They were lucky, however, since the Gladiators were low on fuel; they had already closed up behind Pat and were on their way home.

During the morning of the following Sunday, 4 August, the detachment received a signal from headquarters requesting 'B' Flight to provide four Gladiators to escort a Lysander from 208 Squadron, which was detailed to fly across the border to Bir Taieb el Esem to observe enemy troop movements. Pat decided to lead the escort himself and take with him Pete Wykeham-Barnes, Johnny Lancaster, and Sergeant Rew.

They took off at a quarter past five in the afternoon and within ten minutes had reached the rendezvous point, where they found the lone spotter plane circling at 6,000 feet. Wykeham-Barnes and Sergeant Rew took up a position about 3,000 feet above and immediately behind the Lysander, whilst Pat and Lancaster climbed 1,000 feet higher on the starboard flank, keeping the lower section of Gladiators in full view as they headed towards the border.

The formation crossed the wire twenty minutes later, a few miles south of Sidi Omar, and changed course to follow the sandy track which led directly to Bir Taieb el Esem. Thirty miles inside the border, just as the formation was nearing the target area, the Lysander fired a Very light, signifying that it was being attacked and then headed due east at a low altitude. Pat and Lancaster dived down to find out what was going on, because so far they had failed to spot any enemy aircraft. Wykeham-Barnes and Sergeant Rew had disappeared. A few seconds later Pat heard Peter's voice over the radio-telephone ordering his section to attack and immediately afterwards saw seven Breda 65's, in two separate flights – one containing three aircraft in vic formation and the other made up of two pairs. They were heading east, closing in behind the virtually defenceless Lysander. Before they could get close enough to open fire Pete and Sergeant Rew appeared on the scene and attacked the formation of four Bredas, one of which went down in flames almost immediately. Pat and Lancaster came down directly behind the flight of three and delivered an astern attack. The Bredas dispersed and the four Gladiators became completely separated as they each selected a different enemy machine as a target.

Pat attacked two aircraft which kept close together and turned in a complete circle. As he followed he saw two aircraft spinning towards the desert, each leaving a trail of smoke and flames. One was a Gladiator. A grim determination welled up inside Pat, and his thumb trembled over the firing button, as he was tempted to blaze away at the Bredas, who were now only about 300 yards ahead of him. The wave of anger lasted perhaps for one or two seconds and then his ice-cool brain reasoned that he must get much closer if he was to make certain of hitting them. The Bredas dropped to around 200 feet and each released two bombs, which Pat judged from the explosions must have been twenty-pounders. This was done, he thought, probably to increase their speed and also to affect his aim. In fact, their speed did increase and they very slowly began to creep away from the pursuing Gladiators. Pat was on the point of firing a burst in the hope of slowing down at least one of the Bredas, when quite suddenly they both turned north towards the Italian fighter base at El Adem. Quick to take advantage of the Italian's mistake, Pat cut inside their turn. He closed to within 150 yards and delivered a quarter attack on the nearest Breda. His guns were not working properly, his two port guns ceasing to fire almost immediately. But he had hit the Italian – it slowed down considerably. He swung in directly astern of it and, after a few more bursts from his two remaining guns, saw a puff of white smoke from the starboard side of the engine. The other Breda by this time was half a mile away, and he had not a hope of catching it, so he continued to attack the first Breda, which dropped lower and lower and finally crash landed in a cloud of dust.

Johnny Lancaster had also been having trouble with his guns. After his initial burst all four guns jammed and he spent the next ten minutes frantically pulling his Constantinescu gear pistons and aiming at various C.R. 42's, but without any further bullets leaving his guns. Eventually he was forced on to the defensive and got an explosive bullet in the left arm and shoulder. Because he feared the loss of blood would cause him to lose consciousness, he wriggled out of the fight and with his right thumb pressed tightly against his left radial artery, held the stick between his knees and waggled his way home. In spite of his wounds and the serious damage to his Gladiator, he made quite a smooth landing before losing consciousness. The fitter who came to examine the aircraft shortly afterwards pronounced it too damaged to repair *in situ* and ordered it to be burned forthwith!

The Gladiator that Pat had seen going down belonged to Sergeant Rew, who had attacked the same formation as Wykeham-Barnes. Pete had shot down two of the Bredas, but was then set upon by Fiat C.R. 32's. During this fight his rudder and elevator controls were shot away and he was forced to bale out.

In the meantime Pat had turned towards the border and was attempting, without much success, to clear his port fuselage gun. He was about ten miles south-east of El Adem, when he spotted five C.R. 42's diving towards him from the north-west. He flew on, pretending that he had not seen the enemy fighters, until they were almost in position to open fire and then, with a flick of the wrist and a sharp prod of the foot, shot up and away from the Fiats. It was only a momentary relief, however, for the Italians split up and attacked him independently from all directions. Gradually as the dogfight developed Pat became aware that the enemy was using a set pattern of attack. The Fiats made repeated attacks simultaneously from the quarter and beam, using the speed they gained in the dive to regain altitude after each attack. Pat's own tactics, therefore, were mainly defensive, turning away from each attack and occasionally delivering a short attack on the most suitable target as it dived past. One Fiat on completing its attack turned directly in front of the Gladiator, thereby presenting Pat with an excellent deflection shot at close range. He fired a long burst with his two remaining guns, which caused the Italian fighter to turn slowly on to its back and then spin down towards the desert. Soon after it hit the ground Pat's starboard wing gun packed up, but fortunately at the same time the remaining fighters broke away.

His position, although no longer desperate, was still far from pleasant, for he was alone forty miles behind the enemy lines, and only one gun was still working. He turned towards the border and opened the throttle to the fullest extent that he dared without damaging the engine. Its healthy roar made Pat confident that he would get home safely and he whistled a few discordant notes as he sped along 1,000 feet above the barren, sandy landscape. He was about halfway to the border when he stopped whistling. Directly ahead, barring the way, he saw fifteen Italian fighters – twelve Fiat C.R. 42's and three Breda 65's. The Bredas came at him first, but they seemed afraid to come in too close and Pat had no difficulty in avoiding their clumsy attacks.

After a few dives the Bredas broke away and the 42's took over, employing exactly the same tactics as the earlier five. Within a few seconds Pat's one remaining gun had jammed as the result of an exploded round in the breach, so he attempted to make the border by evasive tactics and heading towards the east at every opportunity. He soon discovered that one of the enemy pilots was an exceptional shot, who made repeated attacks using full deflection with great accuracy. Each time this particular Italian came in, Pat had to use all his skill and cunning to keep out of the sights of the Fiat. The remainder of the Italians as a whole lacked accuracy and did not press home their attacks to a decisive range. Nevertheless, their presence and the fact that Pat had to consider each attack, made the work of the more determined pilot very much easier.

For fully fifteen minutes Pat managed to keep out of harm's way. Then the determined Italian came out of a loop directly above the Gladiator and opened fire again. Pat turned away to avoid the bullets, but flew straight into the line of fire of another C.R. 42. The rudder controls were shot away, so that Pat could no longer turn. He pulled back on the control column, climbed to about 400 feet, and jumped. As he fell the pilot parachute caught in his foot, but he managed to kick it free. The main chute opened just in time for him to make a safe landing off the first swing. Winded by the fall, he lay flat out, gasping for breath, and expecting to be machine-gunned by the Italian fighters, whom he remembered had made a habit of strafing shot-down flyers in the Spanish Civil War. The Fiats, however, flew away to the west. Perhaps they thought the still figure stretched out face down in the dust was already dead, or at least so badly injured that he would not survive very long in the desert.

As soon as the enemy planes had disappeared Pat gathered in the parachute and buried it in the sand. He sat down and suddenly felt quite hungry when he thought about the emergency rations in his Gladiator. He would have enjoyed a piece of that bully beef and some biscuits. There had also been a water bottle and a two-gallon tank of water under the seat. He would have felt a lot happier if he had them with him now, but one glance at the blackened burnt-out wreckage of his Gladiator 200 yards away was sufficient to quell any hopes he might have had of rescuing them.

He looked at his watch. Seven-fifteen. It would be dark in a few hours. He would hide in the sand until he could get his bearings from the stars. As yet, with the sun almost overhead and no compass to guide him, he had no idea which way to go. He calculated that he was about four miles from the border, and that he could reasonably expect to walk this short distance in two or three hours, allowing for the fact that walking in sand is fairly slow, and that he might have to deviate from a straight path so as to avoid any Italian patrols.

As soon as it was dark enough he took the stars as a guide and set out for Egypt. He walked all through the night, and when dawn broke found to his horror that he was walking directly away from the rising sun – deeper into Libya. It was enough to make any man give up, as he was by now dreadfully thirsty and dead tired.

He sat down for a few moments to rest, and then began again to trudge through the sand in the opposite direction. He crossed the wire at the border about midday, struggled on for another two or three miles and then, utterly exhausted and his feet so sore that every step was agony, he lay down to rest and fell asleep at the side of the track. He was awakened by a droll voice inquiring: 'Are you doing this for fun, or would you like a lift?'

Pat looked up and found an officer of the 11th Hussars bending over him. He completed the journey back to Sidi Barrani in the Hussars' armoured car.

Wykeham-Barnes had also been picked up by a Hussar detachment and was already safely back with the rest of 'B' Flight. He was none the worse for his adventure except for a shrapnel wound in the back, a swollen tongue and a pair of very painful blistered feet.

Pat arrived at Sidi Barrani at about six o'clock, more than forty-eight hours after taking off. He was dead tired, but forced himself to stay awake long enough to write out a full report.

The next day he heard Pete's story. The others already knew it and Pat had to put up with a lot of leg-pulling and sarcastic comments. It would take him a long time to live down the fact that he who had spent his boyhood on the South African veldt had got lost, whilst Pete, who was a Londoner and whose previous walking experience hardly exceeded a stroll from South Kensington station to Gloucester Road, had come back like a homing pigeon!

Many months later a new and very exclusive association was founded in Cairo. It was called the 'Late Arrivals Club', and its members were awarded a highly prized insignia of a pair of airmen's boots with blue and white enamelled wings. A certificate which went with the badge stated that

This airman when obliged to abandon his aircraft on the ground or in the air as the result of unfriendly action by the enemy, succeeded in returning to his squadron on foot or by other means long after his estimated time of arrival. It's never too late to come back.

Pat and Pete became the first members of this most select band of flyers.

As a result of being shot down and escaping, Pat seemed to change. Outwardly he was still the same, cheerful, full of good spirits and ever ready for a lark, but inwardly he became even more devoted and dedicated to the job in hand. He regarded being shot down by the Italians, although against impossible odds, as a slur on his flying abilities and vowed that it would never happen again. He would make sure in future that his guns would never fail to fire; furthermore he would make sure that he never got lost in the desert again. He flew to Alexandria, bought a small compass, and never again went on an operation without carrying it in the pocket of his flying tunic. The rest of his flight quickly followed his example and similarly equipped themselves.

With the loss of three Gladiators, Sergeant Rew missing, Lancaster in hospital, and Pat and Pete not fit to take part in operations for at least twenty-four hours, 'B' Flight was, to say the least, rather depleted. Consequently Shorty Graham, Frankie Stubbs, Syd Linnard, and Sergeant Hewett flew from Amriya to reinforce the detachment.

78

The Commanding Officer, Squadron Leader Dunn, also flew to Sidi Barrani. He was most anxious to see that the morale of 'B' Flight had been unaffected by the gruelling engagement in the face of impossible odds on 4 August. Paddy wanted to re-establish the moral superiority already gained previously by other squadrons over the Italians. He discussed the situation with Pat, who, needless to say, was most eager to meet the Italians again.

It had been reported by observers that large formations of C.R. 42's had been patrolling a triangle between El Adem, Sidi Omar and El Gobi fairly regularly twice a day, early in the morning and again late afternoon. Paddy and Pat decided that this would provide an excellent opportunity for the squadron to engage the enemy and it was suggested to higher authority that this should be done. Headquarters were all in favour of this aggressive policy and, the necessary permission being granted, Paddy, Pat and Old Man Evers – the commander of 'C' Flight – discussed very carefully the tactics they should employ.

'Headquarters have given permission for this patrol, but have made one proviso,' Paddy explained to his two Flight Commanders. 'The likelihood of there being upwards of thirty Italian fighters in the patrol area, and the fact that the patrol area itself is so far inside enemy territory, has been carefully considered by headquarters, and in order to keep the odds down to reasonable proportions, they have stated quite categorically that the operation can only be carried out with a reasonable anticipation of success, provided that the patrol is made up of at least twelve Gladiators.'

He paused to light up the battered pipe which he had been busily filling as he gave out the news. When the tobacco was burning to his satisfaction he continued. 'The problem is how are the I-ties going to react to the sight of twelve fighters. You have tangled with them, Pat. What do you think?'

Pat chuckled. 'From what I've seen of them so far, sir, I should think that if they saw a dozen British aircraft flying together, unless there were at least sixty of the blighters, they would scamper away like frightened rabbits.'

'Yes, that is exactly what I had been thinking,' agreed Paddy. 'And there appears to be only one solution, as I see it. Headquarters have not said that all twelve fighters must fly together in close formation, and therefore I would suggest that they fly in two separate formations; a small flight of three or four Gladiators flying low and offered as a bait for the I-ties, supported by a second bigger formation flying higher and thereby out of sight of the enemy.'

Pat and Evers-Swindell agreed that it was an excellent plan, but were quick to point out that it would be extremely dangerous for the pilots flying the leading Gladiators, since they would be at a great disadvantage and would undoubtedly have to bear the brunt of an Italian attack before the other Gladiators could get down to support them.

After a lengthy discussion, it was decided that 'B' and 'C' Flights, numbering thirteen machines altogether, would take part in the mission and that they would be divided into four sub-flights. Sub One Flight would fly low at 8,000 feet and slightly in front, Sub Two Flight at 10,000 feet, Sub Three Flight at 12,000 feet, and Sub Four Flight at 14,000 feet. Sub One Flight would be led by Squadron Leader Dunn, the other two positions in the flight to be filled by asking for volunteers. The leader of Sub Four Flight would take control as soon as the enemy was sighted. The plan was briefly that Sub One Flight would engage, or be engaged by, the enemy, do what it could, and Sub Two, Three and Four Flights would be instructed to enter on seeing the trend of the battle.

'C' Flight arrived at Sidi Barrani at half past three on the afternoon of 8 August for the operation. Their aircraft were serviced by the groundcrews of 'B' Flight, whilst the pilots assembled in front of the operations tent to receive their instructions from the Commanding Officer. Squadron Leader Dunn explained the plan in great detail and then called for volunteers for Sub One Flight. Everyone stepped forward, as Paddy had expected, so lots were drawn. The result was that Pete Wykeham-Barnes and Flight Sergeant Vaughan were to fill the two positions on either side of the Squadron Leader. Evers-Swindell would lead Sub Two Flight, supported by Frankie Stubbs and Twinstead Flower. Heimar Stuckey, 'The Keg' (Pilot Officer Dowding), Cholmeley and Sergeant Gregory would be Sub Three Flight. Sub Four Flight would be led by Pat, and he had with him Shorty Graham, and Syd Linnard.

It was the first time during the war that 80 Squadron was to operate at full operational strength and all the ground personnel came out to see the thirteen Gladiators take off in immaculate formation shortly after half past five. They circled once over the aerodrome and then split up into their respective sub-flights. The aircraft in each sub-flight flew in a vic formation, and the four sections were spread out in a broad vic, this being the standard search formation in those early days of the war. They headed towards the west and the Libyan border, each sub-flight climbing to its allotted height. Just after six o'clock the Gladiators crossed the frontier south of Sidi Omar, and immediately Squadron Leader Dunn changed course to head north towards Bir Taieb el Esem. They flew over several burnt-out aircraft partly buried by the quickly shifting sand dunes and Pat wondered whether his old Gladiator was among the wrecks. He could see no aircraft in the sky yet, but he knew that they were in the area where the Italians had been seen patrolling, and he searched the sky in every quarter with an eager eye.

As the Gladiators were approaching Bir el Gobi, Pat spotted the enemy, a large formation of twenty-seven Fiat C.R. 42's in nine sections of three aircraft, the sections flying in a broad vic formation. It reminded him of a training school on a large-scale formation exercise. He switched the radio-telephone to transmit and spoke clearly and precisely into the microphone.

'Sub Four Leader to Sub One Leader. Twenty-seven C.R. 42's on the starboard beam at six thousand feet, flying in an easterly direction. Over.'

Paddy's voice came back: 'Sub One Leader to Sub Four Leader. Okay, Pat. I can see them clearly. It's up to you now. Take control, repeat, take charge. Good luck, chaps. Over and out.'

It was a copy-book attack, in which the Fighter Command attacks, which the squadron had practised so assiduously in peacetime, were put into practice completely in accordance with the Fighter Command Training Syllabus. This was one of the relatively few times that this happened, at least in the Middle East, because battle formation and tactics soon changed with experience.

Until the dogfight started the attack went so smoothly and successfully that it seemed just like a training exercise. Pat led the squadron in battle formation into an ideal position and ordered Sub One Flight to attack. Just as Squadron Leader Dunn's three Gladiators hit the flank vic of C.R. 42's, Pat ordered Sub Two and Sub Three Flights into the attack. The three C.R. 42's of the first vic and two of the second vic were on their way down in flames or out of control before the rest of the Italian fighters realised they were being attacked. It was not until Pat was about to dive his own flight to attack that the Italians started to break formation. He had achieved complete surprise.

The battle had developed into an enormous dogfight by the time Pat's own flight arrived, and it was a case of each man for himself. Pat engaged one of the Fiats, and after a very short skirmish moved into a position immediately behind the tail of the Italian fighter. From a range of about 50 yards he fired two short bursts directly into the fuselage of the enemy machine. It fell into a spin and burst into flames on striking the ground. He counted five more crashed aircraft, three of which were in flames, and then noticed three more C.R. 42's flying very close together below his port mainplane. A quick glance in his mirror to make sure that there were no enemy fighters behind him, and he winged over towards the trio beneath him. The Italians saw the Gladiator coming and broke away by diving vertically towards the ground, only pulling out at a very low altitude. Pat did not follow, for the obvious reason that he would have lost the advantages of height and surprise. As he turned to search for other enemy aircraft he saw two more planes crash and burst into flames, but was too far away to see whether they were C.R. 42's or Gladiators. The sky seemed clear of C.R. 42's, although several Gladiators were still in the vicinity, and Pat was about to turn towards the border, when tracer bullets flashed past his starboard wing. Kicking the rudder bar viciously, he skidded round and saw a lone C.R. 42 100 feet below and flying at right-angles to his Gladiator. With the advantage of height, Pat stall-turned his Gladiator, judged his approach perfectly and came down directly behind the C.R. 42 less than 30 yards from its tail. He fired one brief burst of shells into the cockpit and engine of the Fiat, which instantly exploded into a flaming mass of falling débris.

Seeing no further signs of enemy aircraft over the area, Pat turned towards Sidi Barrani and on his way home was joined by Shorty Graham and Syd Linnard. They landed at ten minutes past seven to find that most of the others were already back.

Paddy Dunn strolled across to meet them.

'Congratulations, Pat. That was a beautiful piece of leading. The Ities never knew what hit them until it was too late.'

'Thank you, sir. Is everybody back yet?'

'No. Flight Sergeant Vaughan overshot when we tackled the first vic, and was shot to pieces by two C.R. 42's. Old Man Evers shot down one of the bastards, and then got a burst in the engine from another. He opened his brolly, and the last time I saw him, he was drifting down towards the desert. Stuckey is also missing.'

Even as he was speaking they heard the sound of an engine; they turned and saw a Gladiator coming from the west. It roared over the field, did a couple of quick rolls signifying that its pilot had met with success, flattened out, landed, and its pilot, Heimar Stuckey, walked over towards them, a wide grin spreading across his face.

'Oh, boy!' he shouted, 'What a fight! Those I-ties will remember today for a long time to come. There will be a few empty places in their mess to-night. The desert was littered with wrecks. I clobbered a couple which went down for certain and another which began to smoke, but I did not see it crash, as I was attacked by two more 42's.'

'Well, that makes five destroyed and five more unconfirmed,' said Squadron Leader Dunn. 'How many did you get, Pat?'

'Two.'

'Yes, I saw both of them go down in flames,' confirmed Shorty Graham, 'and I hit another which spun down.'

'I got two more for certain,' said Syd Linnard.

'That makes nine definites and six unconfirmed for the loss of two Gladiators,' said Squadron Leader Dunn. 'And the chances are that Evers-Swindell might be walking back. Well done, chaps.'

Evers-Swindell walked in from the desert twenty-four hours later and thus became the third member of 80 Squadron to join 'The Late Arrivals Club'.

This was the biggest and most successful combat which had taken place in the Middle East up to date, and received considerable publicity. It was even mentioned in the news on the radio, in the rather conservative way of most news bulletins – 'A Royal Air Force Gladiator squadron stationed in the Western Desert intercepted a superior number of Italian fighters some distance inside enemy territory and succeeded in shooting down fifteen enemy fighters for the loss of two of its own machines.'

The pilots of 'B' Flight were particularly pleased with the result, because it proved what they had known for some time ... that their own Flight Commander was an excellent leader. The skill with which Pat had positioned the squadron for the attack on the Italian formation and the precision with which he had directed the sub-flights into the attack made it quite clear to everyone that as an aerial tactician and formation leader Pat was supreme. It gave the whole squadron the complete confidence in his leadership, which they were to need later on as the tempo of the battle increased. Their faith was such that they would have followed Pat anywhere.

8

Stalemate

For more than a month after their crushing defeat the Italian fighters kept out of the way of the Gladiators. Pat's flight was in the air every day on offensive patrols, or escorting the Blenheims of 211 Squadron, and each time they returned with their gun covers intact. Even a raid by the Royal Navy on the Italian fortifications at Bardia and Fort Capuzzo, for which 80 Squadron provided a protective umbrella of Gladiators, failed to entice the C.R. 42's into the sky. From dawn to dusk flights of four Gladiators patrolled up and down over the ships of the Mediterranean Fleet without interference from enemy fighters. The only aircraft sighted throughout the day was a Cant flying boat which Wykeham-Barnes intercepted as it was flying over Tobruk. He followed the Cant as it flew through the clouds and was about to open fire when his starboard gun came unmounted and ripped through the fuselage, severing a strut and damaging the leading edge of the tail plane. The Gladiator started to roll and, for a moment, it looked as if Pete had lost control of it. But he reacted quickly, put on full aileron to hold up the mainplane and then continued to attack the flying boat; it eventually caught fire and plunged into the sea.

At about the same time as Pete was shooting down the Cant, John Lapsley, who was flying a Hurricane on detachment with 33 Squadron, encountered four Savoia Marchetti S. 79's near Mersa Matruh. He shot down three and the fourth only escaped by hiding in a belt of cumulus.

Little was seen of the enemy for the rest of the month, although 'B' Flight continued to provide many patrols. As a diversion and with the idea of keeping the gun sights checked, Pat organised a sweep among the pilots and the groundcrews, who also took part. Each pilot in the flight tried his hand at shooting at a four-gallon petrol can from the air; the winners being the pilot who scored the most hits and the groundcrew who serviced the winning aircraft. Everyone enjoyed the competition and Pat was personally very satisfied with the results. Although he himself did not win (some of the flight accused him of deliberately aiming to miss), he was delighted to see that the competition was very successful in keeping the pilots in form with their target practice, their sights checked and their guns all in perfect working condition.

The rest of the squadron had been very busily occupied in moving, first from Amriya to Shineifa, which was about twenty-five miles from Mersa Matruh on the road leading to Sidi Barrani, and then back to Sidi Haneish. Several of the pilots, including Paddy Dunn, Evers-Swindell, Lapsley and Wykeham-Barnes were transferred to form a new fighter squadron, so that by the time Pat took his flight back to rejoin the squadron at Sidi Haneish on 1 September they found many new faces in the mess. Squadron Leader Bill Hickey, a tough, rugged, red-haired Australian, was the new Commanding Officer. Two of the other newcomers who were destined to become exceptional performers in a dogfight were Bill 'Cherry' Vale – a good-looking Aussie with dark wavy hair and an Errol Flynn moustache – and Dick Cullen – a thickset, broad-shouldered, happy-go-lucky Englishman who before the war had been an expert motor-cyclist and who was soon given the nickname of 'The Ape' because of his powerful physique.

'B' Flight had been ordered back to Sidi Barrani owing to the increasing concentration of enemy forces at the border. It was obvious to the pilots of 80 Squadron that the Italians were reinforcing their army with the object of making an all-out attack on Egypt. The Gladiators kept a wary eye open for developments, as they went out daily over the ever-accumulating forces of the Italians. There was considerable movement on the ground, but little sign of any action in the air, so the Gladiators used up their ammunition by machine-gunning the transport and troop concentrations assembling in the sandy wastes.

On 13 September, Pat and five other members of his flight were detailed to escort a Lysander on a reconnaissance of the enemy's positions. It promised to be the same as all the other missions they had flown for over a week – uneventful – until they crossed the border. The first unusual thing they noticed was an enormous haze of white dust spreading across the desert and moving fairly slowly towards them. The formation flew lower to discover the cause of the phenomenon and saw a vanguard of scores of Italian motor-cyclists, each equipped with a side-car containing a machine gun. Behind them lumbered a screen of anti-tank guns mounted on armoured cars and tiny Fiat two-man tanks. In the rear were mobile field and anti-aircraft guns and hundreds of lorries containing Italian infantry. This was Marshal Graziani's invasion army moving like a stream of ants towards the frontier. The Lysander and the Gladiators hurriedly swung round to return to Sidi Barrani with the news.

Within a few hours the Italians had passed through the wire defences at the frontier and occupied a deserted customs post at Fort Musaid. They pressed on through Sollum and Buq Buq, meeting little or no opposition until they were on the coastal road to Sidi Barrani. Here a big convoy of lorries forming part of the vanguard was heavily attacked by Royal Air Force bombers and fighters and many Italian vehicles were left in flames. The advance was resumed and on 16 September the Italians captured the village of Sidi Barrani. A few miles farther on and the Italian transport came to a halt. Behind them stretched for 150 miles a narrow road, along which all the enemy's supplies, including the precious water for the parched throats of the soldiers, had to be brought. Much of that road was along the shore in full view of the Royal Navy's ships; very little of it was sheltered from the bombers and fighters of the Royal Air Force. The squadrons in the desert worked harder than ever before, more sorties being flown in the first three weeks of September than in the previous three months. Tons of bombs were unloaded on to the Italians by the bombers, thousands of rounds of ammunition poured from the fighters' machine guns into the crowded mass of men and equipment, and the Fleet kept a continuous stream of shells pumping into the devastation spreading along the coastal road.

Pat's flight spent much of their time in strafing the Italian vehicles, but also managed a few bomber escort patrols and several protective sorties over the ships of the Royal Navy. They saw many C.R. 42's during these patrols and would have enjoyed 'mixing it' with them. But their orders were clear. Their job was to protect the bombers or the ships. They were forbidden to engage the Italian fighters unless the enemy planes attacked them first. This the Italians very rarely did.

Occasionally the Gladiators caught up with a formation of Savoia S. 79's, but seldom did they succeed in shooting down any of these three-engined raiders, because their speed enabled them to outpace the Gladiators. One afternoon, however, Heimar Stuckey spotted a lone S. 79 over Mersa Matruh and managed to get close to it without being seen. He pumped a continuous stream of lead into the bomber silencing the rear-gunner, and putting one of its engines out of action. He continued to fire into the fuselage of the bomber until he had used up all his ammunition. He was most annoyed when it showed no signs of going down. In the end he flew alongside the S. 79 and fired his Very pistol into the cockpit. Immediately the Italian crew baled out and the machine went down in flames.

A few days later, whilst returning from an offensive patrol to Sidi Barrani, Pat, Syd Linnard and Sergeant Casbolt spotted ten S. 79's in two flights of five in vics. Despite the discrepancy in the speeds between the Italian bombers and the Gladiators, Pat manoeuvred his section into a perfect position for an attack on one of the enemy formations. The Gladiators were almost directly above and diving on to a perfect target. Suddenly, when only about 300 feet from the enemy, Pat pulled away and was automatically followed by Linnard and Casbolt, who by now had formed a habit of not firing their own guns until they heard Pat open fire. Immediately Pat shouted over the radio-telephone that his air pressure had dropped, thus preventing his guns from working, and ordered Linnard and Casbolt to attack independently. In those few seconds, however, the advantage had been lost and, although Linnard and Casbolt chased the bombers, they were unable to get within effective range and finally had to break away. In the meantime Pat had been able to build up his pressure, so that his guns were working once more, and proceeded towards the coast near Bardia, where once again he intercepted the five Savoias. He selected the port-flank aircraft of the Italian formation as his target and got in a burst of fire which caused the port engine to issue a cloud of smoke. The S. 79 broke out of formation and Pat chased after it, but immediately the bomber dived steeply, increasing speed, and leaving the Gladiator well out of range. Both aircraft crossed the coast low down, about half a mile apart, with the gap slowly increasing. Pat decided he would never be able to catch the bomber and broke away.

The Italians, although constantly threatening to continue the advance into Egypt, never really got going again, possibly because like the Italian pilots they were never determined in their actions. A stalemate crept over the desert, and 80 Squadron settled in at their new quarters at Sidi Haneish. The engineers arrived, and within a few days had erected wooden huts to serve as a canteen, a dining hall, and messes for the officers and NCOs. Gradually the squadron accustomed themselves to a new routine of uneventful patrols to Sidi Barrani and Mersa Matruh, an occasional party in the newly built officers' mess and, most exciting of all, a series of knock-out cricket matches between the officers, the NCOs and the airmen.

Pat, ever eager to come to grips with the Italians, soon became bored with all this inactivity. He never seemed happy unless he was in the air and consequently he spent a great deal of time during this period practising dogfighting with the members of his flight. The dogfight invariably ended up the same way, with Pat sitting directly behind his opponent's tail and staying there, despite all the efforts of his opponent to get away. But everyone enjoyed the welcome break from the monotony of routine flying, and undoubtedly every member of Pat's flight benefited to some extent from these practices, although as one pilot remarked after a lesson from 'The Master': 'Pat was on my tail in an indecently short time.'

In October, 'B' Flight was again sent on detachment, this time to Bir Kenayis, a deserted spot some forty miles south-west of Mersa Matruh on the road to Siwa Oasis. Mersa Matruh was being battered almost daily by S. 79's, whose speed usually enabled them to escape before the Gladiators from Sidi Haneish could reach them. It was thought that if the detachment at Bir Kenayis could get off the ground at the same time or possibly before Mersa Matruh was raided, they would be able to cut across country and intercept the Italian bombers as they returned westwards towards Libya. It did not quite work out like that in practice, since the Gladiators, their engines worn out by the continuous strain of desert conditions, were much too slow even for them to catch a glimpse of the enemy raiders. However, the mere presence of Pat's flight at Bir Kenayis had the effect of cutting down the number of raids that were made on Mersa Matruh, and as a result it was arranged to keep a flight there more or less permanently, until Mersa Matruh could be defended more successfully by other means. During the time of 'B' Flight's detachment at Bir Kenayis all the pilots, whether officers or NCOs, would mess together. Pat introduced this system because he felt that all the pilots should be able to discuss tactics, mistakes and counter-measures as soon and as openly as possible. The success of the scheme was proved later on when this system of mixed messing was universally adopted by all desert fighter squadrons.

During the months of October and November the squadron was completely re-equipped with Mark II Gladiators. The old Mark I's, worn out by the dust of this arid wasteland and the extreme changes of temperature of the desert, were now very unreliable. But considering the treatment they had experienced and the length of time they had spent in the desert, they had done wonderfully well. Most of the pilots were a little disappointed, however, when they found they were getting only Mark II Gladiators instead of Hurricanes. The Gladiator was already obsolete when the war began, and would have proved no match at all against the modern fighters of the Luftwaffe. That the Gladiators had been able to establish any supremacy in the air at all was mainly due to the fact that the Italians in the Middle East had relied on the Fiat

C.R. 42, a biplane fighter of similar appearance and performance to the Gladiator. If the Italian Air Force had possessed greater quantities of Fiat G. 50's or Macchi 200's, it might have been a different story in the air war over the desert, in spite of the greater skill and courage shown by the pilots of the Royal Air Force. As it was, the Gladiator was almost useless against the faster bombers of the Italians. The only time that they managed to shoot down S. 79's, for instance, was when several Gladiators cornered one of these raiders and managed to get in a few bursts to slow it down. Only then did they stand an even chance of shooting it down. On the other hand, a Gladiator in the skilled hands of such an expert marksman as Pat was always likely to be a menace to any Italian plane, no matter how fast or manoeuvrable it was. But how much more formidable he would have been had he been flying a Hurricane. One pilot of 80 Squadron once said that if Pat could have got his hands on a Spitfire he would have been unbeatable in the air and would have set up an all-time record for the number of air victories. The majority of the flyers who saw Pat in action were in complete agreement.

The pilots had to fly their old Gladiators to Habbaniyah to exchange them. Pat's flight flew there on 5 November and returned to Sidi Haneish with their new Mark II's, two days later. They were greeted with the news that the squadron had been ordered to transfer to Abu Suweir station to prepare their aircraft for a move to Greece.

9

To the aid of Greece

On 28 October, before dawn, the Italian military forces began their invasion of Greece. They swarmed across the frontier from Albania in several places; the main thrusts were aimed eastwards across the mountains towards Florina and southwards towards Yanina. The Greek soldiers in the mountain passes fought desperately to stem the tide and to give the reinforcing troops time to rush to the front. At the same time General Metaxas, President of the Greek Council, appealed to the British Minister in Athens, Sir Michael Palairet, for assistance, mainly in the form of aircraft and ships. Without this aid Greece would have been in a most unhappy state. Her army was mobilising quickly and though by no means the equal of the Italian army either in numbers or in its modern equipment, it was thought to be capable of holding the Italians in the mountainous country where the Italian mechanised forces would possess no great advantage. But on the sea and in the air Greece was no match for the invader. The Greek Air Force for instance consisted of only 200 aircraft altogether, of which scarcely seventy were suitable for operations, and the majority of these were obsolete. With these few old and battered machines the courageous Greek flyers made an heroic but forlorn attempt to protect the Greek soldiers from the continuous strafing and bombing attacks of the 2,000 modern aircraft sent into action by the Italians.

The British Government responded immediately to the Greek request for aid and Royal Air Force Headquarters in the Middle East organised a small force of fighters and bombers to proceed at once to Greece. Under the command of Air Vice-Marshal J H D'Albiac, DSO, this small force, known as British Air Forces in Greece (BAFG) and consisting of two Blenheim squadrons and a Wellington squadron, soon made its presence felt. The bombers concentrated on the enemy's airfields, the supply ports and the lines of communications in Albania, whilst the fighter Blenheims directed their attacks against the Italian soldiers and their mechanised equipment.

Within a week the Italian advance had been halted, and the Greeks began a strong counter-offensive. The kilted Evzones sprang from their trenches, stormed up the difficult mountain slopes and

by-passed the crack Italian legions in the valley below. They brought up their artillery, showered the Italians with a storm of high explosives, and charged at the demoralised enemy with gleaming steel bayonets. Mussolini's prize divisions of Alpinis panicked, threw away their guns and ran like hares. Hard on their heels followed the Greeks, although at times the pace was so hot that they could not keep in touch. So swift was the pursuit that the Greek headquarters lost contact with the Evzones, and the Air Force was called in to drop supplies and equipment.

The Italians were pushed back until there was not an Italian left on Greek soil, save prisoners, the wounded and the dead. Without belittling the magnificent effort of the Greek army, this tremendous victory could not have been achieved without the support of the Royal Air Force. Time and again the Blenheims and Wellingtons attacked the ports of Valona and Durazzo, creating havoc in these two most important ports, through which the Italian supplies were coming by sea and by air. The tiny BAFG, however, greatly outnumbered by the quick-darting fighters of the Italian Air Force, suffered severe losses, and Air Vice-Marshal D'Albiac was forced to ask for fighter reinforcements. Royal Air Force Headquarters, Middle East was building up its resources for the coming offensive against the Italians in Libya, and desperately needed all its aircraft and pilots. It was a difficult problem. Eighty Squadron were refitting and resting when the request came, and since they were in a position where they could be hastily organised, they were allotted the task of establishing a supremacy over the Italian fighters in Greece.

By 8 November the re-equipment with Mark II Gladiators was complete and the pilots of 80 Squadron began checking over the machines, including the alignment of sights and the swinging of compasses. The following day the squadron left Sidi Haneish for Abu Suweir to pack up kit and aircraft spares in preparation for the move to Greece. The pilots were granted forty-eight hours' leave, whilst the ground party, under the command of Flying Officer Ripley and Ape Cullen boarded the cruisers *Gloucester* and *Edinburgh* and sundry cargo boats in Alexandria harbour and set sail for Athens. Shortly after midday on 16 November they disembarked as the first Royal Air Force Fighter squadron in Greece. They immediately set up shop at Eleusis aerodrome, fifteen miles from Athens, where the groundcrews worked through the night in the moonlight, all illuminations being forbidden, to get things ready for the arrival of the flying parties.

At Abu Suweir the squadron was reorganised into two flights, and it was arranged for the flights to proceed independently to Greece. 'B' Flight's Gladiators piloted by Squadron Leader Hickey, Pat, Shorty Graham, Syd Linnard, Johnny Lancaster, Heimar Stuckey, Cherry Vale, Sammy Cooper, Flight Sergeant Richens and Sergeant Casbolt left Abu Suweir just after lunch on 17 November, and flew to Sidi Haneish where the pilots were bedded down for the night; the aircraft were refuelled by the groundcrews of 112 Squadron. Early the next morning the Gladiators, navigated by a Bombay, headed north-east for Crete. A Sunderland joined the formation at the coastline, its purpose being to pick up anyone who might have the misfortune to land in the 'drink'. Fortunately it was not needed and all the Gladiators and the Bombay landed safely at Cardia, where they were refuelled. After a light lunch they took off on the last part of their journey and ninety minutes later were circling over Eleusis aerodrome. As soon as they landed Squadron Leader Hickey went off to headquarters to get his orders, whilst the rest of the pilots went into Athens to see the sights of this centre of ancient history.

The warmth of their welcome by the Greeks in their capital city was overwhelming. The streets were decorated with flags, the people cheered and slapped them on the back, the children whistled and waved as the pilots gave them the thumbs-up sign. Everywhere they went the airmen were greeted with open arms and offers of hospitality. That night the local pubs, the *tavernos,* were crowded, and all the drinks were free to the Royal Air Force. The party was interrupted when Squadron Leader Hickey returned from the Grand Bretagne Hotel, with the news that 'B' Flight was to take off next morning and fly to Trikkala, where they would refuel and then make their first patrol in Greek skies. The pilots drove back to Eleusis and turned in early, sobered by the thought that on the morrow they would in all probability be meeting the Italians for the first time over a scenery very different from the sands of the desert.

The flight arrived at Trikkala about midday to find the pilots of a Greek squadron already operating from there, sitting on wooden benches in the open, less than fifty yards away from their ancient aircraft. They were enjoying a meal of bread and cheese and olives, which they washed down with a very strong-smelling but sweet-tasting wine. After a snack it was decided that the Greeks would take 'B' Flight to have its First look at Albania.

Three Greek high-wing PZL monoplane fighters took off and were followed by nine Gladiators led by Squadron Leader Hickey. The Greeks flew low, taking the Royal Air Force fighters through the densely wooded valleys, with the snow-capped mountain peaks towering high each side of them. As they neared the Italian airfield at Koritza the PZL's broke away to return to Trikkala. With their very small fuel capacity they had reached the limit of their range, and in order to get back without running short of petrol they would have to cruise back in a straight line, their engines set to use the minimum amount of fuel. If they were careful, and if they were lucky enough not to meet any Italian aircraft, they would just about make it.

The Gladiators flew on over Koritza, where they were greeted by the black puffs of smoke denoting that they had been spotted by the Italian anti-aircraft gunners. A few seconds later Pat, as usual, was first to see the enemy aircraft, which appeared in small groups climbing to intercept the Gladiators. Pat, leading the second section, sighted four Fiat C.R. 42's climbing towards them from the starboard beam.

It had been arranged beforehand that the Gladiators would not use their radio-telephones unless it was absolutely essential, because they had discovered in the desert that the C.R. 42's used a similar wavelength; by listening in to the Gladiators, the Italians received prior information of an attack. Pat warned Squadron Leader Hickey of the presence of the C.R. 42's simply by diving past the Commanding Officer's section and pointing his Gladiator towards the Fiats. Hickey acknowledged that he understood by waggling his wings and Pat withdrew to his position at the head of his section. As Hickey's section dived towards the four C.R. 42's, Pat noticed a second group of two more C.R. 42's, and took his section, consisting of Heimar Stuckey and Sergeant Casbolt, to engage these. Pat went for the leading Fiat, which attempted to evade the attack by diving steeply and slipping from side to side. The Gladiator followed, closing in rapidly, but Pat did not fire until the Fiat straightened out and thereby offered a steadier target. From 100 yards astern he lined up the Italian biplane in his sights and pressed the gun button. The fighter steepened its dive; the pilot had apparently been hit, because he fell forward over the control column. Pat pulled away, as the Fiat went straight down to crash about two miles west of Koritza, bursting into flames on striking the ground. Stuckey, following close behind Pat's Gladiator, smiled and gave a thumbs-up signal to Pat signifying confirmation of the 'kill'.

The two Gladiators, now completely alone, climbed up to 15,000 feet immediately over the airfield, and saw a dogfight in progress a few miles to the north. Heading in that direction, they were soon engaged by five C.R. 42's and two Fiat G. 50's. One of the G. 50's came at Pat in a head-on attack, but broke away much too early, the tracers passing yards below the Gladiator. A C.R. 42 had a go next, but Pat quickly snap-rolled, up and over the fighter, and came down perfectly in position fifty yards behind the Italian. A short burst and the cockpit of the 42 became a mass of flames. It fell away burning furiously. Pat looked around. Once again the sky was empty, and Pat wondered what had happened to Stuckey and the other Italian fighters.

He noticed that his air pressure was low, so low, in fact, that when he tried his guns they would not fire. He flew on over the mountainous countryside, climbing all the time, and attempting to build up the pressure. A C.R. 42 and a G. 50 dived towards him, but broke away before coming into range, and for once he was thankful, for his guns were still not working. After a quarter of an hour cruising around the mountains, Pat had built up his pressure so that he could at least use his guns for a short period. He noticed a Fiat G. 50, one of Italy's newer fighters, a radial-engined monoplane with a performance similar to a Hurricane. It was flying 1,000 feet higher than Pat's Gladiator, and consequently Pat was at a great disadvantage. But the G. 50 made no attempt to attack and Pat, becoming curious to find out what this monoplane could do in a dogfight, climbed towards it. Immediately the G. 50, using its superior speed, climbed to keep out of range. Pat could not see any other aircraft about, so he carried on in an endeavour to get the Italian to fight. He finally became so convinced of his own supremacy over the Fiat that he positioned his Gladiator immediately below and ahead of the G. 50, a sitting duck, but even then the Italian would not come down to fight.

Lack of fuel finally forced Pat to give up the fruitless attempt, and he turned towards the south. Seeing no other Gladiators about, he dived almost to tree-top height, where the brown and green of the Gladiator merged into the landscape, making it almost impossible for him to be seen from the air. Although he only flew at cruising speed, he kept very low, and it felt as if was flying much faster than usual. He tore along the valley of the River Aoos, climbed to get over the Metsovo Pass between the cloud-covered peaks on either side, and dropped down again to follow the railway line from Kalabaka to Trikkala. A few minutes later he saw the airfield, put down his flaps, and came in low and fairly slowly over the trees. He felt a slight bump as his wheels hit the ground, automatically let up the flaps, and taxied over to the other Gladiators. Already the Greek groundcrews were busy manhandling them towards the trees at the edge of the airfield, where they covered them with branches, to hide them from the eyes of any snooping Italian spotter plane.

Pat pulled off his flying gloves and rubbed his cold hands briskly. With fumbling fingers he unbuttoned his mask, containing the microphone. He pulled back the hood, hauled himself out of the cockpit and jumped awkwardly down to the damp grass of the airfield, hampered by the parachute, his thick Irvin flying jacket and his fur-lined flying boots. He unbuckled the parachute harness, slung it into the cockpit, and stamped his cold feet on the soft earth. He set off towards the light-coloured square building which served as the operations room.

The others were gathered round the warm, cheerful-looking stove in the middle of the room, chattering like a lot of excited schoolboys, when Pat entered.

'Late again, Pat! Did you get lost in the mountains?'

Pat smiled. 'No, sir. I met up with a G. 50, and spent a useless fifteen minutes in trying to persuade it to fight.'

He glanced around the dimly lit room and saw that Stuckey's smiling face was absent. He was about to inquire of his whereabouts when Hickey continued.

'Stuckey saw you get a 42 in flames, shot down another himself, and then got a bullet in his shoulder and another in his leg. The Doc is having a look at him now, and then he will probably go back to Athens in the Junkers. He'll be as good as new in a week or so. Everybody else is back, though a couple of Gladiators caught a few I-tie bullets.'

The squadron had shot down nine Italian fighters for certain, and possibly two more which could not be confirmed, and Headquarters were delighted with the result. The Greeks regarded it as a great victory, welcoming it as a sign that soon the hated Italians would be driven from the skies of their beloved motherland. They could not do enough for the squadron. All the pilots were found comfortable quarters in the best hotel in Trikkala, and the local school was closed and converted into billets for the ground staff – much to the delight of the local youngsters, who spent most of their time gaping at the pilots or their aeroplanes.

It had been arranged that 'A' Flight should fly to Trikkala the next day, and that the whole squadron would make an offensive patrol over the Albanian frontier, but instead the pilots had their first experience of the atrocious weather conditions which were to prove such a tremendous handicap to the Royal Air Force in Greece. It started raining during the night, and at dawn, when Pat was awakened by his orderly, it was still pouring. When he looked through the window of his room, and saw the rivers of water gushing over the cobbled stones of the street, he realised that the chances of getting airborne were very slim indeed. But nevertheless he dressed quickly, had breakfast, and drove out to the airfield with several other pilots. Torrential rain had already turned the field into a quagmire and one look was sufficient to convince them all that even if the rain stopped straight away the Gladiators would never be able to take off through the pools of water and the squelching patches of mud that covered the airfield. They went back into the town and spent the rest of the day drinking the rough wine in the local restaurant, and cursing the wretched weather which prevented them going out to help the unfortunate Greek soldiers at the front, who, in spite of the weather, still trudged through the mud in pursuit of the retreating Italian divisions.

It rained continuously for forty-eight hours, and then for two more days the cloud was so dense, with visibility down to a few yards, and the airfield itself was still so soft, that any flying was out of the question. But on 25 November, although conditions were only slightly better, Pat and his flight volunteered to try to take off.

'After all,' Pat joked, 'we shall have a reasonable excuse if we tip the Gladiators into the mud.'

Six of the Gladiators did manage to get into the air and patrolled over the Koritza area, but found no enemy aircraft about, which was not surprising considering the conditions ... the Gladiators were probably the only aircraft flying over northern Greece that day. There was some consolation for the pilots when they got back to Trikkala, since a convoy had somehow managed to find its way from Athens, after three days of sliding and skidding through the treacherous mud and on the narrow mountainous track. The same journey by air took barely an hour.

Air Headquarters in Athens rang up Squadron Leader Hickey the following day and he called the pilots together in the operations room and gave them the news.

'I thought you would all like to know that tomorrow the squadron is moving up to Yanina on detachment. The airfield there, so I am told, is drier than here, and also it is much nearer the front line, only about forty miles or so from the Albanian frontier. That should give us more time to find the I-ties ... especially bombers. As you know, the Greeks are taking a battering from the Savoias, and Headquarters want us to try to knock down a few of them. You will find that most of the bomber flights will have a swarm of C.R. 42's around them and you will always be outnumbered. Try to avoid the fighters, if possible, and remember the bombers are what we are after, but don't go taking any unnecessary risks.

'You will take off at 1100 hours, patrol over the Koritza area, and return direct to Yanina.

'You, Tap,' he said, turning towards Flight Lieutenant Jones, 'will be in charge of the squadron at Yanina until I can get there.

'One other thing,' he continued, 'you will have to rely on the Greek groundcrews there for a few days. It will be impossible to get any of our own ground staff up there by road with conditions as they are. Skeleton crews will be flown up as soon as we can get the Bombay to transport them.'

The weather was clear next morning with not a sign of a cloud in the sky and conditions were ideal for flying, that is if one disregarded the bitterly cold wind which blew directly from the north. The twelve Gladiators had all been warmed up by the early-rising groundcrews, and the engines were ticking over healthily when Pat and the others jumped from the truck which had skidded most of the way along the track from the town to the airfield.

Pat hurried towards his aircraft, pulled his fur-lined Irvin jacket close to keep out the cold and slipped quickly into his parachute harness. One foot on the mainplane, a hand on the edge of the cockpit, a push on the springy turf with the opposite foot and he was up and easing himself down into the cockpit. He pulled on his helmet, adjusted the mouthpiece containing the microphone, and settled his feet on the rudder pedals. A gentle prod with either foot to make sure that the rudder was swinging properly, and then he moved the control column and watched the ailerons and elevators. He checked the throttle lever and brakes, waved away his fitter and rigger, and began to taxi round the field. When in position he braked and waited for the rest of 'B' Flight to form up behind him.

The other flight was already spread out into a flattened vee with Tap at the apex. Heading directly into the wind, they moved forward, slowly at first, but gathering speed until the tails lifted, and finally the six Gladiators were airborne. They climbed easily out of the valley, followed a few seconds later by Pat's flight.

The Gladiators eased out into a loose echelon, climbing all the time to get over the Metsovo Pass. The pilots, although not expecting to meet any Italian aircraft so far south, nevertheless kept their heads turning. It was monotonous flying, cruising along at a set speed with nothing to see but the green wooded hillsides, and the deep valleys occasionally carrying a thin winding track which was the main road through the mountains. It would have been easy to doze off, but the nagging thought that this clear weather would bring out the C.R. 42's in large numbers kept the pilots wide awake, their eyes relentlessly searching in all directions.

They were north of Yanina when they spotted the enemy, a flight of three Savoia 79's escorted by a dozen C.R. 42's. Immediately Tap led his flight down to tackle the bombers, whilst Pat's flight headed for the fighters. Pat watched the first six Gladiators screaming down in a curved line towards the S. 79's and then led his own flight into the gap between the S. 79's and the C.R. 42's. He would at least keep the Italian fighters away from Tap's flight and give them an uninterrupted opportunity of knocking down some of the bombers. At first it seemed as if the C.R. 42's were going to keep well away, because they swung round at right-angles to their original course, and headed away from the area.

Pat was on the point of leading his flight down to give Tap's flight a helping hand, when quite suddenly the C.R. 42's peeled off and attempted to get back towards the bombers, by diving directly below Pat's flight. At once the Gladiators rolled over and in line astern dived steeply on to the C.R. 42's. The fight, if it can be called that, was over in less than a minute. A few seconds of blazing lead from the six Gladiators, and two of the C.R. 42's continued to dive, enveloped in flames and smoke, whilst the rest of the Italian fighters pulled up and hurriedly made off towards the north.

Pat levelled out at 4,000 feet and flew over the deserted countryside until the flight had reassembled around him. There was no sign of Tap's flight, and one glance at the petrol gauge was sufficient to tell Pat that they could not afford to hang around much longer. He set course for Yanina.

When they landed Tap's flight was already there. After their initial dive on the Savoias, during which a lot of lead had been fired into the bombers with no apparent effect, the Italians had 'pulled the plug' and left the Gladiators standing. In future Tap decided that he would employ the method advocated by Pat. The South African had already made up his mind that there was little to be gained by trying to do astern attacks on S. 79's. Their extra speed and heavier armament made it most unprofitable. His plan was to attack the bombers head-on, with his flight in line abreast, thereby bringing to bear a combined firing force of at least twenty-four machine guns.

The aerodrome at Yanina was nothing more than a large reasonably flat field of rough grass, kept fairly short by the constant grazing of a flock of sheep that wandered aimlessly over its surface. There were no runways and no hangars; the Gladiators had to be dragged by the Greek groundcrews to the perimeter of the field, where they were hidden from the prying eyes of Italian reconnaissance machines by the simple expedient of covering them with bushes, branches and undergrowth.

A large mud-bespattered coach that had been at its best many years before the war took the pilots into the town, which in the summer season was set in an ideal spot at one side of a lake amidst a superb mountain scenery. In the late autumn, however, in the middle of a war, it was a dirty, damp village, filled with soldiers, mules and Greek peasants.

They got off the bus at the corner of a block of white buildings, graced by a sign which informed all and sundry that this was the *Acropolis Hotel*, this would be their living quarters whilst they were in Yanina. Within a few minutes they had dumped their kit and set out on a sight-seeing tour. As they walked along the narrow, crowded streets, everybody stopped and stared and then, realising who the visitors were, shouted and clapped and cheered. By the time they reached the restaurant their backs were sore from the slapping and their ears rang with the echoes of *Inglisi*. The food was the same as at the restaurant in Trikkala, oily and spicy, and was followed by the inevitable sweet aniseed wine. Pat knew he would never become fond of this typical Greek meal, but the patrol had used up all his energy and created an appetite which had to be satisfied. He tried to eat without tasting or smelling the food, but this did not work, so he endeavoured to drown it with the wine. This was even worse and he was glad when the meal was finished. The air was thick with smoke from cigarettes and cigars, and the smell, a mixture of oils, spices and tobaccos, was nauseating. He was glad to get outside to breathe fresh air again.

He had never seen so many Greek soldiers before, all bearded and in dirty muddy clothes. Then there were the mules, thousands of them, all carrying heavy packs and bundles of an assortment of equipment from boxes of ammunition to complete machine guns, all moving slowly northwards from this important 'feeding' town towards the Albanian frontier.

Pat moved on through the dirty crowded streets until he finally arrived at a place which was to become the greatest attraction for the squadron during their frequent visits to the town. It was the public washhouse, and to men of the armed forces the charge was only half price … five drachmae. He went inside, and for the first time since he came to Greece he was able to cleanse himself with gallons of hot water and bundles of towels.

Then he returned to the hotel and slept the clock round.

The following day his flight was rested, but shortly after lunch he went out to the airfield to welcome the other flight, who had been detailed to patrol in the Delvinakion sector. It soon became obvious that they had run into trouble, when not one of the Gladiators had returned at the estimated time.

Anxiously he searched to the north, but all he could see was a cloudless sky and the snow-capped peaks of the mountains. Several times he fancied he heard the sound of an approaching aeroplane, but it was only his imagination playing tricks on him. He sat down on a wooden crate and, glancing at his watch, saw that the Gladiators were now twenty minutes overdue. Their fuel tanks must be getting low by this time. He pulled a packet of cigarettes from the pocket of his tunic and his cold hands were still fumbling with the flap when he heard the sound of an aircraft engine. He sprang to his feet and far away to the north-west his keen eyes picked out three shapes. They dropped lower as they passed the ridge of mountains, and for a few moments he lost sight of them as they dropped below the horizon and their camouflage mingled with the forested hillsides. When he picked them out again he was easily able to identify them as Gladiators. Two more, flying very close together, came over the mountain-tops, whilst the first three side-slipped towards the field. He could see no sign of the sixth Gladiator.

The first three came straight in and taxied across the field towards him. He could see that all three had bullet-holes through the mainplanes. They came to a standstill, the pilots vaulted from the cockpits and Pat recognised Twinstead Flower, Price-Owen and Hosken. The other two fighters were now making their approach and Pat could see that one of them was badly knocked about. Pieces of loose fabric were flapping and the perspex hood was splintered into a thousand fragments. By the time it stopped everybody was dashing towards it. Sergeant Gregory, the pilot of the other Gladiator, was first to get there. He fought back a feeling of nausea when he saw the crimson blotches of blood, splashed all over the cockpit, but was reassured by the cheerful grin on the pilot's face.

'It's all right, Greg. I should have ducked a little quicker.'

It was Tap Jones, and he had got a bullet clean through the fleshy part at the back of his neck. It had bled profusely and looked much worse than it really was. But he had to be flown down to the hospital in Athens, which seemed to be the only place in Greece where there was an adequate supply of drugs and bandages.

When Tap had disappeared inside the truck decorated with an enormous red cross, which alone distinguished it as an ambulance, the others gathered together to make out their reports for the Intelligence Officer.

The six Gladiators had encountered twenty C.R. 42's right over the front line near Delvinakion and had shot down seven of them. Sergeant Gregory had sent three down and Tap had shot two more off the tails of Gladiators before he was wounded. Flying Officer Flower had flamed another, and Hosken and Price-Owen had each got one unconfirmed. The sixth member of the flight, Bill Sykes, had collided with another C.R. 42 and he had last been seen spinning towards the treacherous mountains near Delvinakion.

The condition of Tap's Gladiator had to be seen to be believed. It was riddled with bullet-holes, the dashboard and instruments being a mangled mess, and even the tyres shredded to ribbons. It looked as if it would collapse at any second, and it seemed a miracle to the pilots that Tap had been able to bring it back so far. But aircraft in Greece at this time were worth their weight in gold and the Royal Air Force groundcrews who had flown up in the Bombay were soon in action reassembling the wreck. In spite of the lack of proper tools, they worked wonders and in less than a fortnight the Gladiator was ready once again for the fray.

With Tap Jones out of action and Squadron Leader Hickey still at Trikkala, Pat took over the duties of Commanding Officer. He would have liked to send out a patrol immediately to look for Bill Sykes, but common sense told him that he must not risk the remaining six Gladiators, because they would be needed the next day to escort the Blenheims of 84 Squadron for a raid on Tepelene. All five of the Gladiators that had returned that day would need a thorough check, in addition to a bit of patching, before they could be classified as ready for immediate use. That would take at least twenty-four hours with the limited resources that the squadron had at its disposal.

When he got back to the hotel Pat found the rest of the squadron in the bar. They had heard that 'A' Flight had been in a fight and were anxious to know all about it. Pat outlined briefly all that had happened and then told them what he had decided to do about the next day's operation. The orders were to escort nine Blenheims of 84 Squadron for a bombing raid on the enemy's supply dump near Tepelene. Pat would lead the escort of six Gladiators, which would fly in three groups of two aircraft. The first section, consisting of Shorty Graham and Sergeant Casbolt, would fly at the same height as the Blenheims, but about 100 yards to the port side; the second section of Johnny Lancaster and Flight Sergeant Richens would be to the starboard side and 1,000 feet higher, whilst Pat and Cherry Vale would act as lookouts to the rear of the bombers and 2,000 feet above them. In this way Pat would be in a position where he could not only keep an eye on the bombers and Gladiators below, but where he could also act as top cover for the entire formation and thereby prevent it from being surprised from above.

He emphasized the fact that their job was to escort the bombers safely to the target and back again. They were on no account to leave the bombers, even though they might be tempted to do so. No matter how inviting a formation of Italian fighters might appear, the Gladiators would not engage them unless the enemy attempted to attack the Blenheims.

'We will protect the bombers until we have seen them safely out of harm's way. Then ... and only then, will we be able to go and have some fun.' He paused for a moment, to give time for his orders to sink in, and then continued:

'When we have brought the bombers back this side of Delvinakion, then we will split up and search the area for some trace of Bill Sykes's aircraft. If by some chance you should then encounter any Italian aircraft, make sure that you get into an advantageous position, and then give them hell.'

There was very slight high cloud and a following wind the next day, the sort of weather that delighted the fighter pilots, but which could not be considered ideal for the bomber boys. They always welcomed the presence of thick clouds, in which they could take cover if they were attacked. But the pilots of 84 Squadron were not unduly worried that day, because they knew that they could rely on Pat and his boys to give them the fullest possible protection from any interfering Italian fighters.

Everything went off perfectly. The Gladiators met the Blenheims at the rendezvous point dead on time, positioned themselves exactly as planned, and watched over the bombers with the infinite care of guardian angels. The fighter pilots admired the skill of the bomb-aimers, as they saw the bombs explode directly in the middle of the target, and envied the quiet courage of the bomber pilots as they flew steadily on through the barrage of anti-aircraft shell bursts. Then they were turning and heading back towards friendlier skies. The C.R. 42's were apparently engaged elsewhere, since not a single Italian fighter was sighted during the whole of the flight.

Soon after passing over the village of Delvinakion, Squadron Leader Dudley-Lewis, the Commanding Officer of the Blenheims squadron, gave a thumbs-up signal to Pat, which meant that the Gladiators could now go off and enjoy themselves. The Gladiators, in pairs, rolled over and dived towards the autumn-tinted hillsides to begin the search for the crashed Gladiator.

Pat and Cherry Vale, however, did not dive with the others. Pat had already spotted two formations of aircraft coming towards them. He pointed them out to Vale, and then began to climb into the sun directly in the path of the approaching machines. He could already make out that there were half a dozen, two- or possibly three-engined aircraft, probably bombers, but as yet could not distinguish their type, or even if they were friendly or hostile. They were flying in two groups of three, the first group slightly in front and just below the second three. Pat brought his Gladiator round into a position where he could nose straight down out of the sun. Cherry Vale was just behind him and a few yards to the right. Pat stared intently at the rapidly approaching formation, taking in every little detail … three engines … tall single fin and rudder … the long nose … he was sure now. They were Savoias.

The nose of his Gladiator dipped and he sped like an arrow towards the leading bomber. The Savoia, unaware of the danger hidden in the blinding rays of the midday sun, flew blissfully along its steady course. Pat had the engine at the front of the bomber right in the middle of his sights now, but he held his fire until he could clearly see the faces of the pilot and the co-pilot. He squeezed the trigger button on the control column and felt the whole plane shudder with the recoil of the four machine guns. The Savoia was blurred now, but he held his finger on the gun button until it seemed that he must crash head-on into the bomber. He pulled hard on the stick, and as the black monster passed beneath him he could hear Cherry's guns still firing into it. The leader of the second flight was now almost directly on top of him, and the gunners were sending a hailstorm of white tracer towards him. He fired again, and just had time to see his own tracers burying themselves inside the belly of the Savoia before his Gladiator stalled and fell away. By the time he had regained control of his machine the Savoias were half a mile away and he knew he could never hope to catch up with them again. He looked behind and saw Cherry's Gladiator just coming up to join him. Cherry had seen Pat's Gladiator spin down after attacking the second Savoia, and he thought that Pat had been hit by the gunners. He had broken away and followed Pat down.

Pat glanced again at the now rapidly disappearing enemy bombers and wondered how many of them would get back to their base. He could see plumes of smoke billowing out behind the leaders of each trio. If only the whole of his flight had been behind him when he had attacked they would not have got off so lightly. Or better still if he and Cherry had been flying Hurricanes, with their greater firepower and superior speed, they might have downed the lot on their own. When were they going to get those Hurricanes? Surely Headquarters did not expect them to go on flying their veteran biplanes for ever.

The sight of the snow-capped mountains, now frighteningly close to his starboard wing tips, brought him back to reality. He climbed quickly and headed towards Yanina.

The other Gladiators landed soon after Pat and Cherry had got back, but they had not encountered any enemy aircraft. Neither had they been able to find any trace of Bill Sykes or his Gladiator.

10

Bad weather

Pat showed tremendous concern over the welfare of the men whom he had been entrusted to command, whether they were pilots or groundcrews, officers, non-commissioned officers, or aircraftsmen second class. Both on the ground and in the air he advocated the use of teamwork as the only successful way of winning the war, and whenever any man of his own team was lost he always felt the loss most severely, although he was most careful at times when the occasion demanded to hide his feelings. Pat had no greater attachment to Bill Sykes than to a hundred other men belonging to 80 Squadron, but since Sykes was a member of the team which Pat now commanded, in the absence of Squadron Leader Hickey, Pat was most anxious to find out what had happened to him.

Two days after Sykes had failed to return from a mission there was still no news. The weather had deteriorated again, all operations being cancelled because of the low cloud and the rain. It was too bad for any flying at all really, but nevertheless Pat called for volunteers, and took off with two other Gladiators and an ancient Greek Breguet of World War One vintage. They flew to Delvinakion, where Sykes had last been seen spinning down, and crawled around the mountains for an hour, in spite of the mist and the rain. They failed to find any trace of a crashed aircraft.

The weather was even worse on 1 December, with a howling wind and persistent rain showers, and Pat could not risk sending another three aircraft on a search mission. Consequently he set off alone, the only member of the squadron to leave the ground that day at Yanina. He remained over the Delvinakion area, investigating every nook and cranny for some slight indication of a wrecked aeroplane, until his fuel was so low that he had to give up the attempt and return to Yanina.

That same evening a Greek officer brought the news that Flying Officer Sykes had been killed. He had been found by Greek troops in the burnt-out wreckage of his Gladiator, a few hours after crashing, and had been buried at the side of his machine. For some unknown reason the Greek soldiers had failed to notify their headquarters until three days after the crash.

Squadron Leader Hickey rang up from Air Headquarters in Athens early the next morning. He had gone there for a conference with the Headquarters staff. The Greeks wanted more support from the fighters, but, as Hickey pointed out, it was a physical impossibility to get the Gladiators off the ground when they were based at such waterlogged airfields. If only they could be given a decent, well-drained airfield, half a dozen Hawker Hurricanes to replace their worn-out Gladiators, and a few days of good weather, he would guarantee to keep the Savoias away from the Greek positions. Headquarters were very sorry, but they could not promise any Hurricanes yet, and neither had they any control over the weather, but they had arranged with the Greeks that 80 Squadron could move up to the bigger and better station at Larissa, although they would have to share it with a couple of Greek squadrons already stationed there.

'I shall fly up to Trikkala later today,' continued Hickey, 'with a bunch of chaps from 112 Squadron who are bringing up a few extra Gladiators for the Greeks at Larissa. I'll arrange for the rest of the squadron at Trikkala to move by road to Larissa, and I'll expect you to bring the detachment back tomorrow.'

Pat replaced the telephone and went outside to have a look at the weather. It had stopped raining, and the sun was trying hard to pierce the clouds, which were thinning and lifting. He drove out to the airfield, and called to his groundcrew to get his Gladiator ready for take-off. The airfield was still covered with pools of water, but the sun was quite warm now, and if the wind kept up the field should be dry enough to risk a take-off in a couple of hours.

Just before eleven o'clock he took off alone to carry out a weather test. He headed up the valley towards Argyrokastron, and was almost in sight of the town when he caught sight of another biplane also flying towards Argyrokastron. Pat opened his throttle to full power and as he drew nearer attempted to identify the aircraft. It was evidently a reconnaissance machine, because it was flying so slowly and so straight, but Pat did not recognise its type until he had drawn up right behind its tail. Then he saw that it was an R.O. 37 Army Cooperation aircraft, probably spotting for the Italian artillery. It flew along steadily, neither the pilot nor the observer seeing the Gladiator until bullets were shattering the engine of the R.O. 37. It burst into flames and crashed near the road about five miles south of Argyrokastron.

Satisfied that the weather was suitable for flying, Pat headed back for Yanina to organise a patrol.

It always took time to refuel the Gladiators at Yanina, because the fuel tanks had to be filled manually from drums of petrol which were hauled around the field by Greek army trucks. They were still waiting for the petrol bowser which would have been able to pump the fuel into the tanks in a few minutes. It was stuck in the mud somewhere between Trikkala and Yanina.

When the refuelling was complete the mist descended again, but Pat decided to risk a take-off, because he knew how important it was for the Greeks in the front line to have some support from the air. The mere sight of a dozen Gladiators over their positions would be morally uplifting, if nothing else.

At half past two Pat led his twelve Gladiators into the mist, and breathed a sigh of relief. The cloud layer was only 100 feet thick and they had emerged into brilliant sunshine. The Gladiators pointed their noses towards the Albanian border and opened out into their normal search formation. Pat's own sub-flight, consisting of the young baby-faced, ginger-haired Sammy Cooper and the steady reliable Flight Sergeant Richens, flew fairly low through the valleys, covered by another three Gladiators who were a couple of thousand feet higher. Another 2,000 feet above them, Flight Lieutenant Jimmy Kettlewell, leading the other six fighters, kept a wary eye open for the slightest sign of trouble.

They knew they were over the front line when the anti-aircraft guns opened fire but apart from this there was no other indication that this area was any different from any other part of the heavily wooded hillsides. There was no sign of any movement at all below them, but every Gladiator pilot knew that down there the hardy Greek warriors and the crack Italian Alpini were bitterly slogging it out, in deadly hand-to-hand combat, in the middle of a morass of mud.

For three-quarters of an hour the Gladiators flew to and fro along their allotted patrol line. Many Greeks must have been heartened by the sight of the twelve robust fighters keeping the skies clear of the hated Savoia bombers, though many more would have been delighted if the bombers had appeared. Their confidence in the Royal Air Force fighters was such that they knew the Gladiators would have torn the enemy formations to shreds.

The Gladiators were at the end of the patrol line near Premeti, and about to turn around for the last time prior to returning to Yanina, when Pat sighted two aircraft flying 1,000 feet below his section. Signalling to Cooper and Richens to follow, he dived towards the pair. He levelled out just behind and beneath the left-hand aircraft, which he quickly identified as an R.O. 37. He waited for Sammy Cooper to get into position astern of the second unsuspecting R.O. 37, and then both fired simultaneously. Each of the Italian reconnaissance machines fell to the ground enveloped in flames, although one of the occupants of Cooper's R.O. 37 managed to bale out and parachute safely to the ground.

Pat's section re-formed and continued to patrol for a further ten minutes without, however, sighting any more aircraft.

They landed at Yanina at four o'clock, which just gave them sufficient time to make out their reports for the ever-inquisitive Intelligence Officer, before collecting their ration of the eternal tinned 'meat and veg'.

Then, their work finished for the day, the pilots went off to visit the many Greek wounded soldiers housed in shocking conditions in the local hospital. It was so overcrowded that there was hardly room to move between the closely-packed beds. There were few drugs and little equipment, while disinfectant seemed to be unknown to the doctors and surgeons, who amputated legs and arms day and night. It was the only treatment they could use to prevent the spread of infection and disease.

The pilots shared their cigarette rations with the unfortunate Greeks, and brought some cheer amidst the miserable surroundings. The wounded loved these visits, and though few could speak English, their smiling faces were ample reward for Pat and the others, who in spite of their own hardships were comparatively well off.

The tears in the eyes of these cheerful, hardy people, and their sincere cries of 'Good luck, *Inglisi'*, touched the hearts of these hard-bitten fighter pilots and made them more determined than ever to defeat these swaggering overconfident Fascist bullies, who had brought all this misery to such pleasant, peace-loving peasants. This bitter determination was the key to the outcome of all the battles fought between 80 Squadron and the Italians. It gave the pilots that little extra incentive and dash which made all the difference in any unequal battle. It enabled the pilots, although outnumbered by as many as six to one, to turn on the enemy with such ferocity that invariably they were left victorious on the battlefield while the Italians made off for the safety of their base.

Next morning Warrant Officer MacLachlan carefully checked off each one of the groundcrews, and every item of equipment as it was loaded into the old Junkers, which was now used as a transport aircraft by the squadron. 'Mac' was responsible for the correct loading of these worn-out planes of Hellenic Air Lines and, knowing the difficult type of country over which it would be flying, he had to be absolutely certain that the Junkers would not be overloaded. According to his calculations he could not afford to allow even an extra pound above the limit, otherwise the ancient airliner would not be able to stagger around the mountains. Heavily loaded as it was, it would be a sitting duck if pounced upon by the nippy Italian fighters. For once he welcomed the heavy mist which hung over the airfield, for this would at least offer some protection in that it would undoubtedly keep the C.R. 42's on the ground. Their pilots seldom left the ground when the weather was so miserable.

Mac gave a thumbs-up to the bearded Greek pilot, climbed into the Junkers, and closed and locked the door. A few seconds later the huge transport lumbered across the airfield. Its engines roared, and everything on board shook and rattled, including the knees of the groundcrews as they anxiously waited for the plane to become airborne. The enormous wings bent into a crescent shape when they took the whole weight of the Junkers as it left the ground and just managed to scrape over the trees at the end of the field. It disappeared into the mist, still struggling for the necessary height to get over the mountain ridges.

Back on the airfield, Pat and the others climbed into the twelve Gladiators and prepared to take off. They, too, were going to Larissa, but what to them was an easy routine flight of about forty-five minutes' duration would be a nightmare ninety minutes of nervous tension to all aboard the Junkers.

The weather was kind, however, in that it remained unfit for flying, at least for the Italians, and both the Junkers and the Gladiators completed the trip to Larissa safely.

After lunch another nine Gladiators arrived. They had come from Trikkala, flown by Squadron Leader Hickey and eight pilots from 112 Squadron. Four of the Gladiators were handed over to one of the Greek squadrons at Larissa, whilst the other four Gladiators and their pilots, Flight Lieutenant Fry, Flying Officer Cochrane, Pilot Officer Smith and Second Lieutenant Geratty, were attached to 80 Squadron as reinforcements.

There were no operations and the squadron spent the rest of the day in settling in at their new quarters. Then, duty complete for the day, came the usual sight-seeing tour of a new town. Larissa was very similar to Yanina, except that it was bigger and not so crowded either with soldiers or mules. A peasant town, with old white stone buildings and cobbled streets, it had some new buildings along the main street, which was also the highway leading to the north. The pilots soon got bored with their touring and adjourned to the restaurant, with the usual wooden floor, hard-topped tables, and the inevitable smoke, grime and smell of aniseed.

It was fine the next day and soon after dawn eleven Gladiators of 80 Squadron, the attached four Gladiators from 112 Squadron, and the overloaded Junkers with the groundcrews, returned to the advanced landing-ground at Yanina for operations.

Fourteen of the Gladiators led by Hickey then went off to do an offensive patrol over the Tepelene area. One of the Greek column, though hampered by a fall of snow during the night, was pushing towards the important town of Premeti. The Greek warriors could not be reached by the mountain tracks, which were blocked by snow and the Wellingtons of 38 Squadron were out in force dropping food and supplies. The Blenheims of 84 and 211 Squadrons were all busily engaged in battering the Italian troops and communication in the area. This had brought out scores of tiny Fiat Fighters, who were just about to pile into the bombers when the Gladiators appeared on the scene.

Squadron Leader Hickey, leading the lower section, turned towards a large formation of twenty-seven C.R. 42's on his port side and was soon engaged.

Behind him, Flight Lieutenant Charlie Fry, leading the four Gladiators from 112 sighted another bunch of Fiats and dived into the midst of these.

Pat, leading the third section, came up astern of another group of five C.R. 42's, and with Casbolt and Cooper backing him up, made an unobserved approach from out of the sun. Pat chose the port flank aircraft as his target, and fired two short bursts directly into the fuselage. The Fiat dived steeply towards the ground, but flattened out at about 2,000 feet. Pat dived towards it and this time, after firing another brief burst, the C.R. 42 crashed into side of a hill a few miles north of Delvinakion.

Pat climbed back into the dogfight and found Squadron Leader

Hickey hard pressed with several C.R. 42's milling around him. One was coming in from astern with an easy no-deflection shot; the pilot was concentrating so hard on his sights that he never saw Pat close in quickly from the beam. A moment later Pat's tracers sliced into the Fiat and the Italian pilot lost all interest in Hickey's Gladiator as he struggled to get away from the hail of death from the rear. His cockpit filled with smoke and a tongue of flame licked along the fuselage. Pat pulled away and saw the pilot bale out of the doomed blazing fighter.

The sky was filled with wheeling Gladiators, but Pat could not see a single enemy aircraft. A few hundred feet above he could see the cloud base, and acting on an impulse, the result of experience gained in a dozen dogfights, he climbed up to investigate. It was only a thin layer of cloud, and as he broke through it into the clear blue sky above, he was not altogether surprised when he found all the enemy C.R. 42's flying round in circles 1,000 feet above him. Their tactics were obvious. They were hoping the Gladiators would climb up through the cloud to attack them, and as the Gladiators emerged from the cloud layer the 42's would be able to see them clearly against the background of white, and could attack as they pleased from a superior altitude. Already several of the Italian fighters were diving towards him. He rolled over and dipped back out of sight into the now friendly-looking clouds.

Unfortunately he picked a rather thin patch, and before he could do anything about it one of the Fiats had got in a well-aimed burst which put several holes through the Gladiator's main petrol tank. Then the cloud closed in round him and saved him from further damage.

He flew around in the cloud for a couple of minutes, changing direction several times. When he was sure that he was rid of any unwelcome followers he decided to have another look above the clouds. He was determined to make the Italians pay dearly for that damaged petrol tank. The nose of the Gladiator lifted as he pulled gently on the stick, and quite suddenly he emerged from the cloud. A shadow descended upon the mainplane, and glancing upwards Pat clearly saw a C.R. 42 flying almost immediately above him. Obviously it had not seen the Gladiator, otherwise it would have already dived to attack him.

Pat throttled back, so that he was hidden from the Italian pilot by the tailplane of the Fiat, and looked in his mirror to make sure there were no more enemy fighters behind his own tail. Then he pulled up the Gladiator into position slightly below and astern of the C.R. 42 and, taking careful aim, pressed the gun button for only a fraction of a second. The biplane turned slowly to the right and Pat saw the incredulous look on its pilot's face as he scrambled out of the cockpit and tumbled head over heels right in the path of the Gladiator. He missed the port wing tip by inches, as the startled Pat shot past him, and a second later disappeared into the cloud layer.

Several more C.R. 42's now appeared, apparently attracted by the petrol vapour streaming out behind the Gladiator, and Pat once more had to resort to the clouds for safety.

When he again came out for another look around he found two more C.R. 42's flying parallel to his course a quarter of a mile away at the same height just on top of the clouds. He pulled the Gladiator round towards them. They had evidently seen him, since they were also turning, and now the distance between Pat and the Italians quickly diminished as a head-on attack developed. The pilots of 'B' Flight had already learned during practice with the Master that it was useless ever to try a head-on attack on Pat. His split-second timing, his ice-cool nerve and his grim determination to succeed always enabled him to hang on longer and make his opponent break away first; as a result, Pat could do a breakthrough manoeuvre which enabled him to get on to the other's tail. So it was with these two Italians. They broke first, in different directions; in a flash Pat had viciously whipped up and round and was on the tail of one of the Fiats. Bluish black smoke gushed from the doomed fighter and it began to spin towards the clouds.

The other Fiat was now attacking Pat from the port quarter, and one of the wing struts snapped as a well-directed burst smashed into it. Pat pulled upwards with his throttle wide open, and saw two more Fiats diving towards him. He was going to Immelmann out of it, but quickly realised this would only set him up as a perfect target for the two coming down on him. He kicked the right rudder viciously and at the same moment pulled the stick right back. He stall-turned, and the two C.R. 42's roared over him, their guns still spitting tracers into the spot where he would have been but for his split-second reaction. Pat was now diving towards the first C.R. 42, but the Italian saw him coming and headed into the cloud layer. Pat gave it one quick burst before it disappeared and then wrenched the stick back once more. He blacked out momentarily, levelled out and saw that the sky was filled with Italian fighters, and not a single Gladiator anywhere. Two C.R. 42's were coming at him from the side, and another was diving towards his tail. He pulled up hard again, got away from the pair, but the one on his tail was still gaining on him. He dived fast, pushed the throttle wide open, and then pulled like a madman into a fast almost vertical climb. As his speed fell he rolled over and dived again. He saw a C.R. 32 dead ahead, fired a quick burst, which caused it to stall and spin into the clouds, and then stalled himself and also went into the cloud.

His fuel was dangerously low, so he stayed in the clouds and set course for Yanina. He felt satisfied. The three Fiats destroyed and the other two probably destroyed were ample revenge for the few holes he had sustained in the fuel tank and the smashed wing strut.

He half expected to find some of the squadron missing when he landed. But they had all returned safely and once again proved that determination and skill were more than a match for mere numerical superiority. In addition to Pat's victories, Sergeant Hewett had got two C.R. 42's and a G. 50, and Sergeant Gregory and Sergeant Barker had each destroyed a C.R. 42. Others also claimed probables, so that, when the balance sheet was made out, it was a most satisfactory result ... eight aircraft destroyed for certain, another seven unconfirmed, a possible loss to the enemy of fifteen fighters, and every Gladiator had returned safely, although several of them were riddled with bullet-holes.

The squadron escorted the Blenheims four times during the next two days, but failed to spot a single enemy aircraft. They met plenty of fierce anti-aircraft fire, however. After the fourth sortie the old Gladiators had taken such a hammering from the flak that there were only three aircraft considered suitable for operations. Consequently after the last patrol on 6 December the detachment returned to Larissa, the pilots for a few days' respite from operations, and the Gladiators for extensive major and minor repairs. Several of the Gladiators had to be written off completely; Jimmy Kettlewell, Shorty Graham and, a recent addition to the squadron, Pilot Officer Tulloch took off to fly to Athens, prior to embarking for Egypt to ferry new Gladiators to the unit.

Under normal conditions the repairs to some of the fighters were so extensive and difficult that they would have been sent back immediately to a Maintenance Depot. But the Salvage Unit which usually transported the unserviceable aircraft was unable to get to Larissa because of the bad state of the roads in Greece. Squadron Leader Hickey had no alternative but to order the whole of the squadron, including himself, to be put at the disposal of the Equipment Officer, whose task was the unenviable one of organising everything so that no time was lost in making the aircraft available for operational requirements.

Warrant Officer MacLachlan, the officer in charge of maintenance, and his team of non-commissioned officers and men worked like Trojans for more than a week on the Gladiators. Despite the non-stop showers of alternating rain, sleet and snow, the freezing temperatures, the bitterly cold wind and the great inconvenience of not possessing sufficient tools or the correct jigs for the job, they cheerfully stuck to it. They deserved far greater credit than the thanks of the Commanding Officer, sincere though they were, when they had accomplished their task and the squadron was once more classified as fit for operational service. Skilled as they were, no one could have blamed them if they had failed to do the job considering the task they had been allotted and the conditions under which they worked. It was only their great conscientiousness, determination and devotion to duty which kept the Royal Air Force fighters in Greece from being grounded for a much longer period. No praise could be too high for their courageous spirit.

The squadron was due to return to Yanina for operations at the earliest possible moment, but it was, in fact, more than a fortnight before they were able to do so. There was a week's delay whilst the

Gladiators were rendered serviceable and then a further delay owing to the bad weather, which prevented any flying at all for more than a week.

Thick clouds overhung the whole of northern Greece, causing a most depressing atmosphere, and torrential rains swept down, converting the airfields and roads into squelching morasses of mud. The rain turned to sleet and hail, and finally to snow, which slowly crept down the mountains surrounding Larissa. The temperature hovered around freezing-point for several days.

The pilots adjourned to the restaurant, where the main topic of conversation was the Greek advance into Albania. Never for a single moment had the Greeks relaxed their pressure, in spite of the bitter weather and the very nature of the rugged terrain. And there was nothing the Italians could do to stop the gallant little Greek army. Town after town fell before the onslaught. Argyrokastron, the Silver Fort, had been the first to fall on the very day that Pat had scored his triple victory. The Greeks wasted no time in occupying the town and pushed on along the road towards Tepelene. About the same time, some twenty miles across the mountains, another Greek division had captured Premeti. The Italians suffered an even worse blow in the coastal sector, when on 5 December they were forced to evacuate the port of Santi Quaranta. This was the place which the Italians had renamed Port Edda, in honour of Mussolini's daughter. In the northern region the Italian retreat continued and by the middle of the month the front line ran across the mountains in a meandering, jagged course. It was by no means a continuous line, for the very character of the country, with its precipices, gorges and rushing streams, could not allow for a connected system of machine-gun posts or strong-points. Himara, Tepelene and Kelcyre were now the objectives of the Greek armies, and if these fell, then the great port of Valona would be at the mercy of the Greeks.

A couple of American war correspondents came into the restaurant and gave the squadron a more personal side of the story. They had passed countless supply convoys on the mountainside.

'We saw,' one of them explained, 'open carts, pulled by sturdy little mules, and driven by cheerful Greeks, protected from the driving rain and wind by a single piece of canvas, ploughing through the mire. Here and there a cart was held fast by the clinging mud, and old men and women, and even small children, were scrambling around the hillsides searching for stones and branches to make the road passable again. In another place, some six thousand feet above sea-level, where the snow was knee deep and the temperature fifteen degrees below zero, we saw Greek soldiers without even a blanket or greatcoat. Their boots, too, were worn through after weeks of clambering over the rocky surfaces. And yet, for all the suffering and hardships they had to endure, they were always cheerful, and their morale is as high as that of any army.'

The two reporters then left for Athens, to plead to the readers of their respective newspapers for more aid from America in the form of food, clothing and medical supplies.

No. 80 Squadron waited with increasing impatience for the weather to improve.

Pat managed to catch up on his correspondence, which had been rather neglected since the squadron had come to Greece. He had the time now to think about his father and mother, whom he had not seen for nearly ten years, and he felt homesick. Both of his parents were now over 50 years of age, and if it had not been for the war he would have been at home bringing some comfort to their old age. They had sacrificed so much in order to give him the chance to become a flyer, and he had not even been able to say thanks, except in a letter, and that was not the same somehow.

He forced these thoughts into the background and took out his notebook, which quickly brought him back to the reality of war. Ever since that first aerial combat way back in the desert in August he had been jotting down notes about the science of air fighting. He had meticulously made out details of the weaknesses and strongpoints of every type of enemy aeroplane that he had encountered. His study of the enemy had enabled him to work out different rules of procedure for dealing with each type of enemy aircraft that he had engaged. For example his notes on the Savoia 79 advised a head-on attack, because it was too fast to allow an astern attack unless it was unseen. Then aim at one of the engines, which would slow down the bomber and enable an astern attack to be carried out. Silence the rear-gunner next, and then aim at the petrol tank situated in the starboard wing root. If this could be pierced, and the petrol forced to stream out behind the bomber, it was then a simple matter to fire a few tracer bullets into the vapour and cause the bomber to ignite.

Pat regarded air fighting as a science in which every little thing had to be taken into consideration.

'If you obey the rules,' he would say to his flight, 'air fighting is as safe as crossing the street. Use the clouds and sun to make an unseen approach, and when fighting always manoeuvre to get the enemy at a disadvantage by a full appreciation of the advantages and disadvantages of your aircraft as opposed to the enemy aeroplane.'

With his score standing at eleven confirmed victories plus a share in the destruction of two others, he now held the Middle East record for the number of enemy planes brought down by a single pilot, and consequently his advice was sought, accepted without question, and put into practice with much success by all pilots in the squadron. Pat's teachings were undoubtedly one of the key factors to the many great achievements of the squadron in combat.

11

Some of our aircraft did not return

For a few days the weather improved to such an extent that the old Junkers was able to get through to Yanina. It was followed by fourteen Gladiators. Thirteen of the fighters flew low over the airfield, and then carried on to do a patrol over the Tepelene area. The fourteenth landed and the pilot made his way to the operations hut. It was Pat, and he was miserable. He had a temperature, a buzzing head and a running nose; to make matters worse, he had been grounded by Squadron Leader Hickey, on the advice of the Medical Officer, in spite of the obstinate protests from Pat that he was 'well enough to take on the bloody I-ties'.

He hung around the airfield until the Gladiators returned, and he could tell immediately that they had been in action from the way they drifted back in twos and threes. Only ten of them returned.

Owing to the absence of any Gladiators over the front line for a fortnight, the Italians' morale had been boosted and they had sent up large numbers of both bombers and fighters. The Gladiators had attacked five S. 79's over Tepelene and had managed to shoot down one of the bombers before they had been set upon by scores of C.R. 42's and G. 50's. Almost immediately Sammy Cooper's Gladiator had been set on fire, and he had been forced to bale out. As he descended an enemy fighter had fired at the helpless pilot swinging beneath the parachute. Hickey had shot down the C.R. 42 and then had gone down himself. The rest of the Gladiators, by the sheer skill and determination of their pilots, had managed to extricate themselves from a difficult position, without further loss. On the way back, however, Sergeant Hewett's

Gladiator, which had been severely damaged in the fight, was forced to land some twenty miles north of Yanina.

The same evening, soon after Hewett had returned unscathed, Leland Stowe and Ed Stevens, two American war correspondents, arrived in Yanina. They had seen the whole of the fight from the ground.

After shooting down the Fiat biplane, Squadron Leader Hickey had landed in a water-logged field near Argyrokastron. He had taken possession of a Greek truck and set out to find Sammy Cooper. Hickey had found Sammy lying seriously wounded in an area which might be considered a No-man's-land, for it was the centre of a region swarming with both Greek and Italian troops. In the face of heavy artillery fire, he had carried the injured pilot across a swollen, rushing river back to his truck and then driven to the hospital in Argyrokastron. But his tremendously courageous effort was all in vain, for the youngster had lost too much blood. He died later that same evening.

Hickey returned to Yanina at half past nine the following morning, just in time to see Pat taking off with nine Gladiators for a patrol over the Kelcyre sector. The object of the patrol was to cover the return of the Blenheims of 211 Squadron and to engage any enemy aircraft in the area.

The Gladiators should have met the Blenheims at half past ten midway between Tepelene and Kelcyre. They were fifteen minutes early, so Pat opened out the formation into three sections echeloned away from enemy territory at a height of 10,000 feet, and proceeded to fly up and down the patrol line. The air was clear and frosty at this height, and Pat held the stick between his knees so that he could beat the cold from his tingling fingers. His head was continually on the move, searching above and below, to the left and to the right, looking for some sign of the bombers or of the C.R. 42's which he knew could not be far away. But all he could see were a few traces of flimsy cloud 5,000 feet higher, and his section tucked in close beside his port wing tip. Sergeant Casbolt, as usual, was next to him, his head also turning, and on the far side of Casbolt was Richens. Farther away the other two sections were also neatly tucked together.

Below, the undulating countryside looked very rough, with snow-capped mountain peaks, valleys crowded with trees, deep narrow gorges with streams foaming white as they rushed over rocky beds. Pat did not fancy making a forced landing in this treacherous area, and for a few seconds he listened to the old Mercury engine to make sure that it was still running smoothly. The healthy roar, the whirling propeller and the whistle of the wind through the struts and wires, reassured him, and he continued to scan the sky for some sign of the Blenheims.

He glanced at his watch. Ten-forty. The bombers were ten minutes late already. They must have run into trouble.

Quite suddenly he noticed to the north-west condensation trails of white vapour showing clearly against the bright blue sky. It could be the nine Blenheims of 211 Squadron, but it might also be enemy aircraft; as a precaution, he took the Gladiators up another couple of thousand feet and prepared them for combat.

He could now make out nine aircraft in the approaching formation and they were definitely multi-engined, but he was still uncertain whether they were friendly or hostile.

The Gladiators were in a perfect position to make an attack, when Pat's searching eyes discovered the expected C.R. 42's. There were eleven of them flying about 8,000 feet above Pat's formation. However, they appeared not to have noticed the Gladiators, since they flew steadily on. Pal hoped to engage the bombers, which were now very close and easily identifiable as Savoia 79's, without being disturbed, so he ordered the third section to remain and keep an eye on the Fiats, whilst he led the other six Gladiators down in a line-astern dive towards the Savoias.

Pat was halfway down, with his speedometer registering 300 miles an hour, when he realised that the first section of bombers would pass before he could get within effective range. He therefore swung round and attacked the second section of three from ahead and slightly to one quarter. As he closed he opened fire and kept on firing as he swung through the beam, and completed his attack from quarter astern. He broke away less than 50 yards from the S. 79 on the right of the formation, which emitted a puff of black smoke from the starboard engine. The other five Gladiators were firing at the remainder of the Savoias.

The bomber which Pat had attacked and disabled now fell behind the rest of the Savoias, jettisoned its bombs and turned right towards Tepelene. The Gladiator swung in dead astern of it at a range of about 100 yards; setting about the task in the manner advocated in his notebook, Pat fired short bursts at the fuselage in an attempt to put the rear-gunner out of action. A fire broke out just in front of the bottom turret, whose guns had now ceased to fire, and a few seconds later the nose of the Savoia dropped. Pat slopped firing, and followed the bomber down. A hatch in the front of the fuselage flew open, and three small figures toppled into space, their parachutes blossoming like enormous mushrooms as Pat's Gladiator whipped past them.

A fourth figure fell out just before the bomber dived straight into the top of a mountain about five miles south-east of Tepelene. It exploded with a terrible sheet of flame which melted the snow and scorched the earth for 50 yards around.

Five minutes later Pat was back over his patrol line and the Gladiators were re-forming behind him. Two of them, damaged by the withering cross-fire of the Italian bombers, were forced to return to base, but the other seven continued to patrol between Kelcyre and Tepelene.

Pat again spotted the C.R. 42's, this time about eighteen of them, but they remained at a safe distance. They must have witnessed the attack on the Savoias, but had made no attempt to intervene. A Gladiator shot past Pat, and waggled its wings. It was the Keg, and he was pointing upwards with violent gestures. Evidently he had seen the Italian fighters, too. Pat merely nodded and then carried on, ignoring the 42's. It was only on returning to Yanina that he discovered that Dowding had seen another large formation of C.R. 42's, making over forty altogether.

Another formation of bombers was approaching. They were Savoia 81's much slower than the 79's and therefore easier to attack. There were six of them, in two sections of three. Pat attacked the middle aircraft of the leading section from the rear, closing right up behind it. Almost as soon as he pressed the gun button the enemy bomber jettisoned its bombs and its speed increased. Pat soon caught up with it again, and aimed at the starboard engine and fuel tank. Petrol streamed from the damaged tank and was a perfect target for a few rounds of incendiary bullets. Unfortunately Pat's wing guns which contained all his supply of incendiary ammunition, were already empty, so he concentrated the few remaining rounds from his fuselage guns towards the port engine of the Savoia.

Short puffs of smoke came from the engine and the Italian bomber turned back towards Albania. With no ammunition left, Pat formated just above and behind the 81, hoping another Gladiator would come and finish it off. But they were all busy elsewhere.

The bomber slowly lost height, and after flying about five miles the starboard engine packed up completely. It seemed impossible for the bomber to carry on much longer and Pat could visualise the Italian pilot searching for a place to put down his mangled aircraft. About fifteen miles north of Kelcyre the Italian spotted a friendly looking field in a valley and attempted to make a forced landing. Unfortunately for him, the field was much too small for the big bomber to land safely, and it finally ended up against a tree, its tail stuck high into the air, its nose buried in the soft earth, and its starboard wing and engine completely severed from the fuselage.

Satisfied with his day's work, Pat returned to Yanina and discovered that Cherry Vale had brought down another S. 81.

Squadron Leader Hickey was delighted and straight away rang up Headquarters in Athens.

'We got three bombers today, two 81's and a 79. But three Gladiators will need some patching up.'

'Good show!' came the reply from Headquarters. 'But you will have to do better than that. The Greeks are being badly knocked about by the Savoias, and you will have to try to keep them away. Can you manage to get in two patrols a day?'

Hickey hesitated before replying. He was furious.

'We can if you can let us have some replacement aircraft and some spares. At the moment, after today's effort, there are only six Gladiators fit for operations; and it takes hours to refuel them with the obsolete equipment that we have up here. Can you let us have a petrol bowser?'

'I will see what I can do, but I can't promise anything for certain with the roads as they are. It might take weeks to get a bowser through the mud. I have three Gladiators here that have just flown in from Abu Suweir and I will get them up to you as soon as possible.'

'Thanks,' said Hickey, 'but we'll need more than that. How about some Hurricanes?'

'I'm afraid that's impossible. All the Hurricanes are needed urgently in the Western Desert at the moment. That was a good effort of yours yesterday, going after Cooper. You will be pleased to hear the AOC has recommended you for the DFC. Pity about Cooper. He was a fine officer.'

'Yes. He will take some replacing.'

'Pilot Officer Lancaster arrived from Egypt today. He's fully recovered, and I'll send him up with one of the replacement Gladiators. Flight Lieutenant Jones will also be joining you in a few days. He is out of hospital, where I'm told he was looked after by a member of the Greek Royal Family. I'll expect to hear from you again tomorrow. Tell the chaps it was a good show today.'

Next morning ten Gladiators were fit for operations, thanks once again to the strenuous efforts of MacLachlan and the groundcrews. At ten-thirty precisely they roared across the airfield and, led by Squadron Leader Hickey, set off towards their patrol area between Tepelene and the coast.

They climbed rapidly to clear the low range of mountains around the airfield, and then pulled out into battle formation, an echelon to starboard in three sections. The first section contained four Gladiators, with Hickey leading, and behind him, in a stagger running to the right, Flying Officer Hosken, Sergeant Gregory and another pilot who had only recently joined from 112 Squadron, Flying Officer Price-Owen. A few yards behind the first section and farther to the right Pat led the second section, with Sergeant Casbolt and Flight Sergeant Richens close beside him. Still farther away Syd Linnard at the head of the third section had Cherry Vale and Flying Officer Ripley tight behind him.

They continued to climb until they reached 10,000 feet, which was a safe height to get over the snowy tips of the Pindus Mountains. The cloud was patchy and low and only occasionally was Pat able to catch a glimpse of the ground to check a landmark. Here and there an isolated snow-topped peak pierced the cloud and gave warning of what was hidden beneath the layer. Above the Gladiators the sky was clear and the sun strong and glaring, the ideal spot, Pat thought, from which to expect the C.R. 42's to attack.

Hickey's flying was good, simple and straightforward, and this made it easier on the others following behind. The cloud began to thin as they penetrated deeper into Albania and they picked out the river flowing at the side of a winding road which led to Argyrokastron. This was a popular bombing target for the Italians nowadays, and Hickey was hoping to meet the Savoias as they began their bombing run. This was the most dangerous part of any bombing raid, at least for the bomber, since whilst running up to bomb a target it had to fly straight and level, the pilot concentrating on the directions being given by the bomb-aimer. If, as Hickey hoped, the Gladiators could hit the Savoias at this particularly vulnerable moment their chances of success would be enhanced 100 per cent.

They were a mile or so north of Argyrokastron before Hickey waggled his wings, and Pat, looking down and straight ahead, picked out three Savoias. Hickey gave the Tally-ho and rolled over and down towards the Italians, followed at closely spaced intervals by Hosken, Gregory and Price-Owen. Pat peeled off next, but, as usual whilst diving towards the bombers, kept a wary eye searching for the escort fighters. In doing so he spotted another formation of three Breda BR. 20's approaching the port beam, and as these were in a much more favourable position for an attack he turned his section towards them. He looked over his shoulder and saw the faithful Casbolt and Richens following close behind, and in the same instant spotted the escort fighters dead astern and 10,000 feet higher. They had already peeled off and were diving in line astern towards the Gladiators. Pat shouted a warning into the microphone, giving the number and position of the C.R. 42's, and then slammed the throttle to full boost in an attempt to engage the BR. 20's before the Fiats arrived on the scene.

The three Italian raiders scattered in a bomb-burst as the three lethal biplanes tore through their formation. For a fraction of a second one of the Bredas flashed into Pat's ring sight, and he pushed viciously on the gun button. Then he was past the bomber, tugging at the control column, and shouting like a madman to fight off the blackness spreading in front of his eyes. For a second or so he succumbed to the terrific force of gravity draining the blood from his head, then his eyes cleared and he rolled over at the top of the loop. His eyes confirmed what he had expected to see, though he was a little surprised when he realised how many Italian fighters were diving straight towards him. There must have been at least fifty of the blighters, all in wicked trios in line abreast. He glanced over his shoulder and was again reassured by the heartening sight of the Gladiators of Casbolt and Richens coming up quickly to formate behind him.

He pulled up to meet the first attack, saw the vicious orange flashes of the Fiats' guns, and sensed the hail of bullets passing harmlessly beneath him, for the range was still too great for accurate aiming. The enemy fighters broke away at least a quarter of a mile from the Gladiator, and Pat gave them a look of contempt before gritting his teeth to meet the next three. Again the nimble C.R. 42's broke off before coming into shooting distance. The next three repeated these tactics, and so did the following trio. For fully five minutes these continuous and indeterminate attacks were carried out in quick succession, but without much success. Pat was becoming bored with the whole business, for in spite of the great numerical superiority of the Italian fighters they were getting nowhere because of their lack of determination; Pat was not able to get in an attack himself, except at too great a distance to do any appreciable damage.

He decided to change his tactics. He watched the next three very carefully as they swung away, and saw that they levelled out 1,000 feet below and then climbed up again, presumably to take their place in the queue for the next attack.

He would take a risk with the next trio by following them down and round. It would mean that he would be directly in the path of the following attack, with his back towards it, but he was counting on Casbolt and Richens to back him up and keep his tail clear.

The next three Fiats were on their way down. It was now or never. He snapped into a roll, viciously forced the throttle wide open, and came down in a hell-dive, closing in rapidly behind the last of the 42's. At point-blank range he fired a short burst into the belly of the fighter. It shot up vertically, stalled and then spun down towards the foothills, leaving a trail of smoke and flaming débris behind it.

Tracers flashing past his wings warned Pat of the danger behind in the form of the next diving Fiat. He slammed on full rudder and as he skidded round saw the 42 zoom past with Sergeant Casbolt less than 50 yards from its tail. Casbolt's tracers were already ripping into the Italian fighter, tearing it apart. There was a blinding flash as the petrol tank exploded, and the next moment the plane became an inferno of flaming fabric and melting metal.

Half a mile away to the right and much higher there was a mass of whirling, mixed-up biplanes, most of them C.R. 42's, though Pat did pick out one Gladiator hurtling down behind two enemy fighters. He saw its orange and yellow flashes of tracer slice into one of the C.R. 42's, which shot upwards, hung for a moment, its propeller clawing at the air, and then fell away into an ever-quickening spiral dive.

Way ahead Pat could see another Gladiator descending in slow, flat circles, with two C.R. 42's firing straight into its cockpit. He was on the point of turning to go to its aid, when another Gladiator rocketed down and pulled up for a perfect shot beneath the tails of the Fiats.

Another Gladiator flaming furiously just missed the port wing of his plane, and Pat could see the still figure in the cockpit slumped forward across the control column. It was Flying Officer Ripley. He had only been with the squadron for a few weeks.

Pat looked upwards, searching for the C.R. 42 that had got Ripley, and saw the Italian fighter winging away, with Cherry Vale's Gladiator going after it. Cherry closed in right behind the Fiat, and clung to it like a leech, pouring burst after burst into the fighter, until it finally began to burn.

Most of the Italian fighters were still thousands of feet above Pat's head, and realising that he was ineffective unless he could reach that height, he wriggled out of the fight. He flew south towards Argyrokastron, climbing until he had reached 18,000 feet. He turned and with the sun behind him flew back towards the dogfight. He quickly discovered nine C.R. 42's circling over the town at the same height, but could see no sign of any Gladiator and the fight seemed to be over. He singled out the nearest C.R. 42 as his target, but unfortunately when still more than 300 yards from the enemy plane the Italian pilot saw him and dived towards the ground. The rest of the Fiats quickly followed him down. Apparently they did not relish the idea of being attacked by a Gladiator from the same height, although they had such a terrific advantage in numerical superiority.

Pat circled the town of Argyrokastron for another five minutes, but the sky was now empty. He set course for Yanina.

He could see three Gladiators on the airfield as he came down and rolled low over the boundary fence. He put down his flaps and glided in. His fitter and rigger came walking towards the Gladiator as he taxied towards a corner of the field.

He walked towards the ambulance, where he could see Richens, Casbolt and Cherry Vale sitting on the running board with Doc Astbury, the Medical Officer.

'What's happened to the others?' Pat inquired as he neared the group.

'We don't know,' answered Richens, 'except that Cherry saw Squadron Leader Hickey bale out.'

Pat was surprised. He looked inquiringly at Cherry Vale.

'I saw him come out of a mass of 42's. His engine had stopped and he jumped over the side and opened his brolly. The next moment one of those bloody bastards came in and fired at his parachute. I got the 42, and two others, one of them a flamer, but by that time Hickey's chute was blazing furiously. He didn't stand a chance.'

Pat was shocked. This was the second time in three days that the Italians had fired at a defenceless human being swinging beneath a parachute. It was a cowardly, inhuman way of fighting, and brought home to them all the murderous nature of war.

Two more Gladiators came in and the pilots, Hosken and Price-Owen, came over to join them.

A third Gladiator appeared. It was coming in much too fast.

'His flaps have gone.'

The Gladiator smacked the ground and bounced. It came down again and skidded across the field, coming to a stop on the edge of the field, just short of the area where the grass was thick and long. The pilot did not get out. It was Syd Linnard.

The ambulance was already on its way, the pilots standing on the running board and clinging to the doors. They lifted Linnard from the cockpit, saw the splashes of blood on his trousers, and gently carried him into the ambulance, where Doc Astbury took over. They waited outside and talked about the combat.

Pat was summing up: 'Only Sergeant Gregory is missing now. Did anyone see him?' He looked at Hosken and Price-Owen, who had been flying with Gregory in Hickey's leading section.

Both shook their heads. Hosken said: 'We all got split up after the initial attack. The last I saw of Greg he was going after three Fiats. I tried to follow him, but another couple of 42's came between us.'

'What happened to the rest of you?'

Richens began: 'Well I got one 42 for certain and then I saw Vale get two more.'

'I got three altogether,' said Cherry, 'and I also saw Richens get his.'

'You got one off my tail, Casbolt,' said Pat. 'Did you get anything else?'

'Another 42 possibly. It was still spinning and shedding pieces when I last saw it.'

Hosken and Price-Owen claimed a probable each.

Doc Astbury climbed down from the ambulance and reported to Pat, who would have to take charge now that Hickey was gone.

'Linnard will be out of action for several months. There are several bullets still in his left leg and he will have to go back to Athens for an operation. I have given him a shot of morphia to ease the pain and cleaned up the wounds as well as I can. He will have to go back to Athens as soon as possible.'

'Thanks, Doc. I'll arrange for one of the Blenheims to fly him there this afternoon.'

They heard the sound of another aircraft approaching. It must be the missing Gregory. The Gladiator's engine sounded terrible, and it came straight in, downwind, without the usual demonstration roll. It taxied right up to them. Gregory looked a mess. His face was caked with blood. They rushed over to help him down from the cockpit, and half-carried and half-dragged him across to the ambulance.

Again they stood around in a group, silent this time, and waited for the Doc to do his job.

MacLachlan came over, saluted, and gave Pat a rough check on the planes. All would need a thorough check, and it would be impossible to get any of them ready in time for another patrol before tomorrow. Two of them, Linnard's and Gregory's, would not be ready for a week at least, and three others would need plenty of sewing.

The Medical Officer climbed down from the ambulance. Sergeant Gregory was with him, looking much better, with a large bandage wrapped round his head, nearly covering up his right eye, but not hiding the grim smile that spread across his sunburnt cheeks.

'You can't get rid of me that easily,' he chuckled.

He had had a gruelling time in the dogfight and only his grim determination in the face of terrific odds had enabled him to get out of it in one piece.

Later that evening Pat picked up Gregory's combat report. As he read it through ne realised how fortunate he was to be in the company of such men; and how unfortunate were those who had to put up with the company of men who would kill a defenceless man descending under a parachute.

Sergeant Gregory had sighted three Fiat C.R. 42's which he had immediately attacked. His report described it in detail.

Turning round in a stall turn I observed the leader [of the 42's] diving vertically whilst the remaining two had split, No. 2 going up, No. 3 down. As I had the advantage over the lower aircraft I decided to attack this first. He attempted to come up under me but as I was near to stalling, I had no difficulty in bringing my sight round to get in a deflection shot and then turn astern on him.

I followed him down. At the same time I observed the leading aircraft crash on a hill and burst into flames. This dive was very sleep, so much so, that I very nearly hit the ground with the 42. When I pulled up sharply out of this dive the third 42 came past and then pulled up underneath me into such a position that we could both get in quick deflection shots.

This happened three times and each lime we missed colliding by inches, so that after each attack I had to find him again. Quite naturally this developed into a head-on attack, the first of which I slid out of. As the following attack was also head-on I became rather worried. I brought him into my sights, fired, ducked down behind my engine for cover, at the same time pulling back on the control column.

Immediately after this my right eye became warm and I found I had lost my sight in this eye. It took me some seconds to get used to this, as I would try to look towards the rear on the right side, but all I saw was the extensive damage to the centre section, starboard lower plane and a flying wire that had broken. I seem to remember at this point that he came at me from below and we had another deflection shot at each other, but as I had seen him so often in this position it may have stuck in my mind. However, I do remember I decided that my position was desperate and I weighed up the ground that was to receive me below. When I was overcome by a wave of determination, possibly due to the fact that when I was hit and saw the blood I turned my oxygen on at full strength. I pulled up in a loop and rolled off the top into a tight turn back into the direction I had come from. I looked at my compass but it seemed blurred.

Although I could see the sun, I could not convince myself which direction to fly.

Diving down into the valley seemed to be the only means of escape. I was unable to look behind, as this brought on pain in my eye.

At one period my sight was so blurred that I could not decide whether I was being chased by a 42 or if it was A.A. fire. Fortunately it was the latter. I discovered my position to be ten miles north of Valona at four thousand feet. As I could use only sixteen hundred revolutions due to damage to the rocker arm, causing excessive vibration, it took forty minutes to return to base, where a landing was made under difficulties due to damage to eyesight and to undercarriage.

Pat placed the report on his desk and decided there and then to recommend Gregory for a Distinguished Flying Medal when he rang up Headquarters later that day. He did not expect them to be overjoyed, since the squadron had failed to down a single bomber, and had lost two pilots as well, but what else could they expect with the veteran planes they were flying. Eight confirmed victories, and five more unconfirmed, against odds of more than five to one, did not seem such a bad score to him, but then he was only a flight lieutenant taking part in the action. The others at Headquarters, wing commanders, squadron leaders and so on, might well ask the impossible, whilst still flying a desk behind the safety of the four walls of the Grand Bretagne Hotel. Let them come out here into this frozen outpost and see if they could do any better.

Pat was not normally bitter towards anyone. In fact, if anything he was the contrary, forgiving and always ready to go out of his way to apologise if he thought he had hurt anyone, intentionally or not. But the events of the past few days had made him so tired that he did not seem to be able to think clearly. At any other time he would not have thought such things about the Staff at Headquarters. Group Captain Willetts, Wing Commander Paddy Coote and Squadron Leader Cryer were all first-class pilots, who would have been far happier taking a more active part in operations than passing on the orders of their superiors to the squadrons in the field. They were only doing their job and, like it or not, there was little that could be done about it except to get on with it.

Pat was upset emotionally. His mind was clouded with the incidents of the last few days; the shooting down of two fine and courageous men swinging defenceless beneath their parachutes; the loss of their smiling, ginger-haired Australian Commanding Officer; the shooting up of Linnard and Gregory; and only that afternoon the funeral service of the popular young Sammy Cooper. The mess would not be quite the same without them.

He was so tired that he did not care about anything. His head dropped forward on to the desk, the pen slipped from his unfeeling fingers, and he fell fast asleep.

12

A welcome break

A relief squadron of Greek Gladiators was due to arrive at Yanina, so that the detachment could return to Larissa for Christmas. However, the weather again took command of the situation and, although the Greek fighters managed to land at Yanina, the snow came down so thick and fast that it was impossible for any aircraft to take off.

When it became obvious that they would have to spend Christmas at Yanina, Pat began to organise things so that it would be as enjoyable as possible in spite of the lack of home comforts. There were no turkeys available, but the local Greek peasants were very generous and provided a supply of chickens. They also gave the squadron a large Christmas tree which was fixed up in the mess and decorated with candles and souvenirs from shot-down Italian aircraft.

Pat organised a duck-shooting party on Christmas Eve and they went out on to the frozen lake. They all thoroughly enjoyed the hunt, which, however, was not such a huge success as far as subsidising the Christmas larder was concerned, for they all returned empty-handed. The ducks were even better than the Italians at hiding themselves from the guns of the Royal Air Force pilots.

Christmas morning was quiet. They all stayed in bed later than usual, except the bombastic Sergeant Battle, who had been given the task of finding sufficient quantities of the precious beer for the party.

There was a short church parade, during which they sang carols with great gusto but little harmony. Then they adjourned to the local restaurant for the banquet, which was a huge success. Although it was by no means a traditional English dinner with turkey and plum pudding, the chickens were very tasty and made a pleasant change from the eternal bully beef, especially when served by the officers in the traditional Royal Air Force manner. The arrangements made by Sergeant Battle were excellent, with plentiful supplies of the 'airmen's beverage', though no one ever found out how the giant sixteen stone sergeant had managed to acquire such an enormous quantity of the coveted liquid. Pat gave a short speech, in which he complimented everyone who had helped to make it such a gay occasion, and ended by calling for three hearty cheers for the red-faced and by now high-spirited Sergeant Battle.

Later in the afternoon everybody was invited to the Christmas Tree Party organised by the Greek Youth Movement. Each of the airmen received a small souvenir and a liberal supply of wine, after which they joined enthusiastically in the songs, games and dances. The party ended in the early hours of the morning, with Pat preserving his dignity and respect as the Officer in Charge of 80 Squadron, by walking unaided and without a single falter back to his quarters.

It stopped snowing on Boxing Day and the following morning conditions had improved so much that the Gladiators were able to take off. Twinstead Flower had to make a hurried return to the airfield when his engine cut at 200 feet after take-off, but the others carried on to Larissa to rejoin the rest of the squadron. When they got there they were informed that the airfield was overcrowded and were ordered to continue to Eleusis aerodrome in Athens.

They stopped overnight in the Greek capital and flew back to Larissa the next morning. The Italians had already made two raids on the town that morning and, when the ten Gladiators arrived over the airfield, the alarm had just been sounded for the third time. Pat was told over the radio-telephone to continue to search for enemy aircraft. The Gladiators carried on for another thirty minutes looking for the enemy raiders, but failed to find a single aircraft. However, soon after Pat's formation had landed, Ape Cullen, in another Gladiator which had taken off from Larissa when the alarm went, came back with better news. He had flown out over the sea to the east towards the peninsula of Kassandra, where he had found a three-engined Italian bomber. He had set one engine on fire with his first attack and after several more onslaughts had sent the S. 81 diving into the sea west of Kassandra.

When Pat landed he found that Tap Jones had returned from convalescence and had been made Squadron Commander. Heimar Stuckey and Johnny Lancaster, fully recovered from their wounds, were also back and the mess was once again more like it used to be. In fact, conditions had eased so much that the squadron was able to enjoy a few days' rest from operations; Pat himself was granted ten days' leave.

He was fed up with the cold and the snow and when he learned that one of the Blenheims from 211 Squadron was returning to the warmth and sunshine of Cairo he immediately thumbed a lift. Whenever it was possible he always spent his leaves at the Evers-Swindells' bungalow. He and Old Man Evers were the greatest of friends; they seemed to have the same likes and dislikes. Besides, Old Man Evers's wife Muriel was so good at looking after him. She darned his socks, made his favourite cake and, generally speaking, gave him a little of the home life that he had missed for so long.

Those few days of peace, warmth, happiness and contentment were over all too soon, but they were an invaluable few days to Pat, for he felt fighting fit and once again intensely eager to come to grips with the enemy.

He flew back to Eleusis aerodrome and found most of the squadron's Gladiators around the perimeter. The squadron had been ordered to return to Yanina for operations, but the snow and ice, and the temperature, which rarely rose above freezing-point and at night frequently fell to minus 20 degrees, had prevented the squadron from getting over the pass. They had remained at Larissa until 112 Squadron flew in; the station had then become so overcrowded that most of the pilots of 80 Squadron had been forced to fly to Eleusis. Half a dozen airmen, the Medical Officer and Adjutant, who had left a few days earlier in a staff car and two lorries, had somehow managed to find their way through the snowstorms and were now stranded at Yanina. Squadron Leader Jones and a token force of men remained at Larissa, whilst the bulk of the groundcrews, who had left Larissa bound for Yanina on 15 January, had reached Trikkala. They had been ordered to remain there by Squadron Leader Jones, when he heard the news that the mountain road was blocked by snow.

At dawn on the 17th the main convoy was able to proceed once more, but unfortunately, on approaching the snow level in the Katara Pass, a blinding snowstorm brought the lorries to an abrupt standstill. The airmen huddled together for warmth behind the thin canvas covering on the trucks and watched helplessly as the Greek snowplough driver toiled energetically against great odds, with an aged machine, to do the impossible, to clear the tons and tons of snow covering the road through the pass. In the end he had to give up the hopeless task; the groundcrews heard a rumour later that he was severely punished because of this. They were of the opinion that he should have been given a medal for his great devotion in sticking at the job for so long in such fantastic conditions.

When it was realised that the convoy would have to remain in the mountains indefinitely the officer in charge, Pilot Officer Patullo, immediately made arrangements to evacuate the airmen to the village of Malekas, a tiny hamlet eight miles away at the foot of the mountains. The local villagers, tough sturdy peasants, received the men with open arms, providing them with bowls of hot, steaming soup, thick black boiling coffee, and warm blankets in front of a blazing fire. Without this help, most willingly given by the cheerful, hardy people, some of the men would almost certainly have perished in the arctic conditions prevailing in the mountains.

To supplement the meagre food reserves of the villagers, which were never intended to replenish the appetites of so many hungry airmen, Warrant Officers Casey and MacLachlan set off up the mountain towards the snowbound vehicles. They dug out some tinned foods, made a sledge from the wooden baseboards of one of the lorries, and loaded up the rations. They commenced the return journey, dragging the sledge behind them, but the snow was so deep and treacherous that they could only make slow progress, and when darkness fell they became hopelessly lost. They trudged on through the snow, not daring to stop, in case they fell asleep and froze to death. Eventually, after an agonising length of time, they sighted a tiny light on a wayside shrine, which helped them to find their way back to their billets just as daylight was breaking.

When the temperature fell to thirty-two degrees below freezing point a maintenance party led by Sergeant Farley had to return to the convoy to drain the radiators and turn the vehicles. They were accompanied by several of the local peasants. These people set a wonderful example of courage in adversity, the women working equally as hard as their menfolk, as they all struggled to turn the heavy vehicles on the snowbound, precipitous road, where the slightest slip could have cost a life, or a vehicle – with its valuable load. They pulled and pushed in unison, amid enthusiastic and infectious laughter, and soon all the trucks had been turned, and were ready to proceed back down the pass as soon as conditions improved.

On the 20th one of the drivers remaining with the vehicles complained of a pain in the stomach, and two other airmen began to show signs of suffering from the bitter cold. An improvised sledge was constructed from an old tin bath and the three sick airmen were dragged ten miles to a point from which they were evacuated to Trikkala by car.

Later the same day boxes containing documents and files, and other equipment urgently needed at Yanina, were unloaded from the lorries and most of the groundcrews boarded the trucks and returned to Larissa. As they drove away down the mountain track the airmen looked back and saw the Greek villagers wearing long black cloaks with pointed hoods, in Walt Disney cartoon fashion, toiling up the mountainside in a long crocodile, their backs bent beneath the weight of the heavy boxes containing ammunition, supplies and equipment. Under the watchful eye of Corporal Steele, this mass of material was carried many miles over the dangerous, slippery way and arrived at Yanina many days before the rest of the party, who had to make their way by the southerly route via Lamia, Agrinon and Artae.

Probably never in the history of the whole of the Royal Air Force have airmen undergone such an experience and, although great discomfort was suffered by everyone, not a single word of disobedience or even discontent was uttered by the groundcrews – one more tribute to the devotion, determination, courage and comradeship of this fighter squadron.

The war was still going on, but there was very little fighting along the Albanian front line. Snow and bitterly cold winds kept the Greeks in their mountain hideouts, and for most of the time all aircraft were grounded. It was impossible to keep either bombers or fighters in the air for very long without great danger from ice forming on wings and airscrews. Even instruments froze solid and aircraft were just not able to maintain sufficient altitude to clear the mountains.

Greek casualties steadily mounted, not as a result of the efforts of the Italians, but on account of the extreme weather conditions.

In Athens Pat watched hundreds of ill-equipped Greek soldiers arriving at the hospital. The majority of them had suffered severe frostbite, and many had lost arms and legs which had been removed by the Greek surgeons in the front line. Amputation was the only cure when neither drugs nor equipment were available to the doctors.

As he stood on the steps of the hospital the sirens began to wail a warning that an air raid was imminent. Pat turned away and strolled towards 'Maxie's', the restaurant which was the favourite haunt of the aircrews in Athens. He was almost there when he heard the faint sound of an aircraft engine far away and, looking up into the heavens, he soon spotted the small silhouette of an Italian reconnaissance machine flying very high and evidently taking photographs of Piraeus harbour. Pat knew it was packed tightly with shipping, mostly transport vessels and troopships; he also knew what it would mean if that aeroplane managed to get back to its base with the news. The Italians would make every effort to sink as many of these ships as possible before the troops could be disembarked. He hurried back to the aerodrome at Eleusis. It was almost twenty miles away, and took him about thirty minutes in the station wagon. When he drove in past the guard-room three Gladiators were just landing in perfect formation, their gun covers still intact. It was obvious that they had not managed to engage the spotter aircraft.

The sandy-haired flight lieutenant who climbed from the leading Gladiator walked across to Pat's jeep; it was 'Timber' Woods, a rough, superstitious, impetuous Irishman who had joined the squadron whilst Pat was in Cairo. He wore the ribbon of the Distinguished Flying Cross, which he had been awarded six months before, when defending Malta with the famous 'Faith, Hope and Charity' Gladiator flight.

'Any luck?' Pat inquired.

'No,' grunted the Irishman. 'With these bloody worn-out chariots, we were lucky to catch a glimpse of the I-ties. If we don't get some Hurricanes soon, these poor old Glads will fall apart in the air.'

Within an hour the signal Pat had expected arrived from Headquarters. It gave orders that all pilots of the detachment at Eleusis would be required to stand by with their aircraft from dawn to dusk on the following day, to defend a convoy in the dock from an anticipated attack by Italian bombers.

The raid did not materialise until midday, when a message was given over the tannoy system that Italian bombers were approaching from the west. Immediately three Gladiators took off to take up position over the ships in the harbour, whilst another two took off five minutes later to patrol fifteen miles south-west of Athens at 20,000 feet. Another two Blenheims from 30 Squadron also took off on a standing patrol over the city. The rest of the fighters were kept in reserve on the aerodrome, to deal with any further attacks.

A formation of four Savoia 79's bombed the harbour from a height of 13,000 feet and then got clean away without being intercepted. The three Gladiators on patrol in that area had received orders to fly at 10,000 feet, and so had no chance of catching the raiders, although they chased them far out to sea. Timber Woods, leading the other two Gladiators, received no instructions at all regarding the course of the Savoias and consequently failed to spot them.

When a second formation of Savoias came in to unload their bombs the first three Gladiators had turned back towards the harbour and climbed to 15,000 feet. They were in a good position when they sighted the raiders, and immediately attacked them head-on. Heimar Stuckey, Number 3 of the formation, scored a hit on one of the Savoias and in the best Pattle style immediately fell in astern and endeavoured to silence the rear-gunner. But the Italian gunner was too quick for him, and got in a burst of shells which damaged the Gladiator and caused Stuckey to dive almost to sea-level. He headed for the small coastal landing-ground at Hassani, south of Athens, and prepared to make a hurried landing. Unfortunately another aircraft was just taking off, making it necessary for Stuckey to do another circuit.

He was just gliding over the hangars for the second time, when the groundcrews on the aerodrome were horrified to see flames shooting out from beneath the petrol tank. A moment later the flaming Gladiator exploded and Stuckey was killed.

In the meantime Timber Woods had attacked the Savoia damaged by Stuckey and after his second attack the machine burst into flames. Four of the crew baled out, before the machine hit the sea, but only three landed safely. The fourth went straight into the sea like a bullet. His parachute had failed to open.

Stuckey was buried the following afternoon in the Municipal Cemetery in Athens, but only one pilot was able to pay his last respects. The others, led by Pat, were already on their way to Yanina, having received orders to report there as quickly as possible. When they arrived only a small part of the airfield was fit for use. All the pilots managed to get down safely, but three of the Gladiators were written off completely through landing in soft, muddy patches and turning over on to their backs.

For a whole week they were grounded by the bad weather, but after lunch on 28 January, Squadron Leader Jones was able to take off with all available aircraft, fifteen Gladiators altogether, for an offensive patrol between Kelcyre and Premeti. They sighted and engaged four Breda BR. 20's and Five Cant Z. 1007's. Pat's section consisted of himself, Sergeant Casbolt and a new arrival named Trollip, who had joined the squadron after a spell in the hospital in Athens. Trollip was a young officer from Rhodesia, whose African accent revived pleasant memories of home for Pat. Trollip was still inexperienced in the art of air fighting and Pat had especially asked for him to be put into his own section, because he felt a kind of brotherly responsibility for a fellow countryman.

Although this was Trollip's first encounter with the Italians in Greece, he proved to be an ardent pupil, keeping close between Pat and Sergeant Casbolt, and generally giving the impression that he would prove a real asset to the squadron. They did a line-astern attack first of all against one of the Cant bombers, which went down in flames after a single burst of gunfire from each of the trio. Then Casbolt engaged another 1007 whilst Pat, with young Trollip clinging to his tail, went after one of the Breda BR. 20's. One brief burst of shells smacked into the starboard engine of the Breda, and caused it to slow down with smoke gushing from the damaged engine. Pat pulled off to one side and signalled to Trollip to go in and finish the job.

The youngster used up quite an appreciable amount of ammunition before the Breda finally went down, but Pat was very pleased with the way he tackled the job. He was not afraid to go in close in spite of the withering fire of the enemy rear-gunner. When Trollip had silenced this menace he followed Pat's orders implicitly, aiming first at the rest of the crew, crowded together at the front of the fuselage, and then concentrating his tracers towards the port engine. When Pat and Trollip last saw the bomber it was diving into the clouds, which covered the mountains near Premeti. It seemed impossible that it could avoid crashing, but since the Air Ministry would not confirm victories unless the plane was actually seen to be destroyed, the young Rhodesian only put in a claim for one Breda BR. 20 probably destroyed. However, later in the afternoon the Greek authorities notified the squadron that two enemy aircraft had crashed in the area around Premeti, presumably as a result of damage sustained in this combat. One of them was the Cant 1007, shot down in the first joint attack by Pat, Casbolt and Trollip. The other was a BR. 20, and apparently this was the one that Trollip had hit, since no other pilot had submitted a claim. Pat was very proud of his protégé when the claim was upgraded to one BR. 20 destroyed and confirmed. In his own modest way he forgot to mention in his own combat report that he had first of all damaged the Italian bomber and set it up for his colleague.

Heavy and continuous rain kept the Gladiators on the ground for the next two days, but the last day of January brought a drying wind and in the afternoon Pat took six Gladiators to the island of Corfu, which had recently been the target of the Savoias. The biplanes patrolled over the island for more than hour, but saw no sign of any hostile machines. Disappointed, they returned to Yanina, where they again had to exercise great care in landing their machines because of the wet muddy condition of the airfield. All got down safely except the enormous fifteen-stone Jimmy Kettlewell. His Gladiator hit a soft spot and the aircraft turned over, with poor Jimmy hanging from his safety straps, upside down, his face immersed in the mud. The Gladiator suffered considerable damage, but the good-natured Jimmy was all right, except that he needed a bath. He had plenty of time to cleanse himself thoroughly, since the heavens opened again and it rained almost nonstop for the next seven days.

13

Swansong of the Gladiators

For the first time for a week dawn broke with a cloudless sky on 8 February, but the airfield at Yanina was still in a very poor state, and the only aircraft to take off that day was Pat's Gladiator when he made a weather-test flight in the late afternoon.

The weather was again perfect the following day, and a forty mile-an-hour wind quickly dried the moisture from the turf. The camouflage was pulled away from the stubby biplanes and the newly arrived petrol bowser began its round of the Gladiators, pumping the vital fluid into the empty tanks. The armourers speedily filled the belts with a mixture of incendiary, tracer and armour-piercing .303 ammunition and by ten o'clock, when the station wagon arrived with the pilots, the aircraft were all ready to go. Squadron Leader Jones had already outlined the day's operation, an offensive patrol to Tepelene, but they all gathered round him for any last-minute instructions.

'You all know how vitally important it is for the Greeks to capture Tepelene. It is the key town that guards the way to Valona and the whole of the coastal area. If it falls to the Greek army, the Italians will have to fall back to the northern part of Albania. The position of the I-ties will be nothing short of precarious, without the aid of a decent harbour at Valona, through which supplies can be fed by sea and air. The Greeks are launching an all-out offensive to capture Tepelene, and it is our job today to keep the sky over Tepelene absolutely free of enemy aircraft. I know that I can rely on everyone to do just that. Good luck and good hunting.'

Squadron Leader Jones turned and walked towards his waiting Gladiator.

Within a few minutes the aerodrome reverberated with the sound of the fourteen Mercury engines, and the Gladiators taxied into position behind the Commanding Officer. They took off in immaculate formation in four sub-flights led by Squadron Leader Jones, Pat, Shorty Graham, and Timber Woods. As they eased out into a search formation one of the Gladiators in the last section suddenly waggled its wings and broke away. It was Price-Owen. His engine had stopped and there was nothing else that he could do but glide back to the airfield.

The others carried on and reached their patrol line without further incident. Within a few minutes they spotted three Savoia 79's coming straight towards them. But the bombers must have sighted the Gladiators at the same time, since they immediately aimed and, judging from the smoke trails coming from the engines, the pilots must have opened their throttles to maximum power. All that 80 Squadron could do was watch the Savoias until they disappeared into the mist far away to the north. Still, all was well, since simply by being in position over their appointed patrol line they had been able to carry out their orders and keep that particular piece of the sky clear of enemy bombers. Nevertheless most of the pilots were disappointed, for they would have enjoyed tangling with those three Italians.

Squadron Leader Jones took the squadron round in a wide arc just north of Kelcyre and led them back towards Tepelene. His engine had been running rather roughly for the last fifteen minutes and now it was beginning to vibrate. He called Pat on the radio-telephone and told him to take over the lead. Then he throttled right back to ease the shuddering. Within a few seconds he was joined by Twinstead Flower, who was also having trouble with his engine. They flew back to Yanina together, their main topic of conversation being the Gloster Gladiator. Both agreed it was a first-rate fighter – five years ago. Now it was obsolete, and certainly not the ideal aircraft in which to fly over such mountainous landscape. The Mercury engines, which had slogged away for hundreds of hours in climatic conditions which could be guaranteed to test the endurance of anything mechanical right to the limit, were now so unreliable that many pilots were concerned about the ability of their aircraft to get back safely to base, without the added difficulty of possible damage to their Gladiators from enemy action. If the pilots were to give of their best in combat, they must be relieved of this nagging nervous tension, otherwise there would be the extreme danger of losing the moral supremacy which they had already established over the Italian Air Force.

Meanwhile Pat and the remaining Gladiators had continued the patrol, and shortly before noon Pat sighted five C.R. 42's far away off the port beam. Using the scattered cloud to keep the Gladiators hidden from the Fiats, his initial approach gave the squadron a great tactical advantage. Unfortunately, just as he gave the order to attack the three C.R. 42's on the right of the enemy formation broke away, having apparently been warned by the sunshine reflecting from the Gladiators as they prepared to peel off. The other two Fiats were caught like rats in a trap. Pat engaged the biplane on the left, which, after his first shots, dived away towards Tepelene. Pat followed closely behind the C.R. 42, firing short bursts every time the enemy fighter appeared in his sights. Soon the Fiat was less than 20 feet above the tree-tops, its pilot frantically manoeuvring to escape the stream of bullets which inched along the fuselage towards his cockpit. In a last do-or-die effort to escape from the clutches of the unrelenting South African, he rocketed barely inches above the flat white roofs of the buildings in Tepelene, hoping that the terrific anti-aircraft fire from the ground would blast the Gladiator away from his tail. Undeterred by the wall of flak which came up at him, Pat hung on grimly less than 50 yards behind the C.R. 42 and, as they shot over the outskirts of the town, got in a burst which ended the chase. The Fiat smacked into the ground at 200 miles an hour and smashed itself into a thousand pieces.

Pat climbed away as if the devil himself was chasing him; as soon as he was out of range of the anti-aircraft fire he checked his machine for any possible damage. All his controls were working properly, his engine was still running smoothly and he could see no obvious signs of damage. He headed south, still climbing, and soon noticed a parachute coming down and a dogfight in progress very high over Argyrokastron.

He climbed as quickly as he could, but by the time he reached the scene of the battle it was all over and no aircraft were in sight.

He landed at Yanina just after twelve-thirty. He had been in the air for more than two hours and he was tired, mentally and physically, after the strain of the operation. But, despite his fatigue, when he heard that Jimmy Kettlewell had been forced down through lack of oil pressure, south of Argyrokastron, he immediately took off in another Gladiator to look for the missing flyer. It was yet another demonstration of his concern for a junior officer directly under his command. Once again he felt personally responsible for the loss, and he could not rest until he had done everything possible to rectify the situation.

He flew almost fifty miles to the area where Jimmy had gone down, searched until he found first the Gladiator and then Kettlewell several miles away outside a local Greek Army Headquarters. Only then was he satisfied and able to return to Yanina with a clear conscience.

Whilst he was away looking for Kettlewell much had been happening at Yanina. At four o'clock a formation of fifteen enemy bombers escorted by six C.R. 42's had come over and attacked the aerodrome. Fortunately they did very little damage to the airfield, and missed the buildings and the aircraft entirely. Not a single person received so much as a scratch, and most of the bombs fell harmlessly into the soft earth surrounding the aerodrome. Almost as soon as the Italians had left seven Gladiators of 112 Squadron arrived. They were the first part of the big build-up of reinforcements which the Air Officer Commanding the Royal Air Force in Greece, Air Vice-Marshal J H D'Albiac, DSO, had promised would take place as soon as the weather improved.

Later in the evening, after Pat and Jimmy Kettlewell had returned, the news came through that Pat had been awarded the Distinguished Flying Cross for great determination and devotion to duty.

In all his engagements [the official citation announced] *he has been absolutely fearless and undeterred by superior numbers of the enemy.*

Of course, they had to have a celebration party after that.

Pat could never understand why the Italians had never raided Yanina much earlier during the war. It was not a large town, but strategically it was of great importance to the Greeks. It was the main terminal point which supplied the soldiers in the front line. In addition it was the base of all fighter aircraft in the forward areas, and was now also used by the Blenheim bombers as a refuelling station. The Greek Army Headquarters were situated in the town, and nearby there were many fuel stores and ammunition dumps. The one and only main road running from the town towards the north, which carried all supplies and equipment for the troops, crossed several bridges, just outside the town. If the Italians had made a determined attack on any one of these bridges, there would have been chaos and the effect on the war extremely serious.

The Italians must have known all about this from the espionage activities of their allies, the Nazis. At this time Greece was not at war with Germany and was anxious not to provoke them. The Greeks had allowed the numerous German 'tourists' much freedom in their country; it was obvious to everyone that the Italians had received advance information on many of the raids planned by the Royal Air Force during the last few months – and it was equally obvious that the information could only have been supplied by the Nazi espionage agents masquerading as tourists.

In spite of this the Italians had chosen to ignore Yanina. It was a great mistake.

The war had been going on for almost five months before the Italian Air Force made its first raid on Yanina on 9 February, but then, as if realising it had made a serious blunder, the attacks increased rapidly in intensity and frequency.

On 10 February the siren sounded for the First time at daybreak, but it was a false alarm. However, it was a warning which could not be ignored, and Squadron Leader Jones immediately arranged for three Gladiators to be kept permanently at standby during the hours of daylight. It was a wise move, since when the air-raid alarm next warned the squadron at half past ten of an impending attack the three Gladiators, piloted by Pat, Shorty Graham and the Keg were able to take off immediately. Although they climbed quickly at full revolutions, they were unable to reach sufficient height before the arrival of Five Cant Z. 1007's. Nevertheless, the mere presence of the three Gladiators on defensive patrol caused the Italian bombers to make a hurried attack on the airfield, which undoubtedly affected their aiming. As it was, most of the bombs burst harmlessly on the west and north sides of the aerodrome, although one bomb exploded near a staff car, causing slight damage to one side of it.

The three Gladiators chased the Cants, but could get no nearer than a quarter of a mile from the raiders. They fired their guns without much hope of hitting the bombers, and they could not see any signs of damage when they finally gave up and returned to Yanina.

The afternoon was practically one continuous air-raid alarm, but a standing patrol of Gladiators over the airfield kept the area free of bombers. Ape Cullen sent five Fiat BR. 20's scurrying home before they could release a single bomb, and soon afterwards made another determined head-on attack against five Savoia 79's. He again prevented the Italians from completing their task, and chased them as far as the island of Corfu, without, however, doing a great deal of material damage to the Savoias. After returning to Yanina, he surprised another five Savoia 79's and this lime he was luckier – sending one of the five into the lake after setting its engines on fire.

More waves of Fiats and Savoias kept up the continuous onslaught, and eventually one flight of BR. 20's escorted by twenty C.R. 42's eluded the defending Gladiators and dropped a number of bombs which damaged three of the squadron's Gladiators, and completely destroyed one of the Greek machines.

Pat, Timber Woods and Sergeant Casbolt hit and damaged at least one bomber each, but were unable to confirm whether they had been destroyed, because they had to dash away to break up further attacks by succeeding waves of bombers. The only other confirmed victory in addition to Ape Cullen's Savoia was a BR. 20 which crashed fifteen miles south-west of Yanina after being engaged by Cherry Vale. The Greeks later on reported the wreckage of several enemy bombers lying in the wild, mountainous country to the north, and it is quite possible that these were the result of 80 Squadron's efforts during the afternoon of 10 February. Unfortunately these crashed machines could not be examined at close quarters, since they were in the most inaccessible places, high up the mountainsides, and consequently were never credited either to the squadron's tally – which was now over seventy – or to the scores of the individual pilots concerned in this action.

The All Clear was given shortly before five o'clock, by which time the Gladiators were circling over the aerodrome. They had already been warned that they would have to proceed carefully when landing because of the bomb craters, so they were not unprepared for the sight which met their eyes, as the pilots brought their Gladiators over the perimeter hedge. But nevertheless they were more than a little surprised when they saw how many holes there were in the landing surface. Originally there had been well over one hundred indentations in and around the airfield, but the hardworking ground staffs had already partially filled in more than a dozen and made a temporary landing strip; on to which the pilots put their Gladiators with extreme care.

The burnt-out wreckage of the Greek Gladiator was still smouldering at one side of the field and, a short distance away, the staff car which had been hit earlier on was a sorry-looking mess. Another Italian bomb had exploded very close to it, flattening the tyres, and removing one of its doors.

The pilots climbed into the station wagon, which drove around the craters and headed for the town. As they drove along the narrow, winding road, the horror and destruction caused by the ruthless, indiscriminate bombing was brought forcibly to their notice. Everywhere they saw the mutilated remains of men, women and children lying scattered among the smoking débris. Others, blood-stained and wounded, were being carried on improvised stretchers, and some, their minds unbalanced by the terrible happenings, were crying, shouting and running round in circles.

In addition to the human suffering there were signs everywhere of the ferocity of the raids. Cars were twisted out of shape, some on their sides, some overturned, some resting on walls or against buildings, and all scorched by the blast. Many buildings were now no more than piles of rubble, some were still burning, and all had smashed windows and splashes of mud over their white walls. The hospital was fortunate, since it showed very few signs of damage apart from powder marks and scratches caused by shrapnel and flying débris. The door of the restaurant was missing and two of the veranda posts had been blown away, but otherwise it was all right. The pilots' hotel was in a sorry-looking state from the front, but their rooms were untouched, and most of the pilots, worn out by the strain of the dogfights, turned in early. They badly needed a few hours' sleep, for they all knew in their hearts that now the Italians had at last found Yanina ... they would come back again.

They did, very early the following morning, before the pilots had reached the airfield.

Twenty C.R. 42's, eluding the Greek observation posts in the mountains, attacked without warning, machine-gunning the aircraft on the aerodrome. The Greek anti-aircraft defences opened fire immediately and hit one of the Fiats, which crashed a few miles south of Yanina. Some of the Greek stand-by pilots made valiant efforts to get their Gladiators into the air, but had to give up the attempt when one of the fighters was blown to pieces as it taxied across the airfield.

For the rest of the day a standing patrol of four or five Gladiators at a time was maintained over Yanina, whilst the groundcrews, ably assisted by scores of Greek peasants, worked tremendously hard to fill in the bomb craters. By the time darkness fell the job was complete and the weary airmen returned to their billets, hoping for a few hours' rest. The pilots, having seen no enemy aircraft at all during the day, also wearily made their way to their quarters. They were greeted by Squadron Leader Jones, who made a startling announcement that caused all signs of fatigue to vanish in an instant.

'I have just been on the blower to Headquarters and I thought you would all like to know that within the next few days we shall be receiving eight Hawker Hurricanes.'

To say that this news caused an uproar would be a grave understatement. The pilots went wild. Within a few seconds the room looked as if the Italians had dropped a bomb right in the middle of it. When the excitement became subdued sufficiently to make himself heard again the Commanding Officer called Jimmy Kettlewell over and gave him orders to fly to Athens the following day in order to test the Hurricanes.

There was a party to celebrate the occasion which did not stop even though the sirens sounded and three C.R. 42's appeared out of a perfect moonlight night to strafe the aerodrome for twenty minutes or thereabouts. Slight damage was done to one Gladiator.

The Blenheims of 211 and 84 Squadrons had managed to carry out their bombing raids successfully without a fighter escort whilst 80 Squadron had been so busy defending their own quarters at Yanina. But the bomber pilots were very glad when the position had eased sufficiently for the Gladiators to resume their role as protective guardians of the Blenheims. They knew that there was less likelihood of them running into trouble with the C.R. 42's when the 'glamour boys' were around.

On 13 February the Gladiators of 80 and 112 Squadrons escorted the Blenheims during two attacks on Tepelene. The morning raid was completed successfully, all aircraft returning safely without sighting a single hostile aeroplane. The afternoon target was a mountain ridge crowded with troops, guns and light tanks. The Blenheims released their bombs and began to turn towards the south. As they did so, Squadron Leader Jones led the Gladiators down in a machine-gun attack on the Italian positions. Orange flashes from the anti-aircraft guns lit up the ground and puffs of black and white appeared all around the diving Gladiators. Holes appeared in the fabric-covered mainplanes as the shells burst into thousands of lethal pieces of jagged, red-hot metal, but the pilots of 80 were determined to give back a little of what they themselves had so recently received and never wavered for an instant. One after another they sent a shower of death and destruction into the Italian positions and then, satisfied that they had avenged some of the unfortunate Greeks mutilated in Yanina, they climbed away to join up with the Blenheims, now on their way home. One of the Gladiators fell behind the others. Its engine, damaged by the anti-aircraft fire, was making a most horrible grinding noise, and the pilot, Sergeant Barker, had to use all his skill to keep the machine in the air. He could have baled out and made sure of saving his skin, but his dogged Yorkshire spirit urged him to try to fly the damaged fighter back. The Gladiator, in spite of all his efforts, gradually got lower and lower, and by the time Barker had reached the front line he was too low to bale out. Forty miles north of Yanina he tried to make a forced landing in a small clearing, but the ground was much too soft, and the Gladiator turned several somersaults before coming to rest. The machine was a complete write-off, but Sergeant Barker was unhurt and returned to Yanina in a Greek army truck, none the worse for his experience.

He was on patrol again the following day when Pat took nine Gladiators on a sweep over the Kelcyre region. It was an uneventful trip and all returned safely to base at half past nine.

Later in the day they received a message from Jimmy Kettlewell. He had tested the Hurricanes and all were satisfactory for operations. However, there were only six, two having been redirected whilst on their way to Greece. He suggested that the six ought to be collected as soon as possible before any more of them were commandeered. Immediately Squadron Leader Jones gave orders for Shorty Graham, Timber Woods, Twinstead Flower, Sergeant Casbolt and Arty Acworth of 112 Squadron to leave in the Bombay for Athens. He could not afford to risk losing those few invaluable fighters after striving so arduously for them.

That weekend Pat and the remaining pilots of 80 and 112 Squadrons had to be content to use their old Gladiators for operations, since the Hurricanes had not arrived. They escorted the Blenheims twice to Buzi, an Albanian village high up in the mountains, which was being used as an advanced headquarters by the Italians. Although there was again vicious anti-aircraft fire, none of the planes was hit and all got back safely. On Sunday afternoon, when they returned from the second mission to Buzi, Pat remained with the six Blenheims whilst they flew back to their base at Paramythia. He was doing so at the request of Squadron Leader Gordon Finlayson, the Commanding Officer of 211 Squadron.

Every time the Blenheims took off or landed at Paramythia, the pilots saw a light signalling from a point near the top of the mountains behind the airfield. They had tried to climb the mountain so that they could rid themselves of this unwelcome observer, but each time had been defeated by the precipitous slopes or the weather. Now Pat was going to see what he could do about it, with the aid of his four machine guns and his nimble Gladiator.

When the formation crossed the ridge of mountains surrounding the narrow valley which was the bombers' base Pat broke away from the Blenheims and headed towards the spot where he had been told the spy was hiding. Before the Blenheims had even begun their approach Pat sighted the flickering light. He kept his eyes glued on the position, in case the signalling stopped, and aimed his fighter at the spot. He fired burst after burst of gunfire at the light, which went out just before he pulled away, dangerously close to the rugged mountainside. He winged over and came back over the spot to try to confirm the casualty, but all was quiet, and he was most annoyed because he could find no trace of an enemy agent. Finally he flew back to Yanina. He heard later that the Blenheims were never again bothered by lights on the hillsides.

Squadron Leader Jones wanted to see him when he returned to Yanina, so he quickly discarded his flying kit and made his way to the Commanding Officer's quarters.

Tap handed Pat a cigarette, lit one himself, settled in his chair and came straight to the point.

'I have just heard that the six Hurricanes will arrive tomorrow afternoon. I was a little loath to risk them operating from this swampy patch, but I have said nothing to Headquarters as yet, in case they said we couldn't have them. But I have arranged with The Bish [Squadron Leader Gordon-Finlayson] for the Hurricanes to use Paramythia as their headquarters. Now, as soon as the Hurricanes arrive here tomorrow I shall instruct the pilots to carry on to Paramythia. I shall then phone Headquarters and inform them of my decision and I feel certain that everything will be all right. The pilots flying the Hurricanes up will become a detached flight and I am giving you the job of looking after them. I shall have to remain here with the rest of the squadron, who will have to continue with the Gladiators until we can get some more Hurricanes.

'I know I can rely on you, Pat, to take good care of the detachment. Get your gear together in the morning and get over to Paramythia as early as possible to make all the necessary arrangements for the Hurricanes when they arrive. You will find The Bish will give you all the help you need.

'When you have settled in get the flight thoroughly used to the Hurricanes. When you feel that they are ready for ops give me a ring, and we will see if we can concoct a little surprise for the I-ties.

'I shall be relying on you, Pat, to put up a good show, so that we can prove to Headquarters what a difference these modern fighters will make up here. Then I hope that it will not be very long before the whole squadron is re-equipped with Hurricanes.'

Pat was sincere when he answered: 'I will do my best, sir. The chaps won't let you down.'

'I know that, Pat. Good luck, and take care of yourself.'

The next day Pat took off in his Gladiator soon after lunch and headed across the mountains, and over the fast-flowing waters of the Kalamas River, to the beautiful valley of Paramythia.

14

The Hurricanes arrive

Thirty miles south-west of the Albanian frontier and midway between Yanina and the island of Corfu was the narrow valley hemmed in by a ridge of mountains which contained the aerodrome at Paramythia. Aerodrome, in actual fact, is hardly the right term, since it contained no runways, no control tower, and no permanent buildings of any kind; landing-ground would describe it better, for it was merely the large, flattish floor of the valley. Its surface was stony and well drained, and in the early spring encouraged the growth of thousands of alpine flowers, indescribably beautiful, particularly at dusk, when the failing light of day blended the hues of the rocks and flowers in delicate harmony.

As a direct contrast, the tremendous range of mountains to the east stood out in stark silhouette against the background of puffy white clouds reflecting the glory of the setting sun and the glow of the rising moon. High up in those mountains lived the wolves and bears, which had thrived in the early days of the war on the bodies of the Italians, rotting there after the blood-thirsty guerilla attacks of the tough Greek farmers, armed with an assortment of pitchforks, plough shares and pruning knives.

The camp, consisting of a dozen teepee-styled tents, was some way up the mountainside, close to the olive groves. Through the middle of it a fast-moving stream poured its waters into a shallow depression, which had been blocked at one end by the pilots to form a miniature lake, in which they could bathe or soak at will. A bath in that water, however, was more of a necessity than a pleasure, for the water, descending from the snowy regions towards the top of the 5,000-feet-high peaks, was icily cold.

Farther down the mountainside more tents were pitched closer to the landing-ground. They were the homes of the groundcrews. Near to these were the station wagons, trucks, bowsers and other vital equipment which had taken seventeen days to travel by road from Athens. The men who operated this equipment had flown up in the Bombay in just over an hour.

The attractive but dirty little village of Paramythia was a few hundred yards to the north, wisely situated on the side of a mountain.

When 211 Squadron had moved into the valley, they had pitched their tents on the floor of the valley, in spite of the knowing glances and whispered warnings of the sturdy mountain folk. Then a rainstorm had turned the valley into a series of quickly flowing streams that soaked the airmen sleeping peacefully on the beds of flowers and washed their tents and equipment away to the far end of the valley. After that they returned to the drier ground, higher up the mountainside.

As a general rule, however, the landing-ground was relatively dry and, unlike the other landing-grounds at Yanina and Larissa, well drained, with the result that very rarely was it classified as unserviceable.

There was no restaurant at Paramythia and the eating arrangements were primitive, but nevertheless pleasant. The pilots sat around on packing-cases and wooden boxes in the warm spring sunshine, and dined on bully beef and tea boiled on the primus stove in the dimly lit tent which had *Mess* scrawled across its flap in white chalk.

Generally speaking, the pilots were a happy and contented lot. The weather was improving, discipline was relatively easy, the Italian bombers never worried them, and sleeping on the ground was not such a hardship when one became used to it. The high mountains kept the valley free from the bitterly cold winds. Washing and shaving in a bowl of water on a tripod outside the tent was quite pleasant in the morning sunshine; most pilots, however, never bothered to shave. They copied the fashion of the times in this typical Greek olive-grove country by growing beards.

The sun was only partly visible above the mountains to the west when

Pat heard the buzzing note of the Rolls-Royce Merlin engines. A few seconds later the six sleek Hurricanes shot across the field in perfect formation and then proceeded to give a superb flying display which brought forth admiring shouts from the bomber boys and a glow of pride into Pat's heart.

His eyes sparkled, and his feet and hands itched to feel the controls, as the Hurricanes side-slipped into perfect three-point landings. He dashed towards them, ran his expert eye over their powerful contours, and patted and fondled them as if he had never seen such things before.

A moment later there was a deeper drone in the sky and five Wellington bombers appeared and set down on the airfield. They had come with loads of equipment and supplies.

Paramythia had never seen so many pilots or aircraft before, and the tents bulged with happy carefree airmen. The beer supply was quickly exhausted, but the Mayor of Paramythia came to the rescue and provided gallons of the sweet aniseed wine which, in spite of its taste and smell, added life to the party.

Pat joined in the celebrations, but as usual in an unobtrusive manner excused himself early and made his way towards his tent. The moon was shining brightly over the mountains and Pat took one last admiring view of the scenery before turning in. He arranged his bedding on the ground, dug a hole for his hip, and went to sleep dreaming of his scouting days in Keetmanshoop.

The pilots of the detached flight had all flown Hurricanes before in the Western Desert, but they needed plenty of practice with them before they could be risked on operations. It was no use going into battle until one was thoroughly acquainted with all the peculiarities of the Hurricane, and capable of using its advantages. The Hurricane also had some disadvantages when compared with the Gladiator, and these had to be taken into account, too, when deciding on the tactics to be employed in aerial combat.

Consequently Pat and his flight spent the whole of their first day with the Hurricanes in finding out what they could do – and what they could not.

Pat's first impression when lie lowered himself into the cockpit of the Hurricane was of the heavy, solid-looking metal all around him. It would certainly absorb much more punishment than the Gladiator, and instinctively he felt the protection offered by the steel armour at the back of his seat. He revved the engine and straight away liked the obvious power hidden away at the back of the instrument panel. He liked the speed of the take-off, too, and the fast climb, whilst the power of the Hurricane in a dive was breath-taking. In level flight the Hurricane was as steady as a rock and he knew it would make a splendid platform from which to aim the guns. Yes, the guns; he had almost forgotten those. Now he had twice the number of guns, and double the rate of firepower. It would take only half the time to send exactly the same number of bullets towards the target. He would not need to keep the enemy plane in his sights for so long to create the same amount of damage. Neither would he have to wait to get in so close to the target, for the cone of fire of the eight guns did not converge so tightly as the Brownings on the Gladiator.

But he missed the quick loops and the tight turns of the Gladiator. The Hurricane could do everything that the Gladiator could do in the way of aerobatics, but it took a much bigger volume of sky in which to do it. A turn in a Hurricane, for instance, was wide and slow compared with the fast wing over of a Gladiator. On the other hand, the speed of the Hurricane in moving in a wider arc was much faster, and the resulting physical strain on the pilot much greater. Pat found himself blacking out almost every time he made a change of direction and soon his legs became stiff and sore.

Three flights, involving some two hours of practice, that first day caused Pat to adjourn to the pool, where the cold water numbed his body, but brought welcome relief to his aching limbs.

The following day the six pilots were a little more experienced and better able to meet the new conditions. Consequently, after another day of intensive practice in formation flying and mock attacks, Pat was able to telephone Squadron Leader Jones and inform him that they would be ready to fly the Hurricanes on operations on 20 February 1941.

Since this was to be the début of the Hurricanes on the Albanian front, Headquarters in Athens decided to go all out and put on an operation which was bigger than anything before attempted in this theatre of war. Five Royal Air Force squadrons and one Greek squadron would be involved, and plans were made for them all to assemble at Paramythia during the afternoon and evening of the 19th and the morning of 20 February. Wing Commander Paddy Coote and Squadron Leader Sevastopulo flew up from Athens to form an Advance Wing to control operations.

The Blenheims of 211 Squadron and the Hurricanes of the detached flight from 80 Squadron were already at Paramythia. Nine more Blenheims from 84 Squadron arrived just before tea on the 19th, followed by two Wellingtons from 38 Squadron and an old Junkers 52 troop-carrier borrowed from the Greeks. Then just as the light was beginning to fade twelve PZL's of the Greek Air Force flew in and almost upset the whole show. These obsolete high-wing monoplanes were difficult to fly at the best of times, but even more awkward to land, especially on a strange airfield. The dim light of the gathering dusk did not help matters either, so it was not surprising that some slight errors of judgement occurred. Most of the Greek aircraft were down safely when two of the PZL's landed at the same time, but from different directions. They came to an abrupt halt in the middle of the field, when they met and twisted themselves into a mangled embrace. The pilots, both unhurt except for minor scratches, scrambled from the wreckage, and began to shout and gesticulate vehemently, accusing each other of making the blunder of landing in the wrong direction. But with typical Greek cheerfulness in the face of adversity, they soon ironed out their differences and hauled the damaged remains to one side of the airfield, where they quickly set about the task of making one good aeroplane from the two wrecks.

By the next morning one patched-up, badly bent, but complete PZL was ready to take part in the day's operations. That it had not been tested to see if it would fly did not upset the pilot one little bit. He was blissfully happy, because it had been decided that he had landed in the correct direction, and could therefore be entrusted with the aircraft. The other Greek pilot, who had landed downwind, looked so miserable that the pilot of the Junkers offered to take him on the mission as a passenger.

The seventeen Gladiators from 80 and 112 Squadrons arrived from Yanina at lunchtime and shortly afterwards three bursts of machine-gun fire summoned all the pilots to the operations tent.

The Station Commander, Squadron Leader Gordon-Finlayson, then outlined very carefully the mission. Briefly the idea was that the two Wellingtons and the Junkers, escorted by the Gladiators, would fly to the Kelcyre area, where they would drop their loads of food and supplies to the isolated Greek troops. They would be followed by the faster Blenheims, whose task it was to attack the bridge at Berat. The six Hurricanes would provide the escort for the Blenheims, whilst the Greek PZL's, whose endurance was only a little over an hour, would meet the whole of the formation as it returned to Greek territory.

The weather report was good, with some slight cloud expected over the target areas. The Wellingtons and the Junkers took off and, as they climbed over the Kalamas River, were joined by the seventeen Gladiators, who positioned themselves all around the three large machines in a protective circle. They disappeared over the ridge of mountains, and the Blenheim crews climbed into their aircraft. Gordon-Finlayson led the nine Blenheims of 211 Squadron in three sections of three into the air, and as these circled around the valley the three sections from 84 Squadron took off. The eighteen Blenheims joined up into a box formation and set course for the Albanian front. Pat's Hurricanes quickly followed and in a few minutes took up station at the side of the bombers. The Hurricanes flew very slowly, weaving about from side to side, so that they did not outpace the Blenheims, which were hampered by the weight of their bombs.

In half an hour the Blenheims were over Berat and each flight picked out its selected target. Pat kept one wary eye open for enemy fighters, and with the other admired the aiming of the bombers. The bombs exploded all over the town, on the military buildings, on the supply dumps, and smack in the middle of the bridge which carried the main road across the river.

The whole of the Blenheim formation had completed its attack and was aiming a few miles to the north of the target when Pat spotted the Italian fighters climbing to engage diem. He led his section straight towards four Fiat G. 50's, and shouting to Sergeant Casbolt and Timber Woods to attack individually, selected the leading G. 50 as his own target. As he approached, the dark green Fiat pulled away into a steep turn, but Pat managed to hold it in his sights until he came into range and thumbed the gun button. It was the first time he had fired the eight guns of the Hurricane and the result was astonishing. The G. 50 exploded right before his eyes, disintegrating into hundreds of small flaming pieces.

The other Fiats had disappeared, but Pat could see the Blenheims leaving the area; opening his throttle, he climbed away to join them. Within five minutes he had caught them and took up his station above and to the starboard side of the Blenheims. Shortly afterwards Sergeant Casbolt's Hurricane came in just off his starboard wing tip. Pat looked across at the fair-haired Sergeant, held up his thumb, indicating that he was obviously very pleased with his new aeroplane, and with a wide smile spreading across his face held up one finger, denoting a victory. Casbolt, with an equally broad smile, showing that he, too, approved of his new mount, held up two fingers!

On the way back the Blenheims and Hurricanes were followed at a safe distance by a number of G. 50's. These were sighted by the Gladiators, who had seen the Wellingtons and the Junkers safely on the way home, and then gone back up the line. During the ensuing scrap one G. 50 and one C.R. 42 were shot down by Ape Cullen, another G. 50 was destroyed by Jimmy Kettlewell, and a third G. 50 was set on fire by Algy Schwab from 112 Squadron. Then the Greek PZL's arrived on the scene and accounted for another four Italian aircraft, one of them being claimed by the pilot of the rebuilt wreck.

Timber Woods also claimed one G. 50 destroyed, to make up a nice round dozen confirmed. All in all, a very successful début for the

Hurricane in Greek skies, especially as every Allied aircraft returned safely to Paramythia.

After the other squadrons had returned to their own bases, Pat's six Hurricanes and the Blenheims of 211 Squadron established a daily service to the Albanian front. Each afternoon, and occasionally during the mornings also, the Blenheims would go off to bomb some Italian target, comforted by the sight of the escorting Hurricanes. Each time when they returned they were able to report successful bombing and no opposition from enemy fighters. It was becoming a monotonous routine, and Pat was getting bored. His natural desire to come to grips with the enemy urged him to pursue a more aggressive policy. Consequently, in between raids, he would go off in his Hurricane, usually with another fighter accompanying him, and search behind the enemy's lines until he found some suitable target, on which he could expend some of his surplus energy. One day it would be a stream of lorries on a road, occasionally a concentration of Italian troops on a hillside, sometimes a bunch of aircraft on an aerodrome, and frequently a machine-gun post or anti-aircraft battery.

One day he took 'Ping' Newton as his 'floater' on a visit to Valona harbour. Ping was an effervescent Rhodesian, with a dark moustache and a well-trimmed beard, who had only recently arrived in Paramythia, with a detachment of Hurricanes from 33 Squadron. He was a brilliant flyer and had already established a reputation for daredevil tactics. But on this occasion he had to play second fiddle to the maestro.

They shot out of the clouds over the crowded harbour, and immediately Pat waggled his wings as a sign that he was about to attack. Ping slipped into line astern and saw Pat dive straight at a big merchant ship, raking its decks with his guns. Ping had a crack next, and then pulled away as he saw Pat coming in for a second attack in a hurtling vertical dive. He did not pull out until he was almost at deck level. He had been firing straight down one of the ship's funnels.

Ping was flabbergasted. When he landed all he could say was: 'It was an amazing piece of flying. If I hadn't seen it with my own two eyes, I would never have believed it!'

The Bombay flew in to Paramythia one morning with a load of large wooden whistles. They were to be attached to the bombs carried by the Blenheims, in the hope that the 'screaming' bombs would create panic in the Italian troops when the bombs were unloaded. They were used solely for this purpose, and fairly successfully, too, until one day in the mess there arose a discussion as to whether these whistles would make sufficient noise if attached to ground-strafing aircraft to frighten the Italians.

Pat borrowed a Gladiator from Yanina, and with the help of several riggers fitted twelve of the whistles beneath the lower main planes. He then took it up on test. He levelled out at about 4,000 feet over the airfield and rolled into a vertical dive at full throttle, aiming directly at the mess tent. The plane hurtled down towards the pilots gathered round the tent, its whistles screaming like the devil. For a moment it seemed that the plane was out of control and must certainly crash. To the onlookers it seemed impossible that any human being could pull it out of that screaming power dive in time. Some scattered in all directions, others just closed their eyes and waited for the crash. But Pat, judging the distance perfectly, eased it out a bare 20 feet above the ground and went hurtling vertically upwards to 4,000 feet again. He repeated the manoeuvre four times, and the last time dived the Gladiator so fast that both gun cowlings were torn off the machine.

That performance was enough to convince anyone that the whistles would be a useful accessory to any dive-bombing or ground-strafing aircraft, but, unfortunately, all the stock of screamers had been fitted to bombs and, since no more were forthcoming, at least whilst 80 Squadron were still using Paramythia, Pat was never able to test them on operations.

Air Chief Marshal Sir Arthur Longmore and Air Vice-Marshal D'Albiac visited Paramythia on 26 February. They stayed for lunch, and had a few words of welcome for Pat and his Hurricane pilots when they got back from a raid on Fieri, where they had shot up an Italian Advanced General Headquarters.

The following afternoon nine Blenheims from 211 Squadron with an escort of nine Hurricanes went off to Valona. Pat's section, consisting of Ape Cullen, Twinstead Flower, Sergeant Ted Hewett and Arty Acworth, flew on the starboard side of the bombers, whilst four Hurricanes from 33 Squadron guarded the other flank. Since 33 Squadron were providing the direct escort on this occasion, which meant that they had to stay with the bombers for the whole of the mission, Pat was at liberty to remain over the target if he considered it advantageous after the bombing had been completed, and carry out a strafing attack or, if the opportunity presented itself, to engage any enemy fighters that might take off from Valona aerodrome.

Over the target a dozen C.R. 42's were sighted approaching the bombers from the starboard side. Immediately Pat's section attacked them. Within a few minutes the sky was full of falling aircraft – all Italian. Seven C.R. 42's went down in flames and two more became so confused after being attacked by Sergeant Hewett that they collided and went down, too. The only damage to the Hurricanes was one bullet-hole through Pat's petrol tank.

The Blenheims and Hurricanes had a most pleasant flight back to Paramythia.

15

Greater glory

On the morning of 28 February orders were received from Headquarters that all available aircraft were to patrol the area between Tepelene and the coast between half past three and half past four, because it was suspected that large numbers of Italian aircraft would be operating over this area during this period.

Pat had already made a patrol and an escort mission before lunch, but, eager as ever to meet the Italians, he took off with eight other Hurricanes at a quarter past three and, climbing to 20,000 feet, reached the patrol area about twenty minutes later.

Nineteen Gladiators from 80 and 112 Squadrons had already arrived and were patrolling 3,000 feet below the Hurricanes.

Pat took the first section of Hurricanes towards the coast. After about fifteen minutes, he caught sight of four aircraft crossing the coast just north of Himara at about 12,000 feet. Almost at the same time he spotted another formation of fifteen aircraft, flying south along the valley from the direction of Valona. This second larger formation turned east behind the first formation and followed at a distance of about five miles.

Pat ordered six of the Hurricanes to engage the second formation, and then dived astern of the first formation, with Ape Cullen and Twinstead Flower following close behind him. As Pat approached to within firing range he identified the aircraft as Italian Fiat BR. 20's, and picked out the starboard aircraft as his first target. He aimed one burst at the fuselage to silence the rear-gunner and another burst at the starboard engine. A third burst of shells pierced the petrol tank in the wing and immediately the BR. 20 burst into flames and fell away. Pat pulled up over the top of the formation and noticed that the starboard engine of the next BR. 20 was already smoking; Ape Cullen was pumping more lead into it from the rear. Twinstead Flower was pulling up beneath the aircraft on the port side of the formation for an attack, so that the only bomber not being engaged was the leading BR. 20. Pat flew into position immediately behind it and once again aimed at the starboard engine. As before, the fuel tank ignited and the BR. 20 nosed down with flames streaming out behind it. Looking back over his shoulder, Pat saw three BR. 20's going down in flames, whilst the fourth was turning steeply to port, with a Hurricane right on its heels. Beyond this the second formation of fifteen aircraft had turned away from the other Hurricanes and was now heading out to sea.

During his last attack on the leader of the BR. 20's, Pat's windscreen had become splashed with oil and by this time he was unable to see through it at all. He reduced his speed and, pulling away in a climbing turn to port, tried to clean away the oil with his scarf. A shower of tracer shot past his head, causing him to kick viciously at the rudder bar and skid out of the way. Looking upwards through the top of the open cockpit, he saw five G. 50's coming down towards him. He pulled up to meet the attack, and immediately the G. 50's broke in all directions. Pat whipped behind the tail of one of them and, although unable to take effective aim because of the oiled-up windscreen, fired several bursts in the general direction of the G. 50. Several times in the general mix-up that followed Pat was presented with the opportunity of firing blind at the G. 50's, and each time he pressed the gun button. But it was impossible to tell whether any of his bursts took effect, because each time he could only estimate the approximate position of the enemy aircraft.

Finally, with no ammunition left, Pat broke away and made for Paramythia at top speed.

Within ten minutes of landing he was back in the cockpit of another Hurricane on his way back to the scene of the fight. The sky was empty, so he carried on northwards along the valley towards Valona, where he soon spotted a formation of three C.R. 42's flying about two miles south of the town. Farther away he could see five more coming into the valley from the north.

Diving out of the sun, Pat drew up immediately behind and beneath the three GR. 42's without being seen. Sighting on the port machine, he held the firing button and swung his sights through the formation from left to right. The two outside C.R. 42's immediately spun away, but the leading Fiat aimed sharply to the right. Pat followed and gave it a further burst. Blue smoke poured from the engine and the C.R. 42 rolled over on to its back and fell into a spin. As it spiralled down Pat fired another burst into it and then, anxious to try to surprise the other five, pulled away and climbed into the sun. Looking up, he saw the occupants of the first two C.R. 42's slowly descending by parachute.

He hunted high and low for a quarter of an hour for the five C.R. 42's which he had seen approaching the valley, but in spite of his efforts failed to find any of them. A little disappointed, he returned to the scene of his attack on the first trio in order to confirm the destruction of the C.R. 42 which he had last seen still spinning and issuing clouds of blue smoke at less than 500 feet. Unfortunately he was unable to locate any of the crashed aircraft in the densely wooded valley. Consequently when he returned to Paramythia he only put in a claim for the destruction of two B.R. 20's and two C.R. 42's. The other C.R. 42, which almost certainly must have crashed – Pat himself was convinced that he had killed the pilot – was credited to him as probably destroyed.

The airfield at Paramythia was crowded with aircraft and the jubilant groundcrews were excitedly adding up the mounting total of victories. The battle had stretched across the whole of Albania, from the mountain ranges in the east to the coast in the west and even over the sea itself, and everyone had the same story to tell, of victories and more victories over the Italian fighters. In the words of the Greek troops, who had a grandstand view of the fight from their trenches, 'enemy aircraft fell out of the skies like flies – dead ones'.

Of the twenty-eight Royal Air Force pilots who took part in this glorious battle, only seven were unable to put in a claim for a victory.

Even Wing Commander Paddy Coote, the officer in command of the Western Wing, had borrowed a Gladiator from 80 Squadron and joined in the fun, shooting down one of the C.R. 42's. Several of the pilots, including Squadron Leader Jones, Cherry Vale and Jimmy Kettlewell of 80, and Charlie Fry and Flight Lieutenant Fraser of 112, claimed double victories, but the pride of place undoubtedly went to Ape Cullen. In his typical reckless manner he had waded into the Italian formations; in just over an hour he had sent down no less than five enemy machines, all of them in flames. Only when he had used up every round of ammunition and was down to his last few gallons of petrol did he leave the fight and return to Paramythia.

When the last plane had returned and the final count was made it became obvious that the Italians had taken an incredible beating. The two Royal Air Force fighter squadrons had destroyed no less than twenty-seven Italian machines for certain and damaged almost as many again. It was the greatest loss to be suffered by the Italians in one battle throughout the war.

The Royal Air Force lost one Gladiator. Dicky Abrahams, the humourist of 112 Squadron, had to bale out soon after shooting down a Fiat G. 50. He landed in the middle of a bunch of Greek soldiers, who mistakenly took him to be an Italian pilot; they just could not believe it was possible for an Englishman to be shot down on that glorious day.

Signals of congratulation came in fast and furiously. The first was from the Air Officer Commanding the Royal Air Force in Greece, Air Vice-Marshal D'Albiac:

PLEASE CONVEY HEARTY CONGRATULATIONS TO ALL CONCERNED IN A FIRST-CLASS SHOW TODAY.

Then from the Air Officer Commander in Chief, Middle East Air Forces, Air Chief Marshal Sir Arthur Longmore:

MAGNIFICENT. CONGRATULATE ALL.

Later in the evening the pilots gathered round the wireless set in the mess tent and listened to a tribute on the Athens Radio:

In an hour and a half a comparatively small formation of Hurricane and Gladiator fighters definitely shot down twenty-seven Italian bombers and fighters and damaged eight others so seriously that it is most unlikely that they were able to return to their base. The flight lieutenant who led the flight of Hurricanes had already been awarded the Distinguished Flying Cross for previous operations in Libya. His successes in Albania have brought his score to over twenty as well as many probables. He shot down two early in the engagement, returned to his base and rearmed, and going back to the battle, shot down two more.

Another flying of officer, who is known as the Ape to his colleagues because of his immense strength, went one better and shot down two Savoia bombers, two Bredas, and one Fiat C.R.42, all of which fell in flames after his vigorous onslaught.

So the story of the Royal Air Force in Greece takes on greater glory as enemy bases are successfully bombed and their aircraft shot out of the sky in ever growing numbers. The Athens Radio is happy to have the privilege of broadcasting this splendid record of Royal Air Force gallantry and prowess in the Greek skies, and also to extend to Britain's brave airmen, so intrepidly and effectively coming to our assistance in defence of our liberty and independence, the whole-hearted thanks and deep gratitude felt by everyone in Greece.

The sixteen enemy aircraft destroyed by the pilots from 80 Squadron during this battle brought their total score of confirmed victories to just over the century mark, but even this fine achievement did not allow the pilots to sit back and rest on their laurels. They went out again the following day escorting the bombers of 30 and 211 Squadrons. Three times they went on raids to Paraboa, Berat and Valona respectively, and yet even this could not satisfy Pat's insatiable offensive spirit. He went out again before supper in the hope that he might come across some unsuspecting Italian aircraft, but returned disappointed, with his gun covers still intact. It was not that Pat was concerned about his score; his first thoughts were the efficiency of his flight and the personal safety of less-experienced pilots. But nothing on the ground could match the exhilaration and the excitement of out-manoeuvring and out-thinking an aerial opponent. And nothing gave him greater pleasure or satisfaction than seeing his bullets smashing to pieces an enemy of his country.

That day the Italians were very difficult to find, but one Hurricane pilot was lucky. Sergeant Hewett found that his undercarriage was not working properly when he took off for the escort mission to Berat and returned to Paramythia to have the fault put right. Within fifteen minutes Hewett was off again, in an attempt to catch up with the rest of the Hurricanes and Blenheims. On the way he was engaged by five Fiat C.R. 42's. Sergeant Hewett turned on them ferociously. In less than a quarter of an hour he had shot down three of the C.R. 42's, and sent the remaining pair scampering for safety into the clouds.

A signal came through on 2 March announcing the award of Distinguished Flying Crosses to Squadron Leader Jones and Ape Cullen for *courageous determination and devotion to duty.* As if to celebrate the award the very next day Cullen went out and shot down four more enemy planes. He and Arty Acworth were flying a couple of Hurricanes on 'local flying practice' when they intercepted a formation of five Cant 1007's south-west of Corfu. The Ape got right behind four of the bombers and in spite of a withering fire which tore through his fighter and put a neat hole clean through his flying boot, he shot down the lot. Acworth downed the fifth. The Hurricanes then reformed and the two victorious pilots were able to count eighteen Italian parachutes floating down towards the sea which, more than two thousand years earlier, had been the scene of the first Greek naval battle between Gorcyra and Corinth.

The Italian Fleet made one of its very rare appearances on 4 March, when six warships sneaked down the Albanian coast and began to bombard the port of Himara, which was being stubbornly defended by the Greeks, in spite of growing Italian pressure.

Immediately nine Blenheims from Paramythia set out to bomb the Italian fleet, escorted by ten Hurricanes from 80 and 33 Squadrons. Pat's section of four protected the starboard flank, while four Hurricanes from 33 stood guard on the port flank, and a further two Hurricanes from 33 Squadron provided additional protection weaving behind the bombers. At three o'clock, just as the formation reached the target, six Fiat G. 50's in line astern came in from the port side and delivered an attack against one of the weavers, which went down in flames. The G. 50's made no attempt to attack the bombers, and Pat, consequently, made no attempt to chase them. He knew that if he did so he would leave the Blenheims unguarded. His primary task was to see that no harm came to the bombers, and no matter how inviting were the efforts of the G. 50's, Pat would not allow himself to be enticed away from the Blenheims.

He kept his section close by the Blenheims until the bombers had finished their job and were safely on their way home again. Then he split up the Hurricanes into separate pairs and turned towards the screen of Italian Fighters roaming about above the Italian warships.

Ape Cullen was Pat's partner and flew just behind and to the right of Pat's Hurricane. As they approached the fleet a single G. 30 aimed towards them and made an attack on Pat's Hurricane from below. Pat aileron-turned on to its trail and, as he opened fire, saw out of the corner of his eye Ape Cullen's Hurricane creeping up from behind, its pilot obviously itching to get at the Italian fighter. But already the G. 50 was doomed. Its undercarriage dropped out, it turned over on to its back, and then it spiralled down to crash into a mountain-top just north of Himara.

Pat pulled up and, looking over his shoulder, expected to see Ape Cullen's Hurricane still formating with him. However, there was no sign of the Hurricane, or of any other aircraft, and although Pat searched for about ten minutes he was unable to locate his colleague. Obviously, the fearless ex-Wall-of-Death rider, not content to watch his Flight

Commander shoot down hostile aeroplanes, had gone off on his own to take on the Italians.

Pat flew on towards Valona and very soon intercepted another lone G. 50, which seemed quite willing to remain and fight. Its pilot was no match for the brilliant flying, cunning tactics and expert shooting of the South African, however, and in a few minutes it was a blazing wreck falling into the sea south-west of Valona harbour. Another G. 50 joined in just before the first enemy machine went down, but as soon as its pilot saw the result of the first combat he dived away towards Valona. Pat raced after it at full throttle and, after one good burst from the eight machine-guns, saw the G. 50 crash on the west side of the promontory and burst into flames.

The anti-aircraft fire came up thick and fast, but Pat climbed away quickly and the shells burst harmlessly way behind his Hurricane. He passed over the edge of a cloud at 15,000 feet, and discovered a crowd of nine C.R. 42's cruising on top of the cloud and just ahead of him. He put down the nose of the Hurricane, and fired a long burst directly into the cockpit of the C.R. 42 on the extreme starboard side of the enemy formation. The other C.R. 42's instantly disappeared into the cloud, but the fighter he had fired at climbed slowly in a steep left-hand turn, with smoke issuing from its engine. Before Pat could get at it again the C.R. 42 stalled and went down into the cloud in a fast spin. Pat was positive that the pilot of this aircraft was out of action and that the C.R. 42 ultimately crashed, but as he was unable to confirm its destruction, again he only claimed a 'probable'.

He spent a further twenty minutes on patrol without sighting any more aircraft and then flew back to Paramythia.

Sergeant Hewett followed him down. He had had a good day, too, shooting down one G. 50 near Himara and then three C.R. 42's out of a formation of eight which he had found dodging in and out of the clouds near Valona.

Ape Cullen, who had only recently had such an amazing run of success, failed to return.

There were many types of courage among the pilots in Greece. Some, like Pat, were tacticians, who regularly outmanoeuvred their opponents in clearly thought-out, well-planned moves, while others, less sensitive perhaps in the risks they took, exploited an irresistible offensive spirit, relying on superb dash and daring to carry them through.

Ape Cullen belonged to this latter category, and feared nothing.

A big, smiling, long-armed giant from Putney, he had built up a reputation as a daredevil racing motor-cyclist at Brooklands before the war. Then he had joined the Royal Air Force and been posted to the Middle East, where for a time he served as a ferry pilot. There was not enough excitement in that job for the swashbuckling Cullen, and he had put in request after request, until finally he had been posted to 80 Squadron in September 1940. It had taken him some time to get used to flying fighters, but after his first confirmed success against the Italians on the last day of December 1940 he had developed into a first-class fighter ace. Within three months he had shot down no less than sixteen enemy machines, nine of which he had destroyed during the last week in two fantastic fights. But he had to pay dearly for his success. He had several scars across his stomach, one across the knuckles of his right hand and another across his shins, where a bullet had passed right through his flying boot.

He was a reckless flyer, to whom tactics meant nothing. The pilots of 80 Squadron reckoned that if The Ape had been flying alone and happened to see the entire Italian Air Force above him he would have pulled back the stick and swung straight into them. He could not last, and they all knew it. He was tremendously popular with everyone and at Paramythia on that day that he failed to return an air of gloom descended on the camp.

During the few weeks that Pat was stationed at Paramythia he became friendly with the young Rhodesian, Ping Newton. The two pilots had very little in common, except that both were brilliant flyers and both had the same burning desire to come to grips with the enemy. Pat was by way of being a philosopher with his own strict code of ethics. Ping, on the other hand, was impetuous and hot-blooded, with a persuasive tongue and a ready wit. The discussions they had at

Paramythia were always lively and informed, a welcome relaxation after the arduous hours of flying. Headquarters staffs and the inane specimens whose various countenances graced the pages of glossy magazines were Ping's particular anathema. Pat was the one who slowed him up. His wise counsel helped a lot in reconciling Ping to his proper place in the war.

'I am not denying that there were worms in our apple,' Pat would say. 'The trouble is that there is scarcely a crime in the moral calendar from cruelty to vulgarity, from lust to corruption, to which war does not give licence. It enfranchises cupidity and greed, and places in positions of power people who trade on the sufferings of others.

'But if we lose this war, nothing in life which a decent man holds to be good will be left for us. So we would not be honest with ourselves if we did not put our utmost individual effort into beating the enemy. It is only when we have annihilated the threat of barbarism that we can return and settle with the worms in our apple.'

Squadron Leader Jones flew in from Yanina with some great news. The squadron had been ordered to hand over their Gladiators to 112 Squadron, and then to return to Eleusis to re-equip with Hurricanes. Pat's flight was also to return to Eleusis for a short rest from operations. Pat was about to protest that his flight did not need a rest, when Squadron Leader Jones told him the rest of the news.

'As soon as you get to Athens, Pat, you had better see the tailor about getting an extra half ring sewn on. My orders are that, from the 12th March, you are promoted to Acting Squadron Leader and are to assume command of 33 Squadron.'

He stretched out his arm and firmly shook the hand of the astonished Pat. 'Congratulations, Pat. Your promotion is well deserved.'

The following day the squadron moved to Eleusis. As they arrived over the aerodrome 33 Squadron were just taking off to proceed to Larissa, where they were to be stationed. Pat was not at all impressed by the very straggly-looking formation of Hurricanes.

Hardly had 80 Squadron set foot on the ground at Eleusis when the news came through that Sergeant Hewett had been awarded the

Distinguished Flying Medal and Pat a Bar to his Distinguished Flying Cross.

The celebration party was held at 'Maxie's' restaurant. Since there were no operations, the party continued well into the early hours of the morning and for once the normally sober Pat had to be helped back to his quarters.

On 12 March, Pat took his leave of 80 Squadron. He had been with the squadron for so long that it was almost like leaving home. The thoughts and sentiments of everyone in the squadron were summed up very well indeed in the operations record book.

Pattle promoted to Squadron Leader and posted to 33 Squadron to command. It was a sad day for the squadron when it had to say good-bye to Pat, as his great skill and determination as a pilot, combined with his sterling personal qualities had contributed in no small measure to the success of the squadron. His promotion is well deserved and the good wishes of all go out to him in his new position.

16

Commanding Officer

33 Squadron had many years of overseas service in the Middle East to its credit and, until the arrival of 80 Squadron in the desert, had been undisputed premier fighter squadron in the command. Unlike 80 Squadron, which was a closely knit unit with a tremendous team-spirit, 33 Squadron's reputation had been established by the sheer brilliance of its pilots as individuals. They were a tough bunch who hated red tape; discipline was practically non-existent. Most of the pilots were pre-war regulars and the wide range of accents confirmed that they had come to the squadron from many distant parts of the Commonwealth.

There was Ping Newton, who always seemed able to find himself the odd spot of bother now and then, such as coming back from a sweep with his undercarriage full of camel thorn.

Another who hailed from Rhodesia, where he had been in the Police Force, was the gay and carefree Frankie Holman. He was the humourist of the squadron, and very popular with everyone. In the desert he had shot down half a dozen of Mussolini's aircraft and had already added to this when flying with a detachment of Hurricanes at Paramythia.

British Columbia in Canada was the home of Vernon Woodward, who was probably the quietest member of the squadron on the ground. But in the air he was a killer, and with twelve Italian aircraft to his credit, headed the squadron's scoreboard.

John Mackie also came from Canada. Tall, dark and good looking, he was most popular with the fairer sex, and his tent was crammed with photographs of women in full dress, undress, and even no dress at all.

Charles Dyson, better known as 'Deadstick', because of his numerous forced-landings in the desert without the use of his engine, came from Jhansi in India. Already he had collected two 'gongs', a Distinguished Flying Cross awarded in September 1939 for operations in Palestine, and a Bar to this decoration awarded in December 1940 after he had shot down six Fiat C.R. 42's in less than fifteen minutes. They had considered changing his nickname to 'Quickstick' after that!

From Johannesburg, where he had been a secretary before the war, came Harry Starrett. Not a brilliant flyer, but a very sound type, Harry could always be relied upon in a crisis, and already had four Italian scalps in his belt.

Kenya had presented the squadron with a real baronet – 'Blue-blood' Kirkpatrick they called him. Very tall, elegant and good looking, his gentlemanly bearing and Oxford accent showed clearly to the others the benefits of an English Public School education. His calm reserve never deserted him, even in the middle of a dogfight, and he was respected for it by everyone.

The Flight Commanders were both English. Flight Lieutenant Littler, the stoutish leader of 'A' Flight, was known to everyone as 'Pop' for some other reason than age – possibly worldly wisdom, size, appetite or even his appreciation of food. The other flight leader, Dixie Dean, was already well known to Pat, for he had been with 80 Squadron at Ismailia. He was a quietly spoken charming character, full of fun, but he took his job seriously and led his flight well. He possessed a terrific wardrobe of pyjamas and unknowingly helped to kit out Pat in night attire, soon after Pat took command of the squadron. Pat had only one solitary pair of rather tattered pyjamas when he arrived at Larissa and his batman, who also looked after Dixie's kit, felt so sorry for his new Commanding Officer that during one of his dhobying sessions he 'accidentally' miscounted and left one extra pair for Pat – and one pair less for Dixie.

Another Englishman, who at this time was an unknown flying officer, but who was to become a group captain with a DSO and several DFCs, was Pete Wickham. An ex-Cranwell cadet who had joined 33 from 112 Squadron, Pete was a very aggressive character, who lived and fought hard. He was to end the war with very nearly a score of 'kills' to his credit.

Of the sergeant pilots attached to the squadron, Len Nottingham was undoubtedly the most experienced. A stocky man from Grimsby, Len had been with 80 Squadron before coming to 33. He had proved his worth in the desert, where he had shot down three Fiat GR. 42's and a Savoia 79. He was to shoot down many more aircraft in Greece and to win a well-earned Distinguished Flying Cross soon after being promoted to warrant officer.

They were a cosmopolitan crowd who had little respect for authority, but as fighter pilots they were first-rate. Already they had chalked up ninety-one victories for the loss of only four pilots in the desert war, and now they had arrived in Greece they were all out to catch up on 80 Squadron's score.

Their Hurricanes had remained in the Athens area for several weeks, and the pilots were getting bored whilst they awaited the arrival of their new Commanding Officer. When they heard that Squadron Leader M T St John Pattle from 80 Squadron was to be their new boss they had at first been indignant. They all felt that one of their own flight commanders should have been promoted. However, they had all heard of Pat's reputation as a fighter pilot, and many of them had flown with him in the desert, so that by the time they assembled at Larissa to meet their new leader they were quite prepared to listen to him.

This is my first command,' Pat began, 'and I intend to make it a successful one. You have done well in the desert, but you are not a good squadron. A good squadron looks smart. You are a scruffy-looking lot!'

Several eyebrows were raised, but Pat met their looks without a waver.

'Your flying, by my standards, is ragged. Flying discipline starts when you start to taxi and doesn't end until you switch off your engine. In future you will taxi in formation, take off in formation and land in formation at all times unless your aircraft has been damaged, or in an emergency.'

Pat then apologised for his lack of experience in a Hurricane. He had, after all, only been flying one for a few weeks, whilst the others had been flying Hurricanes for more than six months. If any of the pilots of 33 would oblige, he would be very glad to get in a little dogfighting practice during the afternoon.

After that berating, here was the ideal chance for the pilots to get their own back. Almost unanimously they selected Ping Newton to take on their new squadron commander. If Ping was not the best pilot among them, he was certainly the most reckless, and would undoubtedly soon put Squadron Leader Pattle in his proper place with a Hurricane, if not with a Gladiator.

After lunch all the squadron personnel assembled on the airfield to see the show. Pat and Ping agreed on a procedure. They would climb up in formation and at 10,000 feet they would separate, coming in for a head-on attack at constant height and power settings. A break to the right and the fight would be on, with neither of them having an advantage.

Ping had worked out his tactics carefully. The two Hurricanes approached and broke away. Like a flash Ping pulled high to the right, slammed on full right rudder with the stick back, flicking viciously and catching the flick on the three-quarter roll mark to go swinging back in a steep diving turn to the left. Ping felt proud of himself. He had never done this manoeuvre better. Pattle should still be aiming to the left and all Ping would have to do would be to pull back for the deflection shot. He looked for his Commanding Officer in his sights, but there was not a sign of him. What had happened? Ping pulled up hard and flicked again. Still no sign of Pattle. Something made Ping look in his rear-view mirror. He could hardly believe it! Pattle's Hurricane was sitting on his tail not twenty yards behind him. This was terrible. Ping gritted his teeth and pulled and pushed and hammered at the controls. His head wanted to burst and there was a red film over his eyes. But every time he glanced in his rear-view mirror there was Pattle's Hurricane, sitting right on his tail. Only now he was so close that he was almost formating with Ping's aircraft.

Ping gave up and they started again with another head-on attack. But

185

it was hopeless. Within seconds of the fight starting Pattle was back on his tail and remained there.

When they landed Pat was smiling.

'You fly quite nicely, Ping, but you are much too smooth on the controls. You've got to be rough with them in a dogfight.'

Ping's head was drumming, and his whole body ached from the exertion of it all.

Pat ignored the silent onlookers. He knew that he had convinced them of his capabilities as a pilot, but psychologically it was not the correct time to press home his advantage. He would let them brood on it for a time.

The next morning he was up early, inspecting dispersals, maintenance, instrument section, armoury and the signals department. Everywhere he was greeted with a smart salute. He had earned the respect of the ground staffs by his example and skill in the air, and they were quite willing to believe that this small man with the steady eye and unwavering square chin would be just as determined and reliable on the ground. Already he had begun to win their loyalty and admiration, which was the first step towards making his squadron smart and successful.

The Hurricanes began formation-flying practice after lunch, and when any aircraft lagged behind Pat's voice was polite and calm, but crisp and firm, and the unfortunate pilot knew that it was meant to be obeyed. Soon the formation flying was perfect.

Cloud flying, practice interceptions, air-firing tests and mock dogfights followed, and within a week the whole squadron had begun to click together as a team.

When they were not flying the pilots were usually sitting in a circle by the operations hut, discussing ways and means, and then flying again to try them out. During these discussions Pat's views on air fighting were stimulating and provided that lively spark which gave all the pilots complete confidence in his ability, both as a fighter pilot and as a leader of men.

'You must be aggressive in the air,' he would say, 'but not to the extent of recklessness. Always be ready to take the initiative, but only when you have the enemy aircraft at a disadvantage. You must be ready to react instinctively in any situation and you can only do this if you are alert both physically and mentally. Good eyes and perfect coordination of hands and feet are essential. Flying an aeroplane in combat should be automatic. The mind must be free to think *what* to do; it must never be clouded with any thought on *how* it should be done.'

Pat himself was perfectly fit, but still continued to train both his mind and body every day, and encouraged all his pilots to do the same, because as he was always saying – 'perfect physical and mental fitness is the basis on which a good fighter pilot is built'.

Several times each day he continued to train his eyes to pick out tiny objects at great distances, and every morning he tested and trained the speed of his reflexes with the help of his batman.

Usually at 5.30 a.m. 'Taffy' Harris would enter the CO's tent with a cup of tea, to find Pat totally enclosed inside his old green sleeping bag, with the flap pulled right down over his face.

'Good morning, sir. Looks like being a nice day.'

Immediately the flap would fly back, and instantly Pat would be alert. Although Taffy experienced this every morning, he was always surprised to find that anyone could ever be so wide awake in such a short time.

'Good morning, Taffy.' Pat was out of his sleeping bag in a moment and sitting on the side of his bed. He took a quick sip of the steaming hot tea, as Taffy picked up a piece of cane, about fifteen inches long, which had been resting against the tent pole. The Welshman then knelt down directly in front of Pat and held the cane horizontally between his palms and about eighteen inches from the ground.

'Okay, Taffy. Whenever you like.'

Taffy waited a few seconds and then, suddenly, without any warning, let go the stick. Pat's hand shot out like a striking cobra and, before the cane had moved six inches, he was holding it and smiling.

'Your turn, Taffy,' he said.

The roles were reversed and Pat dropped the stick. It rattled on the hard rocky ground – Taffy never managed to catch it, no matter how hard he concentrated.

The squadron soon settled down in Larissa, and after the desert enjoyed being 'out to grass'. Even the mess dog, Mr Deeds, a black-and-tan Alsatian, soon became a well-filled handsome hound.

The town of Larissa looked very different from Pat's last impressions of it. Less than a fortnight earlier a violent earthquake had reduced most of the town to ruins and much of what still stood had been unmercifully bombed by the Italian Savoias. With the arrival of 33 Squadron at Larissa, however, the bombing raids had ceased.

The troops salvaged various equipment from the ruins of the town, which helped to make the so-called field conditions a little more bearable. There were soon iron bedsteads to replace the camp beds in the canvas tents, and these were followed by stone fireplaces, built by handyman pilots from the piles of débris in the town. Various livestock found wandering among the ruins were escorted to the airfield and soon a miniature farm flourished behind the cookhouse tent.

On 23 March, Pat led his new squadron for the first time on an operational mission. Thirteen Hurricanes left Larissa soon after half past six in the morning, and after a pleasant forty-five minute trip over the Pindus Mountains arrived in the beautiful valley of Paramythia. They joined forces with eleven Gladiators from 112 Squadron and set out to escort six Blenheims from 84 Squadron on a bombing raid on Berat. After crossing the Albanian frontier the sun disappeared and the clouds thickened to such an extent that the whole formation was forced to fly just below the cloud base at 1,900 feet. The bombers made their bombing am from 1,500 feet, in spite of a considerable amount of antiaircraft fire, and were successful both in hitting their targets accurately and in getting away from the area without a great deal of damage to themselves. The Hurricanes of 33 Squadron were not so lucky, two of them being turned over by near misses, and receiving severe damage to wings and fuselage. Fortunately their pilots managed to regain control and flew back at a reduced speed, guarded by Frankie Holman's section. They managed to escape further interference from the Italians, but the main formation of Hurricanes ran into more trouble near the border. Pat had re-formed the squadron so that four Hurricanes guarded each flank of the Blenheim formation, with Charlie Dyson acting as a weaver in the rear. He was jumped by a Fiat G. 50, which holed his glycol and petrol tanks before he had even spotted his attacker. He immediately warned the squadron and wheeled to face the onslaught, but after one burst of bullets the G. 50 climbed up into the clouds. Although almost blinded by the glycol fumes, Dyson carried on flying towards the south. But he only managed to get back a few miles before the engine came to a grinding halt and he had to bale out. The Hurricane exploded on hitting the ground, and burnt out completely, but Dyson was soon picked up by a Greek patrol, and within a few hours was on his way back to Larissa in a Greek army truck.

After lunch Pat received orders to ground-strafe the aerodrome at Fieri as a reprisal for an earlier Italian raid on Paramythia. It was a tough assignment. Fieri was a long way behind the Italian lines and was known to have very heavy ack-ack defences, as well as a standing patrol of fighters over the field. At the pre-flight briefing Pat was as scared as any of the pilots, but he hoped it would not show too much. As he detailed the way to approach the target, in two sections, making the final approach at a steep glide in order to effect some element of surprise, his mouth was dry, and he licked his lips frequently.

Not one of the ten pilots relished the thought of strafing Fieri, and most of them breathed a sigh of relief when, shortly after starting the final glide on the field from a height of some 25,000 feet, the Hurricanes were attacked by a strong force of about twenty Fiat G. 50's and Macchi 200's. For the next ten minutes it was a free-for-all, during which the Hurricanes 'hammered the hell out of the I-ties'.

They were all split up during the fight and, with fuel running low, they straggled back to Paramythia. One by one they landed and as each pilot recalled his part in the battle excitement mounted. Then someone realised Pat had not returned. They scanned the sky anxiously as the minutes ticked by, knowing that if Pat was still in the air his fuel endurance was almost expired. Then they heard the buzz of a Hurricane in the distance. Pat landed and they all surged around him. In turn he questioned everyone on the results of the sortie.

'I got one of the I-ties who bounced us,' said Frankie Holman with his characteristic chuckle.

'I got one G. 50, and probably another,' reported Vernon Woodward.

'I'm claiming a couple of probables,' said Newton.

Pat listened without a smile. He was white-faced, but it was anger, not fear. 'I am not interested in the dogfight,' he said. 'Your orders were to ground-strafe Fieri aerodrome. How many of you did so?'

Only Vernon Woodward had gone on to the airfield. The others, once they had been jumped, had never given it another thought.

Pat berated them for about ten minutes. The air was blue! Then they heard his story. When the fighters attacked he had immediately set one on fire, and then pressed on to Fieri, where he made three runs over the airfield in the face of a solid wall of flak, destroying three aircraft on the ground and shooting a fourth as it was approaching to land. He saw it roll on to its back at about 200 feet, but as he did not actually see it hit the ground he would only claim this as a probable!

This was very typical of Pat. He knew the risks he was taking; he was as frightened as anyone. But the order was to ground-strafe Fieri and orders were to be obeyed. He would calculate the risk and minimise it by clever tactics, but he would never evade the job to be done.

The latter part of March was fairly quiet and there was not a great deal of flying except for training trips and the occasional reconnaissance flight. Pat, as usual, was not happy in being grounded for too long and, leaving most of the administrative work to his Adjutant, George Rumsey, spent a lot of his time in the air with a group of youngsters who had only recently joined the squadron. Pilot Officers Winsland, Dunscombe, Cheetham and Woods, and Sergeant Genders had as yet not met the enemy in the air and had a lot to learn. They had an excellent instructor in Pat, however, and accepting his advice without question, they all learned quickly. In a short time Pat was convinced that given the chance they would all prove to be sound, efficient and reliable pilots on operations.

Pat was Station Commander at Larissa as well as being the Commanding Officer of 33 Squadron. There were no other personnel other than the squadron based on the aerodrome, except for an Army Liaison Officer, by the name of Captain Churtons. Pat was therefore responsible for everything that happened on the airfield. One thing that worried him was the safety of the Hurricanes, which at first were dispersed around the perimeter of the airfield and covered with bushes and branches in an attempt to conceal them from the air. Pat knew that the Italians would one day pluck up enough courage to strafe the airfield, and that the chances were that many of the Hurricanes would be set on fire – unless they could be moved to another refuge, unknown to the enemy. The problem was to find such a refuge. It had to be sufficiently large and flat for a Hurricane to land, and yet from the air had to look too small to be a landing ground.

After a great deal of searching, Captain Churtons eventually came up with the perfect solution. Six or seven miles south-west of Larissa he found a grass field, much smaller than the airfield at Larissa and relatively flat and well drained. It was of a rectangular shape, with a deep ditch running along one of the shorter sides. When Pat first saw it from the air he had grave doubts as to whether it was big enough to land a Hurricane, but decided to try. By touching down as near as possible to one side of the field, and by using full flaps and very generous application of the brakes, he finished up only a few yards from the ditch. Others then tried and landed successfully, so from then on the satellite airfield came into being and was used daily as a dispersal area. A small tented camp with field-cooking facilities was organised and the site christened 'Churtons' Bottom' in honour of its discoverer.

Pat was most anxious to see that the squadron was never caught unawares by an enemy raid, and after much thought and discussion with his officers organised an 'early-warning system' which was to prove most successful. With the aid of Captain Churtons he established a considerable number of observation posts at strategic positions on hilltops to the north, east and west of Larissa. Each post was equipped with a telephone which was in direct contact with a group or airmen acting as operators in a small wooden hut on the airfield at Larissa. This operations hut had a large table in the centre, covered with a huge map showing each of the observation posts, which were boxed off into squares and identified by using the letters of the alphabet.

When an enemy raid was spotted by the observation post it would immediately contact the operations hut at Larissa, give its own code letter and then the number of aircraft involved, the estimated height and the direction of the raid. On receiving this information the operator at Larissa would place a card giving all these facts at the appropriate spot on the map. The Operations Control Officer in direct radio contact with the stand-by flight would then pass on this information, and within thirty seconds of receiving news of the raid the standby Hurricanes would be taking off from both Larissa and Churtons' Bottom.

From the beginning, the early-warning system, operating daily from dawn to dusk, was most efficient and was a boon to the squadron.

17

Enter the Luftwaffe

On 25 March 1941 Yugoslavia's Premier, Mr Dragisha Tsvetkovitch, pledged his country to the Three Power Pact of Germany, Italy and Japan. In so doing, he said Yugoslavia wanted to ensure her peaceful future in co-operation with the Axis. He was, in fact, following in the footsteps of Bulgaria and Romania, by giving Germany the right to bring her armed forces through his country without opposition.

The reason for this from Germany's point of view was obvious. Hitler had decided that the Italians were not getting on quickly enough with the task of defeating the Greeks, and now that the better spring weather was here he was going to show Mussolini how to carry out a *blitzkrieg*.

At 2.30 a.m. on 27 March there was a dramatic *coup d'etat* in Belgrade. Mr Tsvetkovitch was arrested and Prince Paul, the Regent, was forced to resign. The 17-year-old King Peter took on the role of leader of his country, with General Dusan Simovitch as his Prime Minister. Together they issued on behalf of the Yugoslav Government a proclamation of policy in which it was made clear that Yugoslavia wanted to go back to the position she had occupied before the signing of the Tripartite Pact. In other words they would defy Hitler, and fight, if he attempted to bring his troops on to Yugoslav soil.

The Führer's answer was equally dramatic. Without warning, waves of German bombers struck at Belgrade. The capital of Yugoslavia had been declared an open city, but this meant nothing to the Nazis. In a few hours the Stukas turned the beautiful city on the River Danube into a smouldering mass of ruins, littered with the dead bodies of old men, women and children.

Simultaneously the German Panzers stormed across the frontiers into Yugoslavia and Greece. Yugoslavia, though partly mobilised, was not ready for war, and her inadequately equipped armies were soon overrun by the German motorised units. They advanced rapidly along the valleys of the Struma and the Vardar towards Salonika, and in the west poured through the Monastir Gap and headed for Fiorina. This disastrous defeat of the Yugoslavs caused the British troops, who had taken up a strong natural line of defence running from the sea near Katerini through Edessa to the Yugoslav frontier, to be immediately outflanked. Less than a week after the unprovoked German assault on Greece, General Wilson, the British Commander, had to withdraw his troops to a new line just south of Mount Olympus.

At Larissa, Pat and 33 Squadron heard of the German attack early on the morning of 6 April; instantly all aircraft were refuelled and rearmed ready for immediate take-off. But it was not until after lunch that Pat received his orders to make an offensive sweep over Bulgaria. In the Rupel Pass the Hurricanes met the Luftwaffe for the first time, but were not impressed by the Germans. A formation of twenty Messerschmitt 109's was engaged by the squadron, which quickly knocked down five of them without suffering even so much as a scratch. Frankie Holman had his first experience of flying wingman to Pat in a dogfight, and after landing commented: 'I never had a chance – we came up right behind this pair of 109's – Pat just gave them a left and a right and it was all over. Both went down in flames.'

Len Cottingham shot down another 109, whose pilot baled out. As the parachute floated down another 109 circled round to give protection, but this aircraft was also shot down by the tubby flight sergeant. The fifth Messerschmitt was downed by the aggressive Wickham.

The squadron was still in the air returning to Larissa when the early-warning system was brought into action for the first time. Pop Littler and Kirkpatrick took off, and about five minutes later were followed by Vernon Woodward's Hurricane; his ammunition belts were still being loaded when the alert was given and he had to wait for the armourers to fix the covering panels. When he finally took off only the four guns in his port wing would fire. The other four in the starboard wing were empty.

Little and Kirkpatrick intercepted five Cant Z. 1007's over Volos Harbour, and after firing all their ammunition sent one of the Cants down in flames and chased the others away. Woodward caught up with these four over the Gulf of Corinth, and by means of some excellent shooting got two of them in flames and so seriously damaged a third that it eventually dived into the sea near the western mouth of the Gulf. When Woodward returned to Larissa with not a single round of ammunition in his guns Pat and the rest of 33 were there to greet him. As he told his story all the chaps crowded round to congratulate him, except Pat. He was most annoyed when he learned that Vernon's aircraft had not been fully loaded with ammunition.

'You might have downed the lot if your groundcrew had been more efficient,' he barked at the quiet Canadian. 'Don't let it happen again!'

Then in a softer, friendlier tone, as the astonished Woodward stood speechless in front of him: 'Come on, Woody. I'll buy you a beer.'

They all adjourned to the mess tent, where the beer was quickly supplemented by half a dozen bottles of sherry, which seemed far more suitable to celebrate the squadron's most successful début on operations with the Luftwaffe.

The following morning the miserable weather matched their hangovers, and no one was sorry when all operations were cancelled until the cloud lifted.

By three o'clock the mist had cleared and Pat led six Hurricanes to escort the bombers of 11 Squadron, which had been detailed to bomb a German transport convoy near Strumitsa, The Blenheims and Hurricanes were on their way back, flying at 17,000 feet; below in the haze they could vaguely discern the Struma Pass like a twisted cotton thread. Quite suddenly Pat shouted:

'Bandit dead ahead at about five thousand feet.'

They all searched the indicated spot, but could see nothing, so Pat left them all with the bombers and dived away to deal with the intruder. About thirty seconds later everyone saw the enemy plane, when it burst into flames. Pat rejoined them, took up his station on the starboard side of the Blenheims and then, at the request of the leader of the bombers, informed him that the enemy plane had been a Fiat C.R. *42*.

For the whole of the week the weather was shocking; if the situation had not been so critical, the squadron would have been grounded. As it was, Headquarters requested the aircraft to take off whenever possible in order to give some support to the hard-pressed Greek and British troops, who were striving desperately to hold the increasing pressure from the overwhelming numbers of Nazi invaders.

On the 8th the squadron flew through almost solid cloud over some of the most dangerous mountains in Europe, whilst escorting eight Blenheims from 211 Squadron. They bombed and strafed an airfield near Petrich in Yugoslavia, where they left a number of aircraft blazing on the ground. Not a single German aircraft came up to intercept them. The weather was probably too bad for them to take off.

The following day the weather was even worse and it was impossible even to think of getting the bombers off the ground. Six Hurricanes from 80 Squadron, who had tried to carry out a fighter sweep, were forced to land at Larissa after getting hopelessly lost in the mountains. The only Hurricanes from 33 Squadron which managed to get into the air were those of Pat and Charlie Dyson. By pure chance they came across a Junkers 88 which was heading south towards Larissa. Pat gave it a good burst of machine-gun fire which caused smoke to gush from the starboard engine. As it disappeared into the clouds he was almost sure that he saw flames spurting from the engine. He could not be certain, however, and consequently when he landed claimed only a 'damaged'. After lunch he was delighted when it was confirmed that the 88 had crashed and, since there was nothing else to do at Larissa, he drove out with Frankie Holman to inspect the remains.

The squadron took the Blenheims of 11 Squadron to Betjol in Yugoslavia just before dusk on 10 April, and over the target had to ward off a number of attacks by Messerschmitts. Pat destroyed a 110 which crashed in flames, and a 109 which spun down, after its pilot had hurriedly evacuated his doomed aircraft.

Pat got another two Huns just after breakfast on the morning of Good Friday. He was already in the air on his way to the satellite airfield at Churtons' Bottom when the early-warning system announced the presence of a number of unidentified aircraft flying fairly low near Volos. Within a few minutes he was over the harbour, sighted several Heinkel Ill's and Junkers 88's apparently trying to lay mines in the sea at the entrance to the harbour. He managed to send two of the minelayers into the watery depths before the standby flight of Hurricanes arrived and chased the others away.

With a general improvement in the weather the next day, the squadron was able to fly on two sorties. During the morning they flew an escort mission with six Blenheims, and all returned safely without sighting a single enemy aircraft. In the afternoon Pat led his Hurricanes on an offensive sweep along the Struma valley, during which he shot down a Dornier 215. As the squadron was returning to Larissa they were warned over the radio-telephone from the operations hut to keep an eye open for three Savoia 79's escorted by Messerschmitt 109's. Almost before he had finished acknowledging the message Pat sighted the enemy formation flying some 2,000 or 3,000 feet lower down on the starboard beam. The escorting fighters were flying on either side of the three-engined bombers. Ordering the last three sections of his Hurricanes to keep the Messerschmitts busy, Pat led his own section, consisting of Frankie Holman and Harry Starrett, to attack the Savoias. He chose the leading Savoia as his target, and went about his task in his own recommended way. First he silenced the rear-gunner, then he holed the petrol tank, and finally put a short burst into the escaping fuel, with the result that the bomber ignited and fell away enveloped in flames. Holman and Starrett took a little longer, but between them managed to shoot down a second Savoia. Pat was unable to Find the third Savoia, so he dashed off to help the rest of his squadron, who were actively engaged with the Messerschmitts. Unfortunately he was now very low on ammunition and had time for only a short burst at one of the Fighters, which caused one of its undercarriage legs to fall down, and a panel about a foot square to fall from beneath the starboard wing.

He followed it for a minute or so, hoping that he had damaged it enough to make it crash-land, but a glance at his petrol gauge soon made him break away and head for Larissa.

The early-warning observation posts were connected to the operations hut at Larissa by telephone which had to go through the exchange at Salonika. Consequently when the Germans captured the great Greek port the early-warning system was put out of action. The squadron therefore now had no means of knowing what was happening on the other side of Mount Olympus. As a result Pat had to send up aircraft singly and in pairs on reconnaissance flights.

During one of these lone reconnaissance flights on Easter Sunday, 13 April, Vernon Woodward was intercepted by three Messerschmitt 109's between Monastir and Vive. He put up a magnificent fight in spite of the odds, shooting down one 109 for certain, and damaging a second before breaking away to continue his reconnaissance.

About the same time Charlie Dyson was also making a lone recce north of Salonika when he sighted a huge formation of forty-two bombers escorted by forty-four fighters. The odds being a little too great even for Dyson, he 'withdrew strategically into the sun'. His subsequent radio report to Larissa caused quite a stir.

Pat was in the air three times during Easter Sunday. Early in the morning, directly after lunch, and again just before dusk, he was leading his Hurricanes on escort duty. The Blenheims were conducted to Yanitsa, Ptolemais and Koziani, and each time bombed their targets and returned safely, without meeting the Luftwaffe.

Another raid by six Blenheims from 211 Squadron, for which no escort was available, was not so fortunate. All six Blenheims were shot down in flames before they even reached their target area. Alan Godfrey and Sergeant James were the only survivors. They managed with the aid of an Australian truck to get back to Larissa, where next day Pat was able to fix them up with a lift in a Lysander. But as it took off from Larissa a flight of 109's appeared without warning and shot it down north of the airfield before 33's Hurricanes could do anything about it. Sergeant James was killed instantly, but. Alan Godfrey, minus two fingers from his right hand, scrambled back to the airfield and later in the day was evacuated to the hospital in Athens.

The Luftwaffe was now operating fighters and dive-bombers from forward landing strips in the north of Greece, refuelled and rearmed by scores of Junkers 52 transport aircraft. These would have been juicy fat targets if the Hurricanes could have got at them, but Pat's squadron was fully occupied defending the Anzac positions north of Mount Olympus, when they were not engaged on bomber escort missions.

On 14 April, whilst flying over the Anzac positions, Dixie Dean and Vernon Woodward found six Stukas just peeling off to attack a convoy of Australian lorries. Ignoring the escorting Messerschmitt fighters, Dixie and Vernon played havoc with the Luftwaffe dive-bombers. In full view of the cheering Australian troops, they shot down three Junkers 87's for certain, and severely damaged another two. The escorting Messerschmitts made no attempt to interfere and, as soon as the two Hurricanes climbed towards them after the massacre, quickly turned towards friendlier skies.

Flight Lieutenant Mackie, Pilot Officer Cheetham and Sergeant Genders were on dawn standby the next day. Usually the standby Hurricanes simply warmed up their engines and then shut down. But this morning the engines continued to roar, and the three Hurricanes began to roll across the airfield. John Mackie had spotted fifteen Messerschmitt 109's coming in very low, obviously with the intention of strafing the airfield. The three Hurricanes had not left the ground when the 109's made their first pass, which was completed without a shot being fired. The German leader must have seen the trio taking off, and was deliberately letting them get into the air before he attacked. Three very brave pilots struggled with their controls to pull up the Hurricanes to a height which would give them a chance to make a fight of it, but their altimeters were barely registering 1,000 feet when the yellow-nosed Messerschmitts screamed down behind them with cannons blazing away.

Cheetham was first to go, but his end was a bit of a mystery. The onlookers, all standing in the open outside their ridge tents, such was the tension, saw Cheetham's Hurricane glide down, almost as if under control, and disappear behind some trees.

The Messerschmitt which had hit Cheetham now overshot the other two Hurricanes, and immediately John Mackie fastened on to its tail. He chased it right across the airfield. It was a fatal mistake. Another Messerschmitt came in close behind him. Mackie could have turned away and climbed out of trouble, as Sergeant Genders was now doing, but instead he deliberately hung on behind the 109 and opened fire. The pilot of the Messerschmitt baled out from 1,000 feet, whilst the plane belly-landed perfectly on its own in a field alongside the aerodrome, not far from the officers' mess tent.

As the German pilot floated down towards the airfield, some Greek ground gunners fired at him with their captured Italian Breda guns. Pat was furious. He was unable to do anything about it at the time, though, except to hope that the bullets would miss their intended target. He was most upset about the whole thing and more so when he learned later on that the German pilot had died in the MO's tent.

In the meantime Mackie's Hurricane had been hit. It staggered, went into a steepening dive, and finally flicked over the vertical in a most pathetic way, before hitting the ground and burning.

Sergeant Genders had never taken part in a real dogfight before, but the youngster weaved and climbed away from the Messerschmitts like a veteran. He not only managed to escape with his life, but also shot down one of the Messerschmitts. He landed at Larissa when the yellow-noses had disappeared, without a bullet-hole in his aircraft.

Pat, who had watched the whole thing from outside his tent, was powerless to do anything about the strafing, but now the Messerschmitts had gone he immediately gave orders that no one was to go near the crashed Messerschmitt in case it was timed to explode.

He then drove off in the staff car, with George Rumsey beside him, to try to find Cheetham's Hurricane. It was not far from the airfield, and when they got to it Cheetham's parachute was on the ground at the side of the riddled Hurricane. Pat and his Adjutant searched for more than thirty minutes, but could find no trace of the tall, dark pilot officer. No one ever saw him again.

Pat and Rumsey returned to the airfield, where they walked over to inspect the crashed 109. It had two neat tiny holes in the fuselage just beneath the cockpit cover, and about level with the chest of the pilot.

Not a single Hurricane on the ground had been hit, most of them being safely parked on the satellite field at Churtons' Bottom, but an odd assortment of Greek aircraft, including some old Avro Tutors, a few Gloster Gladiators, and a captured Savoia 79, all went up in smoke and flames.

The groundcrews were busy trying to clear up the mess when the Air Officer Commanding the Royal Air Force in Greece arrived. Sir John D'Albiac had brought some very distressing news. General Wilson, his forces outflanked by the advancing German Panzers, had decided to abandon the positions around Olympus and to move right back to Thermopylae. This meant surrendering Larissa, and all the other airfields in the north. It also meant that there would then be only three airfields available for the whole of the Royal Air Force in Greece, two of them, Menidi and Eleusis in the Athens area, and the third, Amphiklia, just south of the Thermopylae Pass.

Pat realised that the result of this decision could be one of two alternatives. Either the evacuation of the Air Force from Greece or total annihilation on the ground by the Luftwaffe, for it would be impossible to defend adequately just two or three concentrated targets with the limited number of fighters they had at their disposal.

After lunch Pat saw the AOC safely away in a Lysander, escorted by five of the squadron's Hurricanes, whose orders were to remain at Eleusis after completing the escort. Pat then arranged for the remainder of the squadron's Hurricanes, only eight were in a flying condition, to leave for Eleusis as soon as they were ready. George Rumsey was already busy organising the loading up of the scores of lorries with the equipment that had to go with them. The rest of the equipment which had to be left behind was completely destroyed by setting fire to it.

It was almost dark by the time they were ready to leave. Pat asked Rumsey to call the airmen together so that he could speak to them. He climbed on to an empty fifty-gallon petrol drum, looking very tired and disappointed. He spoke slowly and quietly as he tried to explain the situation.

'I am sorry things have turned out like this, chaps, but since the army has decided to retire to the south, there is nothing else that we can do here. Our orders are to move back to Eleusis. We shall move out at 2030 hours, and make a brief halt for a meal and refuelling at Amphiklia. Don't show any lights on your vehicles, and keep a sharp look-out for strafing fighters and dive-bombers.

'Keep your chins up. We'll get a bit of our own back when we get to Athens. Good luck, chaps.'

Pat, tired out by the tremendous amount of operational flying, and disappointed by the trend of events, allowed himself to be packed into the staff car by George Rumsey and Doc Henderson without a murmur. Rumsey climbed into the driving seat and by the time he had started the engine Pat was fast asleep. It was just starting to rain as they drove out of the airfield at the head of the last section of the convoy.

The night was a series of stops and starts with considerable bombing and strafing, but the staff car was lucky and suffered no damage. Pat slept through it all, as Rumsey and Henderson took it in turns to drive along the slippery, mountainous track.

Taffy Harris in another truck was not so lucky. He was in a Ford three-tonner, standing in the rear on look-out, his eyes searching the darkened skies for the slightest sign of trouble, his ears deafened by the snoring of Corporal Dixon, whose legs were dangling over the back of the lorry.

It was a miserable night, drizzling with rain, the clouds hanging heavily around 500 feet; Taffy did not expect to see any Huns that night. He watched the long crocodile of vehicles lumbering over the rocky, winding road and then noticed green and red flashes above and behind the convoy. They curved slowly in a graceful arc towards the lorries, and then streaked past like a flash of lightning – they were incendiary bullets from strafing fighters.

Taffy yelled a warning and dived from the slow-moving lorry into the darkened rocks at the side of the road. He felt a sharp pain in his right forearm, but quickly forgot it as he dodged to miss the bodies now descending upon him from the back of the truck. Cannon shells and bullets ricocheted from the boulders, and then there was a roaring as the Luftwaffe fighters shot over the convoy. They disappeared into the blackness of the night and the silence that followed was eerie. The groundcrews pulled themselves together and clambered back into the lorry, grumbling and muttering about 'the bloody Huns'. Corporal Dixon was still fast asleep, his feet still dangling over the back of the lorry. About six inches above his head the canvas hood had a dozen neat round holes in a straight line – the result of a burst of machine-gun fire. Dixon himself was unhurt. 'Just my luck,' thought Taffy. He had splintered a small bone in his forearm when he had jumped from the truck.

The first of the convoys reached Amphiklia soon after dawn. The troops stayed for a snack of tinned meat and vegetables, and then climbed back on to the trucks, now weighed down with full fuel tanks, and pushed on towards their destination. Pat awoke when the sun was well above the horizon. His head was buzzing, he was shivering and he had lost his voice. He did not feel like eating, but quenched his thirst with a hot cup of tea brought to him by the Doc. He noticed that the tea tasted rather peculiar, but did not grumble about it, because he did not want to put the MO to any more trouble. Very soon his eyes closed and he was fast asleep again. Doc Henderson had dosed the tea with a sedative.

During the day 33 Squadron's Hurricanes, singly and in pairs, appeared frequently over the convoys, and successfully warded off the attacks of the Luftwaffe. In spite of the terrific odds against them, all the Hurricanes were able to fly back to Eleusis without a great deal of damage, although Charlie Dyson had a narrow escape.

He was approaching the end of a convoy, just south of Lamia, and about to drop a message. He was flying very low, just above vehicle height, with flaps down, and was almost level with a straggling three-tonner, when a bomb dropped beside the road and just ahead of Dyson's Hurricane. It was a tremendous explosion and Dyson flew through a part of it. His aircraft was hurled on to its back, and the cockpit hood shaken loose. Apart from this the Hurricane weathered it well, although the hydraulic system was put out of action. It was an extremely near miss for Dyson – his oxygen-cum-microphone mask was torn from his face by a metal splinter, and he was very shaken. But he managed to regain control of the Hurricane and to fly it safely back to Eleusis. It was a terrific struggle to get the undercarriage to lock down on the hand pump, but he finally succeeded and made a good landing. The following morning he had a fever and a high temperature and was chased off to the hospital in Athens.

The convoys began to arrive at Eleusis during the morning of 17 April and the squadron began to sort itself out, all the flying being done by 80 Squadron, who were already settled in at Eleusis. Pat, still sick with a high temperature, took it fairly easy and left George Rumsey to organise things under the general direction of Squadron Leader Tap Jones, who was now acting as overall wing leader at Eleusis.

There was continuous ground-strafing by the Luftwaffe fighters throughout the day, in spite of 80 Squadron's efforts to keep them at bay. At one time the Messerschmitt pilots even threw hand-grenades from their cockpits. The anti-aircraft defences were practically wiped out, but the ground and administrative personnel put up a valiant fight, even though their only weapons were revolvers, rifles and machine-guns.

During the afternoon six Junkers 88's raided a gunpowder factory half a mile from Eleusis, but were caught by 80 Squadron's Hurricanes. In full view of the cheering groundcrews at Eleusis, the Hurricanes quickly shot down three of the Junkers. Ted Hewett chased another away towards the north and bagged it.

Pat looked very drawn and gaunt that night when Taffy went in to make his bed. The Welshman could see that Pat had lost several pounds in weight, and he was not surprised when Pat asked him if he would mind moving the buttons on his tunic. Obviously Pat did not want the others to know that he was not well. He could have eased off and gone into the sick bay, but he knew that this would have had a demoralising effect on the others around him and he meant to put duty before all else and continue to fight on to the end.

18

Backs to the wall

Five Hurricanes arrived from Egypt during the morning of 18 April. One of them was flown by a young flying officer, Noel-Johnson, who had just been posted to the squadron. He was in the office introducing himself to Pat and George Rumsey when the aerodrome was strafed for the second time that morning. As soon as the raid was over Pat and Rumsey drove to the top end of the airfield to where a Messerschmitt 109 had crash-landed. They collected the pilot, who was a quiet young fellow with nothing to say for himself. He had part of his left calf shot away by small-arms fire – which probably accounted for his quietness. Pat relieved him of his gun, a Browning 9 cm. made in Czechoslovakia and stamped with the Yugoslav coat of arms. The 109 was practically undamaged. The pilot could have flown away, but, apparently frightened by the sight of the blood, he had decided to land on the aerodrome.

After the strafing seven of the less badly damaged Hurricanes were earmarked for repair and after dark – in great secrecy, as everyone thought – the repair sections led by Chiefy Salmon and Chiefy MacLachlan pushed the aircraft into a hangar and worked all night on them.

The casualties among the aircraft were so great that the repair services just could not cope with them; many of them were, in fact, beyond their resources anyway. Those beyond repair were robbed of much equipment, to repair those less badly damaged, but wastage was very high, for replacements were now out of the question. Cannibalism and improvisation were resorted to on a large scale.

Fortunately there was a sandbagged pen in which the ground staffs could do some of the work, but this pen seemed to be the main attraction for the enemy and was continuously being strafed by the low-flying Huns. This, together with the spares problem, made maintenance very difficult. The latest aircraft, received as replacements on this very morning, required new technical know-how and different specialist tools, particularly for the new-type propellers. These tools were filed by hand from old metal drainpipes and any old pieces of metal available. These were hopelessly inefficient, but with the aid of hammers and sheer force managed to do the job effectively, although somewhat crudely.

By dawn five of the seven Hurricanes had been patched up sufficiently to be classified as available for operations and Chiefy Salmon was just on his way to Pat's office with the good news when there was a droning from the north-west. A few minutes later fifteen Junkers 88's appeared and concentrated their entire bomb-load on one particular target – the hangar containing the repaired Hurricanes. Both hangar and aircraft were completely destroyed within a few minutes. It was just one more instance of how the Germans were informed about everything that happened in Athens from their Fifth Columnists. The Germans were, in fact, still in charge of the telephone services.

There were no obvious signs of panic even as events grew worse and worse; the ground staffs seemed determined to follow the example set by the pilots, who were magnificent. Everyone, pilots and groundcrews, were lucky to have as their leaders Tap Jones and Pat Pattle, whom everyone knew and trusted implicitly. They knew that neither Tap nor Pat would let them down, and hence the calm, resigned way in which everyone reacted.

Individual acts of bravery were commonplace and much too numerous to mention here, although two of them must be told. Sergeant Battle, the enormous Armament NCO of 80 Squadron, inspired everyone with his disregard for the strafing Huns, and several times during the raids walked nonchalantly around with a Lewis gun under his arm, shooting at everything within range.

Then there were the two New Zealand gunners who rigged up a machine-gun on top of a lorry and, every time there was a raid, drove the lorry way out into the middle of the field. There, completely exposed to the withering fire of the strafing Messerschmitts, they kept their own gun firing the whole of the time and came through unscathed.

After breakfast Pat led seven Hurricanes on an offensive sweep. They followed the main road north towards Lamia, flying above dozens of army trucks, all heading for the Greek capital. The Hurricanes had only been airborne about twenty minutes when Pat's keen eyes spotted a lone Henschel 126 fighter, obviously out on a reconnaissance flight. It was low down, picking its way carefully between the hills and apparently hoping that its camouflage, which blended almost perfectly with the browns and greens of the mountainous background, would enable it to remain hidden from any interfering fighters. It was, in fact, invisible to the pilots of six of the Hurricanes for several seconds, until its position was carefully pointed out by Pat. He continued to lead the Hurricanes straight over and beyond the Henschel, until he reckoned that the Hun had been fooled into believing that the Hurricanes had not seen him. Then, shouting to the first section to follow him, Pat turned and dived almost to treetop level. The three Hurricanes ate up the distance between them and the unsuspecting German. Pat gave his orders.

'Line astern ... go!'

'Okay, chaps, one burst each should be enough ... Let's go!'

Pat watched the wings of the fighter slowly grow inside the ring of his reflector sight, until it showed a range of 100 yards. He pressed the gun button and for half a second eight streams of lead converged towards the Henschel. The Hurricane screamed up and over the fighter as Vernon Woodward sent another shower of ammunition towards it. Pop Littler's Hurricane quickly followed up behind the damaged Hun, from which flames were already licking their way from the engine towards the cockpit. Another brief burst and the Henschel tipped over and smashed into the forested hillside, sending up a shower of sparks and flaming débris.

The three Hurricanes climbed to rejoin the others and continued their sweep towards the north.

They followed the valley containing the main road and railway, keeping a sharp look-out for any more Huns. The valley narrowed and turned due west; quite suddenly, as they banked round the projecting mountains on the left, the Hurricanes came face to face with nine Messerschmitt 109's. There was no time to manoeuvre and no time to aim, in fact no time to do anything unless one had supersensitive reflexes. Only two or three out of all the pilots, both British and German, were quick enough to press the gun buttons before the two formations crossed, miraculously, it seemed, without hitting each other. But now Pat's reactions, working with lightning rapidity, enabled him to Immelmann out and come down behind the Messerschmitts whilst the others, with the exception of Vernon Woodward, were still wondering what to do next. Within seconds Pat was closing behind the Messerschmitt on the extreme left of the German formation. It was flying about 50 yards behind the others. He opened fire, saw his bullets smash into the fuselage of the 109, and out of the corner of his eye saw the rest of the Huns shoot up into the air all around him. The yellow-nosed Messerschmitt he had fired at seemed to shudder, and its propeller slowed until it was revolving like the sails of a windmill. It appeared to glide for several hundred yards and then quite quickly flipped over on to its back and smacked into the ground upside down, causing an eruption of earth and undergrowth.

Pat pulled back the control column and, looking over his shoulder, saw that the sky behind him was full of diving, twisting, turning and climbing aircraft, all interlocked in a dogfight, which was made even more confusing by the concealing camouflage of the fighters. A puff of white smoke, followed almost immediately by a vermilion flame, helped Pat to pick out one of the losers in this deadly game of aerial duelling, but he could not distinguish whether it was friend or foe. He climbed hard and was just about in a position over the top of the mêlée, when he spotted one of the Messerschmitts trying to sneak away along the valley towards Lamia. He opened the throttle to full boost and, pushing the control column into the bottom left-hand corner of the cockpit, curved down behind the 109. The speed of the power dive would have caused him to overshoot the enemy fighter, but he corrected this by lifting the nose of the Hurricane and putting down his flaps. This steadied the Hurricane into a solid gun platform, from which Pat was able to take a very careful aim. The Messerschmitt was still flying straight and level, the pilot obviously believing that he was now out of range of the Hurricanes. Pat took his time. He pulled out slightly to the right, lined up the cockpit in the dead centre of his sights, and gently squeezed the trigger. The Hurricane shuddered with the recoil from the guns, but it was only for a second, because immediately the German pilot's arms shot up in alarm, and then fell back lifeless into the cockpit. The Messerschmitt tipped forward into a steepening dive, which ended dramatically as it tried to bore a way through the rocky ground.

Pat returned to the scene of the dogfight without further incident and found three of the Hurricanes still circling at about 5,000 feet. He joined up with them and over the intercommunication system inquired the whereabouts of the three missing Hurricanes. Woodward said that he had seen Frankie Holman's Hurricane smoking badly and heading south along the valley, but when he had tried to join it, had been prevented from doing so by a couple of Messerschmitts – one of these he had shot down in flames.

The four Hurricanes returned to Eleusis safely and were just in time to see one of the missing Hurricanes attempting a crash-landing. It was Mitchell. The fabric covering the fuselage, torn by cannon shells, was still continuing to tear and blow backwards, until the tail unit was almost completely blanketed. In order to maintain control, Mitchell had to land at very high speed, but he managed it successfully.

The news of the other two missing Hurricanes was not so good. Flying Officer Moir had managed a crash-landing at Amphiklia and was now on his way back to Eleusis in an army truck, but his damaged Hurricane would have to be destroyed, because there were no replacement parts for it. Frankie Holman was dead. This was a real blow, because Frankie was the character of the squadron. A dashing rugby player, always ready for a lark, he enjoyed life to the full and was liked by everyone. He died after trying to land his damaged Hurricane, with wheels down, in a swampy field near Megara. The plane overturned, and Frankie, who had loosened his straps, broke his neck. Later in the day when George Rumsey, his best friend, went to Megara to collect the body, it had been laid out and covered in flowers by the local womenfolk.

In the afternoon there was another sweep, but this time Pat did not take part in it. Tap Jones, warned by the Medical Officer of 33 Squadron, Doc Henderson, that Pat was overdoing it, ordered Timber Woods of 80 Squadron to lead and, in spite of an outburst of protest from the South African, would not change his decision. He made only one concession. Pat could remain at Eleusis on standby and would only be given permission to fly should there be an air raid alarm. Pat finally agreed to this, knowing full well that the Germans would not leave the airfield alone for more than two or three hours at the most.

He returned to his camp bed, gave Taffy explicit orders to wake him immediately an alarm was sounded, and for the next couple of hours tossed and turned in a nightmare of screaming aircraft and barking cannons. The constant action of a month of almost non-stop operations, interspersed with only very short periods of rest, was beginning to play on his nerves. He knew that he had over-exerted himself to make a success of 33 Squadron, which had been taking some hard knocks. He felt tired, both physically and mentally, but he could not give up. This was his first command, and he was determined to make a success of it, no matter what the cost.

He was awakened by the five Hurricanes returning from the sweep.

By the time they had rolled to a stop he was outside, walking towards the pilots, who were laughing and joking. Obviously the mission had been successful.

They had caught a formation of Junkers 87's dive-bombing the aerodrome at Almyros and, disregarding the escorting 109's, had waded in merrily, destroying four of the Stukas right over the aerodrome in full view of an applauding audience of airmen and Anzacs. When the

109's eventually came to the aid of their unfortunate comrades they were soon routed by the five resolute Hurricane pilots, who got one Messerschmitt for certain and probably several others. The only Hurricane which was hit belonged to Sergeant Casbolt. He was most upset; he had just got on the tail of a 109, and was beginning to knock bits and pieces off it, when another 109 put a burst into his engine, and covered his windscreen with oil. By the time he had managed to clean it sufficiently to see through it the fight was over and all the enemy aircraft had disappeared, apart from those on the ground still burning.

Pat walked over to the readiness hut. He picked up a magazine and settled in a comfortable chair.

There was a knock on the door and in walked the ever-faithful Taffy Harris with a tray and a pot of tea. 'How about a nice cup of tea, sir?'

'Yes, Taffy. That would be most welcome,' answered Pat.

Taffy placed the tray on the small, round table, with the creased but clean square of linen that had once been a tea-cloth. He walked over to the battered cupboard hanging on the wall at the side of the window, or rather the window frame, since there were only splinters of glass still embedded here and there around the edges. Taffy put his left index finger through a bullet hole in the door of the cabinet, opened it and took out a cup and saucer. He was almost halfway across the room when the tannoy suddenly came to life.

'Attention, attention. Standby pilots take off immediately. Enemy aircraft approaching from the north-west.'

Pat grabbed his helmet and shot out of the chair.

'Better drink that yourself, Taffy,' he shouted and then he was gone.

'Good luck, sir,' the Welshman yelled, and shrugging his shoulders strolled across to the teapot.

Within minutes Pat's Hurricane was climbing away from the airfield and heading towards the raiders. His radio soon crackled into life and he heard Tap Jones calmly giving all the information he needed – where to find the enemy. He adjusted his course, and when he had reached an altitude of 15,000 feet, which was 3,000 feet higher than the estimated height of the raiders, he levelled off and began a thorough search of the clear blue sky. There was nothing, which was not surprising, because he was still several miles from the raiders. But he continued to look all around him. It was only a fool who did not keep his eyes open these days in Greece.

He glanced at his watch. Fifteen minutes had elapsed since take-off. He could see the harbour of Khalcis just in front of the leading edge of his starboard wing. For a moment he thought he had spotted the enemy, but it was only a reflection on the deep blue waters of the Aegean Sea. He was immediately over the busy port when he noticed a couple of aircraft a mile away to the west. He swung round and as he drew nearer saw that it was a Hurricane chasing a Junkers 88. One of the engines of the Junkers was already smoking badly. Pat closed in nearer to the fight and was soon able to make out the grim, determined features of Sergeant Casbolt. Pat smiled and watched his old wingman go in closer to make sure of his kill. Then thinking that he might find the rest of the Huns somewhere around Khalcis, Pat doubled back towards the port. He looked back once, in time to see the 88 falling in a flat spin, and then found another Junkers 88 going very fast towards the north. It must have unloaded its bombs, for it was now diving towards the safety of its own lines. Pat gave chase, and finally caught up with it a few miles south of Akra. He silenced the rear-gunner with his first burst, and then methodically set about demolishing the Junkers piece by piece, until eventually the crew baled out and the Junkers dived into the sea.

He returned to Eleusis and as soon as it was dark drove into Athens in the staff car. He went round to Tommy Wisdom's little flat in the heart of the city, and for an hour soaked himself in a wonderful hot bath. Tommy, a RAF Press Liaison Officer, was on duty at nine, and for once Pat was glad, for he needed a good sleep in a decent soft bed.

19

The Battle of Piraeus Harbour

A number of pilots were kept at standby throughout the night at Eleusis. It was expected that the Luftwaffe would keep up their attacks throughout the hours of darkness, if only to stop the pilots and the ground staff from enjoying a few hours' much needed rest. Although these attacks did not materialise, the tension was so great that very few pilots were able to doze off for long. Mick Richens and 'Cas' Casbolt played cards for most of the night, and consequently were first off the ground soon after five o'clock when the first alarm sounded on Sunday, 20 April – Hitler's birthday.

Neither Richens nor Casbolt found any trace of the enemy, although they patrolled up and down and back and forth over Piraeus harbour for more than an hour. Below them in a crowded harbour they could easily pick out the red crosses of the hospital ship, on to which were being loaded an almost non-stop stream of stretchers carrying wounded soldiers. So far it had been left alone by the Luftwaffe, but everyone knew that it could not last; it was such an inviting target for the murderous dive-bombers. So, too, were the only two aerodromes in Greece still in British hands: Menidi and Eleusis. With their overcrowded concentration of aircraft, they acted as a magnet, attracting every Luftwaffe machine that became airborne.

When Richens and Casbolt returned to Eleusis it was obvious that some German bombers had managed to get through to the aerodrome undetected, for a Yugoslav Savoia 79 was blazing furiously at the top end of the field. The servicing crews were still hard at it, however, striving valiantly to do the impossible, protected solely by a number of sandbags, which had been heaped up in the form of a pen. Although Richens and Casbolt had seen nothing at all, most of the other pilots had become involved in fights with 88's and 109's. Nobody bothered to count up the victories; everyone was too busy in getting the Hurricanes ready for the next fight. They stopped for a moment, and listened silently whilst Sergeant Bennett recounted how 'Ginger' Still had been shot to pieces near Lamia by three Messerschmitt 109's. Then the Hurricanes were taking off yet again to intercept.

Three or four times during the morning the Hurricanes either harassed the enemy or beat them off entirely. Then the skies cleared. With the situation easing, at least for the time being, Tap Jones actually planned an offensive sweep, hoping undoubtedly that this would give both the pilots and the groundcrews a moral uplift which would help them to survive the onslaught. The sweep was detailed to take off at six o'clock.

At five o'clock the pilots gathered in the readiness hut for the briefing. Pat still had a high temperature and was lying shivering on a couch, covered with blankets.

Suddenly the air-raid siren sounded and a voice over the tannoy announced that more than a hundred dive-bombers and fighters had been sighted, heading directly towards the harbour.

In a few seconds the room had cleared, except for Pat and his Adjutant, George Rumsey. Pat flung off his blankets and started for the door. Rumsey tried to stop him, but Pat was equally determined, and in spite of Rumsey's protests hurried out of the hut, towards the nearest aircraft, which was parked some two hundred yards away. As he ran towards it a Me. 110 swept past, spitting cannon shells. Pat stopped in his tracks. He felt a violent thump on his back and a fitter ran past, shouting:

'Come on, sir, I'll start you up.'

When Pat had the engine running the fitter unplugged the external battery, and then ran way out into the middle of the field, where he stood and waved Pat off. He was indicating that he would not take cover until Pat was airborne. Pat felt very proud – this was typical of the spirit of his squadron, a spirit which had been engendered in every man, through the inspired and devoted efforts of their Commanding Officer.

Fifteen Hurricanes had taken off – these were all the fighters left in Greece – and some of these in less difficult circumstances would have been classified as unserviceable. But because of the size of the German raid, the biggest yet, everything that would fly and fight had to be put into the air.

The Hurricanes had taken off singly, but whilst climbing in different directions had managed to sort themselves out into small sections of two or three.

Squadron Leader Jones's voice could be recognised over the radio telephone from the control room at Eleusis and on his instructions the Hurricanes climbed to 20,000 feet and proceeded to Piraeus harbour.

Ping Newton, Pete Wickham and Harry Starrett were first on the scene. They found the hospital ship in the harbour being dive-bombed unmercifully by about fifteen Junkers 88's. The three Hurricanes caught the dive-bombers just at their most vulnerable moment, when they pulled out of their dives. Five of the Junkers went straight into the harbour, and three more were smoking badly before the Hurricanes had to leave because they had used up all their ammunition. Newton and Wickham returned to Eleusis, rearmed and refuelled and went back into the battle. Poor Harry Starrett was not so lucky. His Hurricane was hit and set on fire. It was not burning too badly, however, and Harry, knowing how desperately short of Hurricanes the Air Force was in Greece, refused to bale out. He flew the Hurricane back to Eleusis and had to make a belly landing, with his wheels up, because his hydraulic system had failed. He made an excellent job of it; the Hurricane had almost come to a standstill when the glycol tank exploded. The plane was enveloped in flames. Harry managed to get out of the fighter, his clothing in flames, and rolled over and over on the ground, but he could not get his burning parachute off.

When they got to him Harry was severely burned and unconscious, but still breathing, and they hurried him off to the hospital in Athens.

He died from his burns two days later. Another brave and unselfish man, who had put duty before all else.

Overhead the battle still raged. Len Cottingham and Vernon Woodward attacked the Messerschmitt 110's who were supposedly guarding the Junkers 88's. Vernon got one 110 for certain and damaged three others before breaking away to return for more ammunition, whilst the tubby flight sergeant set three of the Messerschmitts on fire. He was then wounded by the rear-gunner of another 110 and forced to bale out.

Cherry Vale found thirty dive-bombers circling and taking it in turns to dive on the shipping in the harbour. He made several attacks on the Junkers, and finally had the satisfaction of seeing one of them go down in flames. He attacked another, and watched big chunks breaking away from the wings and fuselage. It was going down vertically with black smoke pouring from both its engines when Cherry broke away to elude a Messerschmitt 109 which had tried to sneak up behind him. He used up all his ammunition on the dive-bombers.

Ted Hewett found himself alone above six Messerschmitt 109's. He dived down behind the last one of the six and got in a burst which caused it to roll over and go down with smoke streaming out behind it. The rest of the 109's had still not noticed the presence of the Hurricane, so Hewett closed up behind the next Messerschmitt; after some attention its pilot baled out. The sergeant then had a go at a third 109, but this time he did not stay to see what happened, because the other 109's turned on him viciously.

Timber Woods had been one of the first off the ground, closely followed by Flight Sergeant Wintersdorf, a Frenchman and new addition to the ranks of 80 Squadron, and the ever-reliable Sergeant Casbolt. They had joined up together and, after climbing to 21,000 feet, had been led down by Woods to attack a formation of circling Messerschmitts. After two or three attacks on these, Timber Woods returned to Eleusis to rearm. Wintersdorf got one of the Messerschmitts and was then himself hit and wounded in the leg and had to bale out. Casbolt got two of the 110's and then was hit by another in the rudder, a piece almost a foot square being shot away. He broke away and was attacked by a Messerschmitt 109, which he easily outmanoeuvred and shot down in flames. He, too, then broke away to return for more ammunition.

In the meantime Timber Woods had climbed back into the fight and spotted another group of circling Me. 110's. This time, however, they were above him, but this did not deter the reckless Irishman, who climbed right up towards them.

Pat had now reached the scene of the fight and was 1,000 feet above a defensive circle of 110's when he saw a lone Hurricane climbing towards them, and at the same time saw one of the Messerschmitts detach itself from the circle and dive towards the Hurricane. Pat knew that what the Hurricane was doing was extremely foolish. All the advantages were in favour of the circling Messerschmitts, but he could not stand by and do nothing. Without hesitating for a single moment, he put down the nose of his Hurricane, and dived down through the middle of the maelstrom of 110's to protect the tail of the Hurricane. He knew that they would follow him like a swarm of enraged wasps, but he kept going and pulled up beneath the first 110, which was now firing at point-blank range into the Hurricane. The 110 burst into flames a split second after the Hurricane began to blaze.

The cannons of the pursuing Messerschmitts were now barking louder and nearer. Knowing that the 110's could outdive his Hurricane, Pat pulled his fighter up and round. The sky seemed full of aircraft, all of them with two engines, black crosses and cannon guns spitting red and yellow flashes. He dived frantically into a space with no Messerschmitts in it, and almost collided with a German which was banking sharply. He pressed the gun button and just had time to see the Hun stall and then fall flaming before he tugged the Hurricane away from another attack.

No one actually saw Pat die except the pilots of the Messerschmitts, but a few minutes later Jimmy Kettlewell arrived on the scene. He saw the Hurricane diving, with its pilot slumped forward across the dashboard. Flames were spreading towards the cockpit and two

Messerschmitts were still firing at it. Jimmy clobbered one of the Messerschmitts and watched sadly as both it and Pat's Hurricane fell almost side by side into the depths of the bay south of Eleusis.

A few moments later Jimmy, too, was hit and had to bale out. He injured his back in landing and for a few months after this had to walk about in a plaster cast.

That night the mess was unusually silent – not because of fear of the dangerous situation they were in. They were all resigned to the fact that the Battle for Greece had now been lost and that they would have to evacuate. They all knew that the best thing for them to do now was to get back to Egypt, to rebuild their strength both in men and material, so that they could hit back at the Hun, and avenge the death of their beloved Pat.

They had always felt that no German would ever be good enough to shoot him down, but they had not reckoned on Pat making the supreme sacrifice in order to try to save the life of a fellow flyer.

*

When they did start talking there was only one topic of conversation.

'Pat was the greatest fighter pilot I ever saw,' said Casbolt. The way he used to send down those Savoias with just a few rounds was unbelievable.'

'Yes,' confirmed Shorty Graham. 'I shall never forget that day at Amriya, when he cut that drogue to pieces and it cost Mick Richens a bottle of champagne.'

'Pat's amazing eyesight,' said Cherry Vale, 'was, I believe, his greatest asset. It gave him that second or so to get into a position from which he took command of a battle. His brilliant leadership gained us all a lot of victories, and saved so many of our lives.'

'I shall always remember that day at Larissa when he took over the squadron,' remarked Ping Newton. 'I had always had a good opinion of my own flying ability, until I was cut down to size by Pat's perfect flying and split-second timing.'

'What you are all trying to say,' concluded Jimmy Kettlewell, 'is that Pat was a fighter pilot "par excellence". But, you know, Pat was much more than that. He was a fine officer and a true gentleman. None of us will ever forget him.'

Combat Record of Squadron Leader M T St John Pattle, DFC and Bar
Date / Type of Aircraft and Result / Place

1940

4 Aug
Breda 65 destroyed – Bir Taieb el Esem
Fiat C.R. 42 destroyed – Bir Taieb el Esem

8 Aug
2 Fiat C.R. 42's destroyed – Bir el Gobi

15 Sept
Savoia Marchetti 79 damaged – Sidi Barrani

19 Nov
2 Fiat C.R. 42's destroyed – North of Koritza

27 Nov
2 Fiat C.R. 42's destroyed (Shared with 11 other pilots) – Teniteon

29 Nov
2 Savoia Marchetti 79's damaged (Shared with P/O Vale) – Tepelene

2 Dec
R.O. 37 destroyed – Argyrokastron
R.O. 37 destroyed – Premeti

4 Dec
3 Fiat C.R. 42's destroyed – North of Delvinakion
Fiat C.R. 42 probably destroyed – North of Delvinakion
Fiat C.R. 32 damaged – North of Delvinakion

20 Dec
Savoia Marchetti 79 destroyed – South-east of Tepelene
Savoia Marchetti 81 destroyed – North of Kelcyre

21 Dec
Fiat C.R. 42 destroyed – North of Argyrokastron

1941
28 Jan
Cant Z 1007 destroyed (Shared with P/O Trollip and Sgt. Casbolt) – Kelcyre

9 Feb
Fiat C.R. 42 destroyed – North of Tepelene
Cant Z 1007 damaged – Yanina
Fiat 13.R. 20 damaged – Yanina

20 Feb
Fiat G. 30 destroyed – Berat

27 Feb
Fiat C.R. 42 destroyed – Valona

28 Feb
2 Fiat B.R. 20's destroyed – Between Valona and Dukati
2 Fiat C.R. 42's destroyed – Between Valona and Dukati
Fiat C.R. 42 probably destroyed – Between Valona and Dukati

4 Mar
Fiat G. 50 destroyed – North of Himara
2 Fiat G. 50's destroyed – Valona harbour
Fiat C.R. 42 probably destroyed – Valona harbour

23 Mar
Fiat G. 50 destroyed – Fieri
Fiat G. 50 probably destroyed – Fieri
3 Fiat G. 50's destroyed on the ground – Fieri

6 Apr
2 Messerschmitt 109's destroyed – Rupel Pass

7 Apr
Fiat C.R. 42 destroyed – Strumitsa Pass

8 Apr
2 Messerschmitt 109's destroyed on the ground – Petrich

9 Apr
Junkers 88 destroyed – Larissa

10 Apr
Messerschmitt 110 destroyed – Betjol
Messerschmitt 109 destroyed – Betjol

11 Apr
Heinkel 111 destroyed – Volos
Junkers 88 destroyed – Volos

12 Apr
Dornier 215 destroyed – Salonika
Savoia Marchetti 79 destroyed – Near Larissa
Messerschmitt 109 probably destroyed – Near Larissa

19 Apr

Henschel 126 destroyed (Shared with F/L Littler and F/O Woodward) – South of Lamia

2 Messerschmitt 109's destroyed – South of Lamia

Junkers 88 destroyed – Khalcis

20 Apr

2 Messerschmitt 110's destroyed – Piraeus Harbour

Messerschmitt 109 probably destroyed – Piraeus Harbour

Epilogue

It never ceases to amaze me that it took you, who never knew him personally, to 'discover' him twenty years or so after his death, when there were dozens of other people who were well aware of his exceptional talents and courage and did nothing to ensure that he was accorded the acclaim, you gave him.

Cecil St John Pattle

The above words made me wonder how in fact I had become interested in the pilots who fought the war in the air. I suppose, like young Pat, I was fascinated by the occasional passing of an aircraft over the places where I played as a young boy, and I shall never forget the day when an old biplane fighter crash-landed in the field fairly close to our house. I began to read Captain W E John's books about Biggies, but this didn't last very long because my teacher very wisely implanted the suggestion that truth was stranger than fiction. Hence my visit to the local library where I discovered Kiernan's biography of Captain Albert Ball, VC, of World War I fame. I became engrossed in the stories of Mannock, McCudden, Bishop, von Richtofen, Rickenbacker and countless other fighter aces of the First World War. But all too soon we were in another world war and as I began to take notice of the daily newspapers I discovered new words like Spitfire and Hurricane and 'Phoney War' and a New Zealander fighter pilot by the name of 'Cobber' (Kain).

My collection of newspaper clippings on the exploits of the fighter aces of the Second World War began at about this time, and was followed by a regular order for copies of *Flight* and *The Aeroplane,* which were read and re-read and kept carefully filed in cardboard boxes, whilst I was studying aeronautical subjects in the local Air Training Corps. I suppose I would have naturally progressed into the Royal Air Force to train as a pilot, but the RAF had too many pilots in training in those days, so I did the next best thing and went into the Fleet Air Arm. I joined a class of forty budding pilots, only to be told I was surplus to requirements. My ambition to become a fighter pilot was frustrated.

My post-war training as a teacher, the writing of theses, and the meticulous keeping of records, inculcated a researcher's feel for putting things in order ... hence I began to collect the details of the numerous clippings, and the countless copies of citations to decorations into chronological order. Eventually when I felt that I had enough information about a particular pilot, I rewrote it in the form of a chapter for a book which was put together for personal enjoyment only and never really intended for publication.

I was at this time, in the early 1960s, regularly reading a magazine *Royal Air Force Review*, one copy of which contained an article about the wartime efforts of No 80 Squadron in the campaign in Greece in the winter of 1940-41. It was the first time I had heard of Pattle, who at the time was a flight commander with the DEC and had several aircraft to his credit. Most of my newspaper clippings were about the fighter pilots who had fought in France and the Battle of Britain and I was intrigued to find out more about the pilots who took part in the air battles over the Western Desert and Greece. There were very few press references to these forgotten pilots and even fewer citations to decorations, but eventually my persistent efforts enabled me to put together a somewhat hazy picture of the RAF's part in the Greek campaign, and in particular the part played by Pattle and 80 Squadron. My story appeared in print for the first time in the same magazine. A few weeks later I was approached by publisher William Kimber, who wanted me to write a series of biographies about 'The Fighter Aces of the Royal Air Force'.

Whilst I was still researching that first book I had met and interviewed a number of fighter pilots, including a survivor of the Greek campaign, Vernon Woodward. It was he who informed that Pattle had been his Commanding Officer when he was a Flying Officer with No 33 Squadron in the Greek campaign in 1941 and furthermore that his CO was the outstanding fighter pilot of the whole of the RAF at that time with a score of well over thirty enemy planes destroyed, and the majority of those shot down whilst flying an obsolescent Gloster Gladiator biplane fighter plane. My curiosity was aroused. I had to find out more about this unknown ace.

The Air Ministry and the Air Historical Branch were most helpful and went to a lot of trouble in not only giving me access to operational record books and combat reports, but also with the assistance of the South African authorities in helping me to eventually contact Pat's next-of-kin, his elder brother Cecil. Imagine my surprise when I finally received a copy of Pat's Certificate of Service to find no mention of his ever having served with 33 Squadron. It soon became obvious that the official records of operations in Greece had been destroyed before our troops were evacuated. My only hope now was that I could find some of the airmen who had served there, and not only survived the campaign but also been able to retain their diaries, log-books or whatever else they had been able to write on. The response to my enquiries was quite fantastic with diaries, records and photographs coming in quantities from places as far apart as Rhodesia and Australia. I travelled all over England and Wales to look at documents which the owners were loath to part with but were quite willing for me to study. Slowly the story was put together and it gradually emerged that, in fact, not only was Vernon Woodward right when he put Pat at the top, but he was also right when he said the story of Royal Air Force fighter squadrons in that dreadful cold winter and spring of 1940-41 should be told in full.

The final parts of the story were put into place when I eventually traced the adjutants of 80 and 33 Squadrons who had kept some records of those final days before the evacuation from Greece. Ted Tyler of 80 Squadron was living in Victoria, Australia and sent in pages of records on the evacuation from both Greece and Crete. He also sent a list of 80 Squadron victories which he had compiled from combat reports and squadron histories at Headquarters, RAF, Middle East immediately after returning from Greece. The adjutant of 33 Squadron, George Rumsey, was a most elusive character for it took more than a year before I made contact with his sister, who gave me his address in Hokitika, New Zealand. But it was well worth the wait, for he was a great help with the movements of 33 Squadron when retreating to Eleusis (he had managed to keep his log-book with him when he flew out in a Sunderland flying boat with 85 others to Crete). In fact he also took with him Pattle's own log-book, which he handed in at RAF Headquarters in Egypt. But he said it would have been of no use, for Pattle had not filled it in since the start of the campaign ... he had left all the writing to Rumsey. He also told me: 'After Pat's death we talked in terms of his score being around 65.' Rumsey provided short biographical notes on all of the flying personnel of 33 Squadron.

Soon after the last amendments had been made to the manuscript and it had gone off to the printers in the summer of 1965, I received an interesting letter from another ex-member of 80 Squadron, Frank Pattullo. He had joined 80 Squadron in Egypt as an RAFVR Cypher Officer in April 1940 and went to Greece with them in the following November. He had remained with them until March 1941 when he was transferred to HQ Intelligence in Athens where he remembered helping to burn all Intelligence records, and other administrative despatches which might have included papers relating to Pattle. One interesting point he made was: 'I was under the impression that Pat was killed when serving with 80 Squadron as a F/Lt', which perhaps further illustrates the fact that not only did the Air Ministry records department not know that Pat was Commanding Officer of 33 Squadron, but also that the paper work on his promotion could not even have reached Intelligence Headquarters in Athens.

As Cypher Officer, Pattullo remembered decoding many signals from Group Captain Willetts reading 'WELL DONE 80 REPEAT 80 Sqn'. His letter showed his high regard for Pattle.

Pat Pattle represented the epitome of excellence both as a man, and as a fighter pilot in the Royal Air Force. His perpetual cheerfulness, mental resilience and guts were I am sure a moral boost to us all. I seem to remember that he was awarded the DFC fairly early in the campaign, but in my opinion if he had also been awarded the DSO and bar it would have been well and tally earned. I well remember the air battle in which he was killed, helplessly outnumbered, over Piraeus, and I still often think of him with sorrow and affection.

Pattullo later on sent a number of photographs he had taken in the desert and others taken during the long hard snowy winter in Greece. His accompanying letter showed his opinion of Pat as a flier.

I well remembered Pat flying a Gladiator over our HQ and Mess in Yanina to drop a message, and looking out of the open cockpit and grinning; yet he was flying so slowly that he must have been only a fraction of a foot per second above stalling speed: he almost seemed to be hovering, and I remember thinking then what a brilliant and utterly casual piece of slow motion flying it was.

A television interview on the day *Pattle: Supreme Fighter in the Air* (the original title of this book) was published, in which I tried to describe some of his exploits, brought several telephone calls from ex-servicemen, and ex-servicewomen who had been in Greece in 1940-41. Roy Barnes and his wife Hilda had got to know Pattle quite well. Both had served in Greece; Roy as a Flying Officer bomber pilot with 211 Squadron at Paramythia, and Hilda as a nurse at the 26th General Hospital. 'We have often said that we have heard too little of the Greek campaign. In the events which followed, Greece seems to have been forgotten, and much of the bravery and courage of the campaign forgotten with it,' said Mrs Barnes. She herself left the country only hours before the swastika was flown over the Acropolis.

A former 33 Squadron pilot and comrade of Pattle, John Darragh commented that Pattle was the ideal leader for a mobile air squadron which travelled at short notice to give support to offensives carried out by the Army. He said, 'Pattle was down to earth in his approach to every member of his unit, never stood on ceremony and hated "bull" as much as the lowest aircraftman.' He concluded, 'I feel that something should be done to recognise his feats. Certainly no man deserved recognition more for his outstanding bravery and skill.'

During the next few days the newspapers took different views ... The *Daily Express* proclaimed This young pilot may have been the greatest ace of air ... The *Daily Mail* asked 'Was he the RAF's top ace?' ... and the *Daily Sketch* concluded 'RAF chose wrong hero'. When they tried to find out more they were told by an Air Ministry official, 'The book gives every evidence of painstaking research ... and one could not quarrel with the conclusions. Pattle was a great pilot.' *Air Pictorial* in its review pointed out, 'After all these years it is fitting to see due tribute made to a gallant South African, who came over to join the RAF in 1936, and whose achievements might never have become known ... It is to be hoped that the exploits of other airmen who took part in obscure and ill-documented campaigns ... might one day be similarly recorded.'

I was amazed at the number of people who had known Pat and took the trouble to write in to add their pieces to the story, even if it was only to confirm some minor detail.

But the most significant letter was written by W J Ringrose, with reference to an article which had appeared in that newspaper on 12 December 1965.

I am an ex-member of 80 Squadron, and have in my possession a complete record of Pat Pattle's "kills" during the Desert and Greek campaign. I joined the squadron at the same time as A/PO Pattle in 1938 at RAF Debden, and was the Fitter on his aircraft. I was in contact with him from then until he was shot down at 1720 hrs on 16.4.41. over Liself. I make his score over 50, these unofficial records are at your disposal should you so desire.

I immediately wrote to Mr Ringrose asking for these records and within a few days received three foolscap sheets which were photocopies of the same victory lists of 80 Squadron that had been forwarded to me more than a year earlier by Ted Tyler, the ex-adjutant of the squadron. But in addition there was another sheet which Ringrose assured me was exactly as he had written it in his diary in 1941.

COPY OF THE NOTES FROM W J RINGROSE'S DIARY
April 2nd joined 33 Squadron S/LDR. PATTLE

April 4th Gs declare war on Greece. Patt on patrol 2 M.E. 109s
April 5th Escort No. 11 Sqdn over enemy transport 1 C.R. 42
April 6th Escort 211 Sqdn on Airfields 2 M.E. 109s
April 7th Raid on our drome Patt took off 1 J.U. 88
April 8th Escort 11 SQDN again at 15.30 hrs TARGET 1 M. E. 109, 1 M.E. 110
April 9th Heavy raids on our drome Patt took off 1 HEIN. 111, 1 J.U. 88
April 10th on drome patrol met and shot down 1 S.79, PROBABLE 109
April 11th Air raid alarm couldn't find enemy
April 12th Big day air raids everlasting. 07-10 1 M.E. 109, 08-43 1 J.U. 88, 10-04 1 M.E. 110, 13-08 1 S. 79, 17-40 1 J.U. 88
April 13th Big day again. 06-35 2 J.U. 88, 1 PROBABLE, 10-12 1 M.E. 109, 14-50 1 J.U. 88, 1 PROBABLE JU87, 18-20 2 M.E. 109s, Retreated at 20-32 hours
April 16th over Eleusis, straffing and bombing at 14-12 2 M.E. 109s, 15-41 1 J.U. 88
Patt was shot down at Liself at 17-20 2 HEINKELS to his credit before they got him.
April 17th Retreated to KADAMATA.

Total: 11 – 109s
       1 – C.R. 42
       8 – J.U.88s
       3 – HEINKELS
       2 – 110s M.E.
       2 – S.79s

FULL TOTAL: 27 – 3 PROBABLES

This was very exciting news, but my first impression was that something was very wrong about the dates. Everyone knew that the Germans had declared war on Greece on 6 April, and in addition many of the entries seemed to be two days before similar entries from other airmen's diaries and letters. When I queried these discrepancies with Ringrose, he assured me that he did not possess a current 1941 diary at the time, and he thought that he might have used the days rather than the dates when he wrote down items in the diary. He went on to tell me that he carried his diary at all times, and he normally completed the notes in his diary, as soon as possible after S/L Pattle had landed from a mission.

But the biggest discrepancies between Ringrose's list and my combat record in the biography are for 13 April to 18 April, when I was unable to confirm any victories at all for Pattle. Certainly from the evening of the 15th to the morning of the 17th Pat was, according to Rumsey, 'prostrate and voiceless ... in the staff car for the retreat south, and there was not a murmur from him.' But from the 18th onwards, Pat led the organised sweeps, whenever he could. According to Ringrose the big days were 12 and 13 April (his list), which I believe were actually the 14th and 15th. These were the final two days the squadron spent at Larissa before beginning the evacuation to Athens and I can well imagine that the airfield would have been continuously attacked by strafing fighters and heavily raided by dive-bombers. This could be the reason why Ringrose insisted that Pat flew five sorties on 12th (14th) and destroyed five enemy aircraft, and the next day took part in four more sorties and got a further six destroyed plus two probables during air raids on Larissa.

Now, if in fact Ringrose's list is a true record of Pattle's victories in air combat, Pat's score would be as below:

With 80 Squadron
24 destroyed plus shared in 3 more
2 probably destroyed
5 damaged

With 33 Squadron

27 destroyed

3 probably destroyed

TOTAL

51 destroyed plus shared in 3 more

5 probables

5 damaged

If we classify these as victories they add up to a total of 64 which is very close indeed to what George Rumsey had quoted to me. He had said: *'After Pat's death we talked in terms of his score being around 65.'*

However, it seems unlikely that we shall ever know for certain exactly how many hostile aircraft Pat Pattle shot down and destroyed, but I am myself convinced that it must have been more than 40. I am also very sure that he shot down more enemy aircraft than any other Royal Air Force pilot during the Second World War.

There is no doubt at all in my mind that the Battle of Britain 'Few' richly deserved all the publicity, and the awards they received for their very gallant efforts which were instrumental in saving the United Kingdom from being invaded by the German aggressors in 1940. But I am also certain that the forgotten airmen of the Greek campaign who responded magnificently against tremendous odds of both men and material in 1941, should have received many more awards for gallantry and bravery. With this thought in mind I wrote to the Ministry of Defence in December 1965 and recommended that an investigation be made, with the possibility of Sqn Ldr Pattle's courageous leadership being recognised in the form of a posthumous award for gallantry and devotion to duty.

A few weeks later I received the following reply:

... Squadron Leader Pattle was awarded the DFC and Bar in 1941 for his services in the Middle East theatre and, as all questions of awards in respect of war-time service have long

*since been closed, it is not now possible to take any further action
in this matter.*

Since the Ministry of Defence had apparently ignored the first part of
my letter in which I recommended an investigation I decided to press
the matter further. I insisted that the case of Sqn Ldr Pattle was not
normal because his personal Certificate of Service was incomplete and
furthermore that the Operational Record Book of 33 Squadron was no
true record. I urged the Ministry of Defence to reconsider, and
promised to make available to them all the data I had collected in my
researches.

My letter was passed on by the Ministry of Defence to the Air
Historical Branch for further action. A reply was soon forthcoming:

*... the destruction of unit records to prevent their falling into
enemy hands is perfectly correct procedure which was not
confined to the Royal Air Force ...*

*Following such instances where it was necessary to destroy
records every effort was made at the earliest opportunity to
reconstruct the unit history from whatever source was available.*

*In view of this, your very kind offer to make available to this
branch the result of several years' research into the activities of
No. 33 Squadron during the campaign in Greece is heartily
appreciated ...*

*It is, of course, quite impossible to investigate further into a
matter for which original records are not available ... You may
not know that the DFC (and bars to the DFC) cannot be awarded
posthumously.*

My records and documents were duly forwarded to the Air Ministry
and several weeks later were returned with the following letter from the
Air Historical Branch:

I am returning herewith the papers on Nos 33 and 80 Squadrons ... I have had a large number reproduced and placed with our official records for the benefit of future historians and other approved researchers ...

I confess that I felt more than a little disappointed. But at least future historians and researchers would be able to consult my 'unofficial records' and obtain a good idea of what happened to 33 Squadron and its beloved Commanding Officer in those last fateful weeks of gallantry and devotion to duty in Greece.

E C R Baker
June 1992

Epitaph

A letter written by Pat's father to a friend shortly after hearing that his son was missing:

It was a great though not unexpected shock to hear that Tom was missing, but knowing the tremendous odds that our lads have been fighting against, we could hardly expect our boy to come through unscathed. Whatever be his fate, my wife and I can thank God that he played the man, and that he has earned the gratitude of his King and Country. What more can any man wish for? Our prayer must now be that his sacrifice has not been in vain. If he be alive or has passed beyond, we can only commend him to the good God Who gave him to us.

C J ST JOHN PATTLE

Acknowledgements

This book could never have been written without the most generous co-operation of Major Cecil St John Pattle. Much of the information contained herein has been extracted from the personal letters of the late Squadron Leader M T St John Pattle, DFC and Bar, and I am greatly indebted to Major Pattle for permission to use them.

My sincere thanks particularly to the following, who have not only contributed very willingly from their store of memory, but who have also been most generous in allowing me to consult personal papers, diaries and flying log-books: Gordon Barker, 'Cas' Casbolt, Charles Dyson, 'Taffy' Harris, Jimmy Kettlewell, John Lancaster, 'Ping' Newton, 'Percy' Oldroyd, 'George' Rumsey and Vernon Woodward.

Further valuable help has been supplied by the Air Ministry, especially the Air Historical Branch, and Department A.R.8B, the South African Embassy and the Commonwealth War Graves Commission.

A great many people have assisted in providing material for this book and I should especially mention: Air Vice-Marshal W A B Bowen-Buscarlet, KBE, CB, DFC; R W Cleary; Air Vice-Marshal J G Davis, CB, OBE; Air Vice-Marshal P H Dunn, CB, CBE, DFC; G F Graham; H Haigh; Group Captain W P Harvey; Air Commodore R C Jonas, OBE; Wing Commander S Linnard, DFC; Squadron Leader J I< McLachlan, MBE; Wing Commander R A Millward, OBE, DFC; N H Pascoe; Squadron Leader F J Pittman; E E Tyler; Air Vice-Marshal P G Wykeham, CB, DSO, OBE, DFC, AFC.

Books consulted include *Wings Over Olympus* by T H Wisdom; *Operation Mercury* by M G Comeau; and *Royal Air Force, 1939-45* by Denis Richards and Hilary St G Saunders.

E C R BAKER

Lightning Source UK Ltd.
Milton Keynes UK
UKHW010658150922
408910UK00001B/292